Moonbeams

A Hadassah Rosh Hodesh Guide

Moonbeams

A Hadassah Rosh Hodesh Guide

by Leora Tanenbaum,

Claudia R. Chernov,

and Hadassah Tropper

edited by Carol Diament

HADASSAH
The Women's Zionist Organization of America, Inc.

JEWISH LIGHTS PUBLISHING
Woodstock, Vermont

Moonbeams: A Hadassah Rosh Hodesh Guide
© 2000 by Hadassah
The Women's Zionist Organization of America, Inc.

Library of Congress Cataloging-in-Publication Data is available.

ISBN 1-58023-099-7

10 9 8 7 6 5 4 3 2 1

Manufactured in the United States of America

Design: Tina R. Malaney
Cover Illustration: Susan Gross

Published by JEWISH LIGHTS Publishing
A Division of LongHill Partners, Inc.
Sunset Farm Offices, Route 4
P.O. Box 237
Woodstock, VT 05091
Tel: (802) 457-4000   Fax: (802) 457-4004
www.jewishlights.com

CONTENTS

FOREWORD

Moonbeams is intended for anyone who wants to engage in the historic Jewish practice of text study, either individually or together with a Jewish women's group. As its title suggests, *Moonbeams* is especially intended for groups that meet on the festival of the new moon, Rosh H̲odesh. Over the past few decades, women's Rosh H̲odesh groups have sprung up all over the United States.

Moonbeams also provides a course of study for adult women who are currently preparing for a bat mitzvah ceremony in their congregations or at a Hadassah Conference. The book is especially recommended for women who have already participated in an adult bat mitzvah ceremony and are now seeking to continue their Jewish education. In 1996 Hadassah sponsored its first bat mitzvah ceremony, and made Jewish study a requirement for all bat mitzvah candidates. The *Moonbeams* study guide is the second volume of a Jewish woman's educational trilogy that began in 1997 with *Jewish Women Living the Challenge*. That book was a compendium of essays on areas of particular interest to Jewish women, accompanied by discussion questions and suggested activities. It explored abortion, breast cancer, aging, interfaith marriage, and contemporary Jewish women's rituals, among many other issues. The third volume of the trilogy will examine Jewish liturgy, and will focus especially on Jewish women's prayer.

Contemporary women's Rosh H̲odesh groups typically gather to pray together and to explore women's spiritual qualities within Judaism. Hadassah's Jewish Education Department, however, has prepared

Moonbeams as nine months of Jewish text study, because we hope that you and your women's group will combine study with Rosh Hodesh prayer. To enable you to do so more easily, Appendix A provides outlines for typical Rosh Hodesh weekday services as well as supplementary readings from the Bible and from Jewish women's poetry, with suggestions on incorporating the readings into a morning Rosh Hodesh service.

Many of the issues explored in *Moonbeams* have particular urgency and relevance among Orthodox women, for example, women's hair covering and modest clothing, women wearing *tallit* and *tefillin*, newly observant Orthodox women. While most readers of *Moonbeams* will not consider themselves Orthodox, the authors and editor seek to raise awareness of some of the issues that remain controversial among Orthodox feminists. In addition, many Jews view Orthodoxy as a world apart. We believe it is important for our readers to gain access to that world and better understand it. (The next book of Hadassah's trilogy, focusing on Jewish liturgy, will explore gender language in traditional Hebrew prayers and in modern translations and adaptations, and will consequently highlight key feminist developments in the non-Orthodox denominations.) It is also our hope that through the study of issues still raging in Orthodox Judaism, readers of all denominational affiliations will acquire insight into their own Jewish practice and thought. To enable readers to learn more about the issues presented in *Moonbeams*, Appendix B provides a list of recommended books.

THE JEWISH MONTHS

The *Moonbeams* course of study is designed to begin during Tishrei, shortly after the High Holidays, and then to meet every Rosh Hodesh until the month of Sivan (around May). The topics for each of the nine chapters often reflect some aspect of the month.

1. Tishrei: The History and Observance of Rosh Hodesh. The introductory chapter looks at the significance of Rosh Hodesh as a women's holiday. This month's study is an introduction and a new beginning, appropriate for Tishrei, which begins with the celebration of the new year. (Rosh Hodesh Tishrei coincides with Rosh Hashanah, and is not observed as a separate holiday.)

2. Heshvan: *Kippah, Tallit, and Tefillin.* Rosh Hodesh Heshvan gives the group its first opportunity to pray together on the new month. Consequently, *Moonbeams* examines Jewish prayer garments and their use by women.

3. Kislev: Modesty. The third chapter analyzes the ideal of modesty in Jewish literary sources, looking at two aspects of this ideal: humility and bodily privacy.

4. Tevet: Jewish Self-Hatred. Rosh H̲odesh Tevet occurs on the seventh day of H̲anukkah, the festival commemorating the triumph of Judaism in a civil war among Jews. This chapter's investigation of Jewish self-hatred illuminates the phenomenon of Jews who hate themselves and who consequently fear and hate other Jews.

5. Shevat: Medical Ethics. The holiday of Tu B'Shevat (the 15th of Shevat) celebrates the new year of the trees and has become a time for Jews to reflect upon the preservation of the natural environment. On Rosh H̲odesh Shevat, *Moonbeams* probes Jewish ethical issues related to fertility drugs, surrogate motherhood, cloning, and autopsies—a few of the ways in which humankind has recently harnessed nature's power.

6. Adar: Claiming a Jewish Feminist Heritage. In the month to come, Jews celebrate Purim, and on Rosh H̲odesh *Moonbeams* explores the personalities of three proto-feminists and one actual feminist: Miriam of the Torah, Vashti of the Scroll of Esther (the Purim story), Beruriah of the Talmud, and the contemporary author Letty Cottin Pogrebin.

7. Nisan: *Ba'alot Teshuvah.* Passover falls on the 15th of Nisan, and it celebrates the redemption of the Hebrew slaves from bondage. In the seventh chapter, *Moonbeams* presents stories of Jewish women who join the Orthodox Jewish community as adults, many of whom believe that they have been redeemed from the bondage of nihilism and cynicism.

8. Iyar: Women and Israeli Law. Israel's Independence Day is celebrated on the 5th of Iyar, so this month's celebration of Rosh H̲odesh is a great time to learn more about the Jewish State. *Moonbeams* examines landmark Israeli Supreme Court cases on women's issues.

9. Sivan: Women Rabbis. Shavuot, the festival of the giving of the Torah, is celebrated on the 6th of Sivan. On Rosh H̲odesh Sivan, *Moonbeams* honors women whose love for the Torah has led to their ordination as rabbis.

Although many of the *Moonbeams* topics are based upon themes related to the Hebrew months, the guide will be valuable when the chapters are studied in any order at all. When using the guide as part of a Rosh H̲odesh study group, however, the authors and editor recommend that you begin with chapter 1, regardless of the month in which you first meet. After your first session, skip to the chapter that corresponds to the Hebrew month in which your second meeting occurs.

On a related note, many chapters have enough material to occupy a study group for two months, so that study groups who wish to do so could certainly hold a meeting every month of the Jewish year. The authors and editor encourage the facilitator (perhaps in consultation with group members) to use her own judgment on the order of chapters, as correlation with monthly themes will be more difficult.

We offer one suggestion for adapting the curriculum to correspond to twelve months. Study chapter 2, "*Kippah, Tallit,* and *Tefillin*" in both <u>H</u>eshvan and Kislev, and then study chapter 3, "Modesty" on Rosh <u>H</u>odesh Tevet, which occurs during Hanukkah. Just as Hanukkah celebrates the preservation of Judaism in the ancient world, so the distinctive dress code of Orthodox women preserves their Jewish identity in the modern world. Study chapter 6, "Claiming a Jewish Feminist Heritage," in both Adar (Miriam and Vashti) and Nisan (Beruriah and Letty Cottin Pogrebin). Passover, occurring in Nisan, connects generation to generation as we retell the story of the exodus. By learning about our foremothers, we connect to earlier generations of Jewish women. Study chapter 9, "Women Rabbis," in both Sivan and Tammuz. During the month of Tammuz, we read the weekly Torah portion of Pin<u>h</u>as, which includes the story of the five daughters of Zelophe<u>h</u>ad (Numbers 27:1–8). Women rabbis, like the biblical daughters of Zelophe<u>h</u>ad, have protested injustice against women. Study chapter 4, "Jewish Self-Hatred," during Av, the month in which we mourn the destruction of the First and Second Temple in Jerusalem. Finally, study chapter 7, "*Ba'alot Teshuvah,*" during Elul, the month in which we spiritually prepare for the High Holidays. Just as we focus on *teshuvah*, repentance and atonement, during Elul, *ba'alot teshuvah* repent their former secular way of life and atone through intensive study of Jewish tradition.

For additional suggestions of monthly themes, recommendations on how to start a study group, or other assistance with the *Moonbeams* curriculum, please feel free to contact the National Jewish Education Department of Hadassah (50 West 58 Street, New York, NY 10019; 212-303-8167; jewisheducation@hadassah.org).

TRANSLITERATION AND THE PRONUNCIATION OF HEBREW

Many Hebrew words and phrases, written with the English alphabet, are included in *Moonbeams*. In transliterating, the Hadassah Jewish Education Department generally follows the practice of the *Encyclopaedia Judaica*. The list below indicates the pronunciation of transliterated Hebrew.

a	father or mama	kh	"ch" as the Scottish word loch
e	celebrate		or the German name Bach
ei	weight	<u>h</u>	"ch" as the Scottish word loch
i	magazine		or the German name Bach
o	stone	tz	ts as in hats
u	Ruth or blue		

(All other letters have the same pronunciations in Hebrew as in English.)

FOOTNOTES

Moonbeams includes footnotes as well as notes placed at the end of each chapter. Notes placed at the bottom of a page are intended to aid the reader in understanding. Notes placed at the end of a chapter indicate the sources of citations.

ACKNOWLEDGMENTS

I am indebted to many people for their contributions to *Moonbeams: A Rosh Hodesh Guide*.

Thank you to the authors Leora Tanenbaum, Claudia Chernov, and Hadassah Tropper. Not only did they write, research, and compile the lively and readable material, but they prepared questions for discussion, suggested activities, and obtained permissions to reprint or to translate. I would particularly like to thank Claudia Chernov, who served as senior editor, and who, in the tradition of the Jewish Education Department, emphasized primary sources, historical analysis, and a broad view of American Jewish life.

I also gratefully acknowledge Cantor Elizabeth S. Berke, one of the *madrikhot* of the Hadassah Leadership Academy, whom I met at a Southern California retreat in May 1999. She wrote the detailed outlines for Rosh Hodesh *ma'ariv*, *shaharit*, and *minhah* services, and offered discerning advice on instructions for prayer groups.

Rachel Schwartz, Jewish Education manager and production editor, deserves special thanks for bringing this work from computer files to bound book. She worked closely with the designer and the Creative Services Department on the cover and on every aspect of the publication, and she also organized and oversaw all proofreading. Debi Averbach, project manager for Jewish Education, Elissa Groskin, administrative assistant, Eda Greenbaum, project manager for *Al Galgalim,* and Miriam Miller, librarian, read the entire text and saved us from many errors. I am grateful to the Jewish Education Department staff for their many insightful comments on the material.

In preparing the work, the Jewish Education Department of Hadassah used the expert talents of Michael Cohen, director of Hadassah's Creative Services Department, Tina Malaney, who designed the study guide, Susan Gross, who illustrated the cover, and Deb Meisels, who proofread the work. Their efforts have helped to make *Moonbeams* inspirational and attractive.

The Jewish Education Department is thrilled to be working with Jewish Lights Publishing in our efforts to reach beyond Hadassah's membership to the broader Jewish community.

Finally, I wish to acknowledge Barbara B. Spack, the past Jewish

Education chair who helped us shape the book, and Sandra King, the current Jewish Education chair, whose support, encouragement, insight, and understanding sustain all of us in the Department.

Carol Diament, Ph.D., Editor

THE HISTORY AND OBSERVANCE OF ROSH HODESH

I am sitting in synagogue on a Shabbat morning, in part savoring the peaceful pause from a hectic week, in part worrying that I don't have enough cholent* to serve everyone at lunch. The people sitting nearby are whispering in quiet conversation, keeping an eye out to make sure that the rabbi doesn't notice them. The Torah and *Haftarah* readings are over and we have just recited the Aramaic transitional prayer *Yekum Purkan*. I am looking forward to the next few minutes, when we will return the Torah to the ark and meditatively recite the silent *Amidah* of the *musaf*** service. But wait! Why isn't the cantor launching into the singsong *Ashrei*? What is going on? All of a sudden the realization hits: Rosh Hodesh, the mini-festival that marks each month's new moon, is coming up this week. That means that we recite an additional prayer today: *Birkat HaHodesh*.

Rosh Hodesh is a symbol of renewal. At the end of its monthly cycle, the moon becomes visually obliterated, only to re-appear as a tiny, luminous sliver of light as it commences a fresh, new cycle. Likewise, we have the opportunity to take stock of our lives and revise our behavior, our commitments, our goals. We, too, have the power to start over.

---

*Cholent is a meat and bean mixture eaten by Jews of Ashkenazi descent on Saturday. The dish is prepared on Friday afternoon before Shabbat begins and is then placed in a slow oven until lunch on Saturday.

**Musaf is an additional selection of prayers recited on Shabbat, Pesah, Shavuot, Sukkot, Rosh Hashanah, Yom Kippur, and Rosh Hodesh. We recite *Musaf* in remembrance of the additional Temple sacrifice offered on those days.

Everyone rises; a hushed silence pervades the air. The cantor holds the Torah scroll for all to see. With pomp and fanfare, the cantor declares that a new moon will be "born" at the moment when the moon is hidden between the sun and the earth. (Six hours after the *molad*, the moon's birth, a crescent of light will reflect off of the moon, making it visible.) The cantor informs the congregation whether this Rosh Hodesh will last for one day or two. (When the preceding month is 30 days, Rosh Hodesh is observed for two days; and when the preceding month is 29 days, Rosh Hodesh is observed for one day.) The cantor is quite specific about the time of the *molad*, down to the exact *heilek* (part of a minute). (The lunar cycle is 29 days, 12 hours, and 793 *halakim*, and each *heilek* is equal to 3 and ⅓ seconds; so an entire lunar cycle is equal to 29 days, 12 hours, 44 minutes, and 3⅓ seconds). The cantor concludes the prayer by requesting that God bless the new month and grant the people of Israel life and peace, joy and gladness, deliverance and consolation. Everyone in the congregation responds, "Amen." Only then do we begin the melodious *Ashrei*.

Birkat HaHodesh is the modern commemoration of the new moon. Today, though, as feminist Judaic scholar Blu Greenberg points out, if you "randomly ask one hundred Jews about this special day that comes eleven times a year, ninety of them will offer a blank stare. There are far more Jewish bird-watchers than there are moon-watchers."[1] But in ancient times, before the Jewish lunar calendar was fixed, the sighting of the new moon was cause for grand festivity alongside grave seriousness. Since every Jewish community was obligated to observe holidays at the same time, all Jewish communities needed to agree on dates, and dates were determined based on the sighting of the new moon.

During the Second Temple period, the new month began when at least two reputable witnesses observed the first sliver of moon. The witnesses were called before the *beit din*, the rabbinic court in Jerusalem, and the judges called each witness separately to testify about the precise location and appearance of the moon. If both gave identical testimony, the *beit din* declared the arrival of Rosh Hodesh. Then sacrifices were offered and incense was burnt. Special prayers were chanted, the *shofar* was blown, and a celebratory meal was eaten. The news of the moon's appearance was communicated to Jewish communities throughout Israel and the diaspora by setting fires on the hilltops of Jerusalem, with each Jewish community that observed those fires then lighting its own fires to alert neighboring communities. Toward the end of the Second Temple period, the *beit din* instead sent messengers to outlying towns and villages to alert them of the appearance of the moon, because the Samaritans* had

---

*The Samaritans, who lived to the north of Judea, were descendants of the tribes of Israel mixed with non-Hebrew peoples. Their religion, though based in some ways

begun to deliberately set fires at incorrect times in order to mislead the Jews. By the middle of the fourth century, the rabbis had established a fixed calendar, and the examination before the *beit din* and the sending of messengers to publicly proclaim the new moon was discontinued.

Today we enjoy no festive meal nor do we blow the *shofar* on Rosh Hodesh. We do, however, continue to celebrate Rosh Hodesh with prayer. Besides reciting *Birkat HaHodesh* on the preceding Saturday, we recite a special *musaf* service on Rosh Hodesh itself. In addition, the *Kiddush Levanah* (sanctification of the moon) ceremony takes place outdoors on a clear night soon after Rosh Hodesh (usually on the first Saturday night that follows). We observe the new moon festival eleven times a year; we don't celebrate Rosh Hodesh for the month of *Tishrei*, which coincides with Rosh Hashanah, since the new year celebration incorporates the new month.

God first commanded us to observe the new moon just as we were ready to flee from the enslavement of Egypt. Rabbi Samson Raphael Hirsch, the nineteenth-century German scholar, noted that since we would soon be liberated from slavery, we could appreciate the moon's emergence from darkness to light. Through the moon's renewal, God is telling the people of Israel: "This is to be the model for your own conduct! Even as the moon renews itself by the law of nature, so you, too, should renew yourselves, but of your own free will."[2] God also commanded us to count the months, so that we could always calculate the amount of time that our people have been free.

Rosh Hodesh has long been considered a special holiday for women. There are a number of reasons. First, according to legend, the holiday was a reward given to the women of Israel because they refused to surrender their jewelry for the creation of the golden calf. Because of their righteousness, the women were exonerated from working on Rosh Hodesh. Second, many people have pointed out that the menstrual cycle is similar to the monthly cycle of the moon. (The English word "menstruation" derives from the Latin word for "monthly.") Third, Penina Adelman, author of the first modern Rosh Hodesh ritual guide for women, points out that the words *Roshei HodshiM*, heads of the months, contain the same letters that form the word *ReHeM*, womb.[3]

Fourth, the status of the moon has often been compared to the status of women. The Talmud recounts a legend that the moon and the sun were originally of equal size and brightness, but the moon asked how two could rule equally; God responded by making the moon smaller. In

upon Judaism, was distinct and separate. When the Jews returned from Babylonia in 537 to rebuild the Temple, they barred the Samaritans, whose influence they feared, from assisting them. As a result, the Samaritans became hostile to the Jews and often tried to sabotage Jewish religious observances.

ancient texts, woman likewise has a lesser status and is subservient to man. Furthermore, the *Zohar*, the authoritative work of the mystical tradition, frequently likens the moon to the *Shekhinah*, the Divine Presence, which mystics consider the feminine aspect of God.[4] Only when the world is redeemed will the *Shekhinah* reunite with the masculine aspect, the *Kadosh Barukh Hu*, the Holy One Blessed is He, and only then will the moon's light intensify.[5]

Rosh Hodesh has long been sacred to women. From the sixteenth to the early twentieth century, the women of Eastern Europe wrote special Rosh Hodesh *tekhines*—personal prayers in the Yiddish vernacular. Over the past three decades, Rosh Hodesh observance has been revived by religious feminists. The book *Miriam's Well: Rituals for Jewish Women Around the Year* by Penina Adelman, first published in 1986, presented the experiences of one of the first women's Rosh Hodesh groups, and provided a template for creative Rosh Hodesh rituals. Adelman describes, for example, an "anointing ritual ... which invokes the messiah in each individual"; creating a small model of the gallows so that participants can hang "the Hamans of women's lives—sexual harassment, low pay, the beauty industry"; and "group wailing" to recall the wailing women in the Book of Jeremiah.[6] In addition to feminist groups focusing on personal spiritual growth, like those that began in the seventies, a wide variety of Jewish women—feminist and non-feminist—now meet to celebrate Rosh Hodesh. Some groups are sponsored by synagogues, others by non-denominational organizations, and a few meet independently. Activities range from reciting the traditional liturgy and sharing a meal to discussing Jewish ethics and working for social change. Some groups, like those following Hadassah's *Moonbeams* guide, set aside Rosh Hodesh for Jewish study.

by Leora Tanenbaum

THE MOON AND ROSH HODESH IN JEWISH LITERATURE

Genesis 1:14-18

In the first Book of the Bible we read of the creation of the moon.

God said, "Let there be lights in the expanse of the sky to separate day from night; they shall serve as signs for the set times—the days and the years; and they shall serve as lights in the expanse of the sky to shine upon the earth." And it was so. God made the two great lights, the greater light to dominate the day and the lesser light to dominate the night, and the stars. And God set them in the expanse of the sky to shine upon the earth, to dominate the day and the night, and to separate light from darkness. And God saw that this was good.

Exodus 12:1-2

Immediately prior to the exodus from Egypt, God commands the Israelites to mark the months of the year.

The Lord said to Moses and Aaron in the land of Egypt: This month shall mark for you the beginning of the months; it shall be the first of the months of the year for you.

Numbers 10:10

The Book of Numbers briefly describes the celebration of Rosh Hodesh.

And on your joyous occasions—your fixed festivals and new moon days—you shall sound the trumpets over your burnt offerings and your sacrifices of well-being. They shall be a reminder of you before your God: I, the Lord, am your God.

Numbers 28:11-15

This passage from the Book of Numbers is chanted during the traditional synagogue morning service each Rosh Hodesh.

On your new moons you shall present a burnt offering to the Lord: two bulls of the herd, one ram, and seven yearling lambs, without blemish. As meal offering for each bull: three-tenths of a measure of choice flour with oil mixed in. As meal offering for each ram: two-tenths of a measure of choice flour with oil mixed in. As meal offering for each lamb: a tenth of a measure of fine flour with oil mixed in. Such shall be the burnt offering of pleasing odor, an offering by fire to the Lord. Their libations shall be: half a hin* of wine for a bull, a third of a hin for a ram, and a quarter of a hin for a lamb. That shall be the monthly burnt offering for each new moon of the year. And there shall be one goat as a sin offering to the Lord, to be offered in addition to the regular burnt offering and its libation.

Mishnah, Rosh Hashanah 2.2-4

The Mishnah describes how torches were lit to provide notification of the sighting of the new moon.

Originally they used to light beacons (to convey the news of the new moon to the Jews in the diaspora of Babylonia). When the Cutheans (Samaritans) adopted evil courses (and lit beacons on the thirtieth day, so as to mislead the Jews in Babylonia), they made a rule that messengers should go forth. How did they light the beacons? They used to bring long poles of cedar and reeds and olive wood and flax fluff which they tied to the poles with a string, and someone used to go up to the top of a mountain and set fire to them and wave them to and fro and up and down until he saw the next one doing the same thing on the top of the second

---

*A hin is estimated as the equivalent of six quarts.

mountain; and so on the top of the third mountain. Whence did they carry the chain of beacons? From the mount of Olives in Jerusalem to Sartaba, and from Sartaba to Grofina, and from Grofina to Hauran, and from Hauran to Beth Baltin. The one on Beth Baltin did not budge from there but went on waving to and fro and up and down until he saw the whole of the diaspora (the district of Pumbedita in Babylonia) before him like one bonfire. (On seeing the beacon fire, the inhabitants used to light torches.)

Babylonian Talmud, *Sanhedrin 42a*

The Talmud associates Rosh Ḥodesh observance with the Shekhinah, *the Divine Presence.*

Rabbi Aḥa ben Ḥanina also said in the name of Rabbi Assi in Rabbi Yoḥanan's name: Whoever pronounces the benediction over the new moon in its due time welcomes, as it were, the presence of the *Shekhinah*. For one passage states, "This month" (Exodus 12:2) while elsewhere it is said, "This is my God, and I will glorify Him" (Exodus 15:2). ["This" here connotes something that could be pointed at with one's finger, and the use of "this" in the two verses suggests that the one who praises God at the periodic renewal of the moon, gives witness to the revelation of divine glory as manifested in natural phenomena.]

Babylonian Talmud, *Ḥullin 60b*

The Talmud recounts a legend of the moon becoming smaller than the sun.

Rabbi Shimon ben Pazzi pointed out a contradiction [in the account of the creation of the sun and moon]. One verse says, "God made the two great lights" (Genesis 1:16), and immediately the verse continues, "The greater light ... and the lesser light." The moon said unto the Holy One, blessed be He, "Sovereign of the Universe! Is it possible for two kings to wear one crown?" He answered, "Go then and make yourself smaller." "Sovereign of the Universe!" cried the moon. "Because I have suggested that which is proper must I then make myself smaller?" He replied, "Go and you will rule by day and by night." "But what is the value of this?" cried the moon. "Of what use is a lamp in broad daylight?" He replied, "Go. By you, Israel shall reckon the days and the years." "But it is impossible," said the moon, "to do without the sun for the reckoning of the seasons, as it is written, 'They shall serve as signs for the set times—the days and the years' (Genesis 1:14)." "Go. The righteous shall be named after you [righteous people shall be named "the Small" after the moon, which had become the small light] as we find, Jacob the Small, Samuel the Small, David the Small.* On seeing that it

---

* Jacob the Small, from Amos 7:2—"How shall Jacob stand? For he is small." Samuel the Small was a renowned first-century rabbi of the Mishnah, called "the Small"

would not be consoled, the Holy One, Blessed be He, said, "Bring an atonement for Me making the moon smaller." This is what was meant by Rabbi Shimon ben Lakish when he declared, "Why is it that the male goat offered on the new moon is distinguished in that there is written concerning it 'unto the Lord' (Numbers 28:15)? Because the Holy One, Blessed be He, said, 'Let this male goat be an atonement for Me for making the moon smaller.'"

Midrash, *Pirkei deRabbi Eliezer* 45 (circa 750)

Pirkei deRabbi Eliezer *recounts legends from the time of Creation until the wanderings of the children of Israel in the desert.*

The women heard about the construction of the golden calf and refused to submit their jewelry to their husbands. Instead they said to them: "You want to construct an idol and mask which is an abomination, and has no power of redemption? We won't listen to you." And the Holy One, Blessed be He, rewarded them in this world in that they would observe the new moons more than men, and in the next world in that they are destined to be renewed like the new moons.

Midrash, *Exodus Rabbah* 15:6 (900–1000)

Exodus Rabbah *is an exegetical and homiletic work on the Book of Exodus compiled in the years 900–1000, including material from much earlier periods.*

You find that if the moon does not appear in the sky at night, the world is so dark that a man cannot walk about even within the city, but as soon as the moon appears in the sky, all rejoice and walk about. So it was in the days of Ahasuerus who decreed that Israel should be destroyed, slain, and made to perish; but Esther came and brought light to Israel, for it says, "The Jews had light and gladness, and joy and honor" (Esther 8:16).... Should you inquire why Esther is compared to the moon, the answer is that just as the moon renews itself every thirty days, so did Esther say, "But I have not been called to come in unto the king these thirty days" (Esther 4:11).

Midrash, *Exodus Rabbah* 15:9 (900–1000)

The rabbis of Exodus Rabbah *comment on the commandment in Exodus 12:2 to mark the months.*

We may illustrate by the parable of a king unto whom a son was born, whereupon he made a joyful celebration; but the son was taken captive and spent a long time in captivity. On his release, the king fixed

---

because of his humility. David the Small, from I Samuel 17:4 — "And David was the smallest [youngest]."

an anniversary. So, too, prior to Israel's descent into Egypt, they counted by years; but after they had gone down to Egypt and become enslaved there, God performed miracles for them, and they were redeemed; and then did they begin to count the months, as it says, "This month shall mark for you the beginning of the months" (Exodus 12:2).

Rashi (1040-1105) on Babylonian Talmud, Megillah 22b

Rashi, Rabbi Solomon ben Isaac of France, is the foremost commentator on the Bible and on the Talmud. Here he discusses a passage from the Talmud about the public reading of the Torah on weekdays, holidays, and new moons.

"New months." There is no absolute prohibition against work, yet women do not perform work on those days.... I learned from my aged teacher, may his memory be for a blessing, that this commandment was given to them [women] because they did not submit their jewelry for the golden calf.

Tosafot on Babylonian Talmud, *Megillah* 22b (12th to 14th centuries)

The Tosafot (literally additions) are commentaries to the Talmud, as well as commentaries to Rashi's Talmud commentaries, written in medieval France and Germany. In commenting on Rashi's notes on Megillah *22b, the Tosafists (authors of the Tosafot) repeat the passage on women and the new month from* Pirkei deRabbi Eliezer, *chapter 45. In commenting on the Talmud passage about the public reading of the Torah, the Tosafists use even stronger language than Rashi on women's observance of Rosh Hodesh.*

"And when there was no prohibition against work as on new months, four read." ... There is no requirement that we celebrate. It is said that on Rosh Hodesh an additional sacrifice is required, yet performing work is permitted.... It is permitted that men work, but women are forbidden to work because they did not submit their jewelry in the making of the golden calf.

Zohar Bereishit, pages 19b-20a (circa 1300)

The Zohar, the Book of Splendor, is the central work of Kabbalah, Jewish mysticism. The main portion of the Zohar is a symbolic interpretation of the Five Books of Moses. To non-initiates much of the Zohar is obscure, as the great scholar of Jewish mysticism Gershom Scholem observes, "It is hardly possible at first contact with the world of kabbalistic symbolism to escape a sense of bewilderment."[7] The Zohar gives each word of Torah layers of meaning above and beyond the literal meaning, thereby enriching and deepening Jewish religious dedication. The Zohar attempts to penetrate the nature of God through a complex system of correspondences between the created world and the divine.

In addition to esoteric knowledge that enables the Jew to spiritually perceive the nature of God, the Zohar includes material from earlier legends, allegories, and homilies. The selections below discuss the female demons Lilith and Naamah, and their connection with the new moon.

"God said, 'Let there be lights'" (Genesis 1:14). The word for "lights" (*meorot*) is written defectively, as if curses (*me'erot*), for the reason that the children's disease, croup, was through them created. For after the primordial light was withdrawn there was created a "membrane for the marrow," a *klifah*, and this *klifah* expanded and produced another. As soon as this second one came forth she went up and down till she reached the "little faces" [the cherubim residing in Heaven]. She desired to cleave to them and to be shaped as one of them, and was loath to depart from them. But the Holy One, Blessed be He, removed her from them and made her go below. When He created Adam and gave him a partner, as soon as she saw Eve clinging to his side and was reminded by his form of the supernal beauty, she flew up from thence and tried as before to attach herself to the "little faces." The supernal guardians of the gates, however, did not permit her. The Holy One, Blessed be He, chid her and cast her into the depths of the sea, where she abode until the time that Adam and his wife sinned. Then the Holy One, Blessed be He, brought her out from the depth of the sea and gave her power over all those children, the "little faces" of the sons of men, who are liable to punishment for the sins of their fathers. She then wandered up and down the world. She approached the gates of the terrestrial paradise, where she saw the cherubim, the guardians of the gates of Paradise, and sat down near the flashing sword, to which she was akin in origin. When she saw the flashing sword revolving, she fled and wandered about the world and, finding children liable to punishment, she maltreated and killed them. All this is on account of the action of the moon in diminishing her light. When Cain was born this *klifah* tried for a time without success to attach herself to him, but at length she had intercourse with him and bore spirits and demons. Adam for a hundred and thirty years had intercourse with female spirits until Naamah was born. She by her beauty led astray the "sons of God," Uzza and Azael, and she bore them children, and so from her went forth evil spirits and demons into the world. She wanders about at nighttime, vexing the sons of men and causing them to defile themselves. Wherever these spirits find people sleeping alone in a house, they hover over them, lay hold of them and cleave to them, inspire desire in them and beget from them. They further inflict diseases on them without their being aware—all this through the diminution of the moon. When the moon was restored, the letters of *meorot* (lights) were reversed to form *imrat* (word), as it is written, "the word (*imrat*) of the Lord is pure, He is a shield to all who seek refuge in

Him" (Psalms 18:31). That means, He is a shield against all those evil spirits and demons that wander about the world at the waning of the moon, unto those who hold fast to their faith in the Holy One, Blessed be He....

When the moon was in connection with the sun, she was luminous, but as soon as she separated from the sun and was assigned the charge of her own hosts, she reduced her status and her light.

"God made the two great lights" (Genesis 1:16). The word "made" signifies the due expansion and establishment of the whole. The words "the two great lights" show that at first they were associated as equals, symbolizing the full name Tetragrammaton Elohim*.... The word "great" shows that at their creation they were dignified with the same name [and] ascended together with the same dignity. The moon, however, was not at ease with the sun, and in fact each felt mortified by the other. The moon said, "Where do you pasture your sheep?" (Song of Songs 1:7). The sun said, "Where do you rest them at noon? (Song of Songs 1:7) How can a little candle shine at midday?" God thereupon said to her, "Go and diminish yourself." She felt humiliated and said, "Let me not be as one who veils herself" (Song of Songs 1:7). God then said "Go follow the tracks of the sheep" (Song of Songs 1:8). Thereupon she diminished herself so as to be head of the lower ranks. From that time she has had no light of her own, but derives her light from the sun. At first they were on an equality, but afterwards she diminished herself among all those grades of hers, although she is still head of them; for a woman enjoys no honor save in conjunction with her husband. The "great light" corresponds to Tetragrammaton, and the "lesser light" to Elohim, which is the last of the degrees and the close of the Thought....

It is fit and proper that two lights should rule, the greater light by day and the lesser light by night. The lesson we derive is that the male rules by day to regulate his household and to bring food and sustenance into it. When night arrives, the female takes command, and she rules the house, as it is written, "She rises while it is still night and supplies provisions for her household" (Proverbs 31:15)—she and not he. Thus the dominion of the day belongs to the male and the dominion of the night to the female. Further it is written, "and the stars"(Genesis 1:16). As soon as the wife has given her orders and retired with her husband, the direction of the house is left to the maidens, who remain in the house to look after all its requirements. Then when day comes the man again duly takes command.

---

* The four letters *yod-hei-vav-hei* constitute the Tetragrammaton. When reciting prayers or reading Scripture, the Tetragrammaton is pronounced Adonai.

Zohar Bereishit, page 169b (circa 1300)

Now on the fourth day the lights were created; but the moon was created without light, since she diminished herself. This is implied in the phrase "Let there be lights," wherein the term *meorot* (lights) is written defectively (minus the letter *vav*), as if it were *me'erot* (curses); for as a result of the moon's diminution, occasion was granted to all spirits and demons and hurricanes and devils to exercise sway, so that all unclean spirits rise up and traverse the world seeking whom to seduce; they haunt ruined places, thick forests, and deserts. These are all from the side of the unclean spirit, which, as has been said, issues from the crooked serpent, who is, indeed, the veritable unclean spirit, and whose mission is to seduce man.... Should a man strive to purify himself, the unclean spirit is foiled and can no longer dominate him. Thus it is written: "No evil will befall you, no plague will come into your tent" (Psalms 91:10). Rabbi Yose said: "'Evil' here alludes to Lilith, and 'the plague' to the other demons, as has been explained elsewhere." Rabbi Eleazar said: "It has been taught that a man should not go out alone at night, and especially when the time of the creation of the moon recurs and it is without light. For at that time the unclean spirit, which is the same as the evil spirit, is at large."

Zohar Vayikra, page 77a (circa 1300)

Sometimes it happens that Naamah goes forth to have intercourse with men and a man is linked with her in lust, and then suddenly wakes and clasps his wife though his mind is still full of the lust of his dream. In that case the son so born is of the side of Naamah, and when Lilith goes forth she sees him and knows what has happened, and brings him up like the other children of Naamah, and he is often with her, and she does not kill him. This is the man who receives a blemish on every new moon. For Lilith never gives them up, but at every new moon she goes forth and visits all those whom she has brought up and makes sport with them; hence this man receives a blemish at that time.

Sefer Hemdat Yamim 1:23b-24a (18th century)

This anonymous work of homiletics and ethics draws upon the Kabbalah.

Women should appreciate the glorious, majestic splendor of the day, in that they observe Rosh Hodesh more than men. Although it is proper for them to completely refrain from work because of their refusal to join the men in the sin of the Golden Calf, there is no actual prohibition of work, as on a holiday, so as not to embarrass the men. Women of every rank and status must observe the day.[8]

Siddur Sim Shalom (1985)

The Hebrew prayer recited on the Sabbath immediately prior to Rosh Hodesh dates to the medieval era. Rabbi Jules Harlow composed the following English translation.

May it be Your will, Lord our God and God of our ancestors, to renew our lives in the coming month. Grant us a long life, a peaceful life with goodness and blessing, sustenance and physical vitality, a life informed by purity and piety, a life free from shame and reproach, a life of abundance and honor, a life embracing piety and love of Torah, a life in which our heart's desires for goodness will be fulfilled.

Questions for Discussion

1. Do you believe that God was justified in diminishing the moon? Is the light that rules at night necessarily of lesser value than the light that rules at day? How did God make amends to the moon? Was the payment adequate?

2. Do you regard the moon as possessing feminine traits and the sun as possessing masculine traits? Why? Why does the Talmud say that the *Shekhinah*, the Divine Presence, is present during the celebration of the new moon?

3. Why did God give the people of Israel the festival of the new month on the eve of the exodus from Egypt? Would giving the holiday when the Israelites received the Torah or entered the promised land have been more appropriate? Why?

4. What is the importance of counting lunar months as opposed to, say, periods of 90 days or 120 days?

5. Why did the Jews of the Second Temple era light fires on Rosh Hodesh? How did they do it?

6. How was Esther similar to the moon?

7. Why did the women of Israel refuse to participate in the creation of the Golden Calf? Is their reward a fitting recognition?

8. The Rabbis have encouraged women to refrain from work on Rosh Hodesh. Do you know anyone who refrains from work on Rosh Hodesh? Would you consider refraining from work?

9. The kabbalists believed that female spirits came out on Rosh Hodesh. Why did this idea originate? What might account for the kabbalists' fear of the new moon? What might account for the kabbalists' fear of female demons?

10. The *Zohar* presents a sexual dualism extending from domestic life to the celestial world to the nature of the divine itself. Discuss.

11. Consider the negative attitudes toward women found in the selections from the *Zohar*. Can Jewish women today reclaim this work of

Kabbalah? If yes, how? Consider the allegorical and mythical accounts of demons in the selections. What allegorical accounts might women compose today?

12. Over the past two decades, Rosh Hodesh groups have sprung up throughout the United States. Should these groups be for women only? Should they be primarily for women? Many Rosh Hodesh groups involve the creation of new rituals and the recital of original benedictions. How do you feel about such innovations? Is Rosh Hodesh an appropriate venue for new rituals?

Suggested Activities and Programs

1. Have all group members close their eyes. Ask: How did the people of Israel celebrate Rosh Hodesh during the time of the Second Temple? If you were an artist, how would you portray the celebrations? Go around the room and have everyone offer her vision. As a group, create a picture of ancient Rosh Hodesh celebrations on poster board. Use ink, charcoal, paint, or any other material with which you feel comfortable.

2. Jane Litman, Judith Glass, and Simone Wallace write:

> The division of symbolic inanimate objects into binary gender roles is unfortunate. The explicit association of men with the sun and women with the moon and the hierarchical positioning of the former over the latter are misogynistic. This division is part of a dualistic way of thinking that tends to value, among other things, the male over the female, the larger over the smaller, rich over poor, youth over age, and day over night.[9]

Debate this opinion. Does it make sense to liken the moon to femininity and the sun to masculinity? Divide the group into two: those who support the contention of Litman, Glass, and Wallace, and those who oppose it. Ask each side to consider the implications of its assigned position. Allow ten minutes for both sides to discuss their rationale, then have each side appoint a spokeswoman to debate.

---

1. Blu Greenberg, Foreword to *Celebrating the New Moon: A Rosh Chodesh Anthology*, ed. Susan Berrin (Northvale, NJ: Jason Aronson, 1996), page xiv.

2. See the translation of Exodus 12:2 and Hirsch's comments on this verse in Samson Raphael Hirsch, *The Pentateuch* (New York: Judaica Press, 1986), page 250. Cited in Susan Berrin, Introduction to *Celebrating the New Moon*, page xxii.

3. Penina Adelman, *Miriam's Well: Rituals for Jewish Women Around the Year*, 2nd ed. (New York: Biblio, 1990), page 94.

4. *Zohar Shemot* 2, pages 51b, 125b, 138a, 143a, 144b, 145b.

5. Refer to Gershom G. Scholem, *Major Trends in Jewish Mysticism* (New York: Schocken, 1961; originally published 1941), pages 229–235, for a discussion of sexual dualism in the *Zohar*.

6. Penina Adelman, *Miriam's Well,* pages 29, 65, and 42.

7. Gershom G. Scholem, *Major Trends in Jewish Mysticism,* page 212.

8. Translated by Arlene Agus, "Examining Rosh Chodesh: An Analysis of the Holiday and Its Textual Sources," in *Celebrating the New Moon,* page 7.

9. Jane Litman, Judith Glass, and Simone Wallace, "Rosh Chodesh: A Feminist Critique and Reconstruction" in *Celebrating the New Moon,* page 24.

KIPPAH, TALLIT, AND TEFILLIN

It was a fine Spring Shabbat morning, and I burst into my Orthodox *shul* (synagogue), breathless after walking the half-mile from home at a rapid pace so as to arrive before the Torah portion. I maneuvered my way through the rows of high heels, silk blouses, and tailored skirts, murmuring "Good *Shabbes*" to the women who looked up at me, and slid into the empty seat next to my mother. I straightened my skirt and opened my prayer book, noting that I had arrived on time.

The *shul* was particularly crowded this morning, and the two hundred seats of the women's section were almost full. I stood on my toes for a moment to peer over the *meḥitzah* (barrier that separates men and women) and find my father in the men's section so that we could share our usual wink. I laughed to myself as he winked at me. Regardless of how many people are present and how many hats block his view, my father always manages to know when I enter the *shul*.

As I lowered my eyes to begin reading from the *siddur* (prayer book), I suddenly saw something that made me sit bolt upright. It was so strange, so jarring, that I blinked just to be sure my eyes were functioning. A woman standing a few rows in front of me, swaying as she listened intently to the words of the cantor, was wearing a *tallit*, a prayer shawl! The *tallit* was draped over her shoulders and the fringes moved as she swayed, just as if she were a man!

"What is she doing? Who does she think she is?" I said to myself, feeling disturbed and angry. Never before had I seen a woman wearing a *tallit*, and it looked wrong, even sinful. "The *tallit* has only been associated

15

with men for as long as I have known," I thought, "How dare she wear it? She is violating the prohibition against women wearing men's clothing, isn't she? And if she feels that she *must* violate the prohibition, acting in a way the Bible calls abhorrent, she should at least do it in the privacy of her own home, and not in public, where she is offending her community! She cannot simply desecrate our tradition."

This took place a number of years ago, and since then I have often seen and heard about women wearing the *tallit*. I have also heard of women wearing *tefillin* (phylacteries), and I now frequently see women wearing a *kippah* (*yarmulke* in Yiddish; skullcap in English).* As women have begun learning more about the Jewish religious heritage and trying to enrich their spiritual lives, a number have begun wearing these male-identified ritual garments. I had originally thought that such women were simply pushing a feminist political agenda too far. Yet as I studied more, I came to realize that accepting any one of these precepts could be a way to increase one's involvement in prayer. Adorning oneself with the *tefillin*, fixing the box of parchment upon one's head and winding the leather straps around one's arm, or pulling the large white *tallit* over one's head can prepare the individual for prayer, giving a sense of readiness to speak to the Creator of the universe. Wearing the ritual garments has the potential to free us from mundane thought and to help us enter into a higher, more spiritual frame of mind. Putting on *tallit* and *tefillin*, and then wearing them throughout prayer, sets the tone for relating to God. Similarly, by wearing a *kippah* we acknowledge that God watches over us and therefore we are constantly reminded to behave appropriately. Thus I had come to feel a certain respect for the innovative and brave woman who wears *kippah*, *tallit*, and *tefillin*.**

Nonetheless, the key question remains unclear: Do these women's actions have a legitimate basis in Jewish law? Though I am not comfortable enough with women and *kippah*, *tallit*, or *tefillin* to wear any of these garments myself, I relish my freedom to decide differently if my future learning leads me in a different direction. I firmly believe that each woman must decide these important issues for herself. Certainly, no Jewish woman should reject *kippah*, *tallit*, or *tefillin* simply because of ignorance.

by Hadassah Tropper

---

* While writing this essay, I was a student at Barnard College, which is located near the Jewish Theological Seminary, the rabbinic school and academic center of Conservative Judaism.

** My initial hostility arose, in part, because of fear of change. An example of such fear is the impassioned hostility of the members of my synagogue to the rabbi's suggestion that the Torah scroll be passed to the women's section before being replaced in the Ark. Even though Jewish law permits it, the idea was so new that a majority of men and women—without any research or study—opposed it.

KIPPAH

Covering the head symbolizes that God is above us, offering us divine protection and demanding our reverence. In our era, wearing a *kippah* has become the most easily recognized sign of allegiance to Judaism. Among observant Conservative and Orthodox Jews, many men always wear a *kippah*, and many others wear a *kippah* whenever they pray, including before and after mealtimes. Earlier in the twentieth century, wearing a *kippah* was hotly debated between Reform and Orthodox Jews. Reform Jews consider covering one's head optional, and until recently most Reform men prayed bareheaded. Over the past twenty years or so, as a part of a larger revival of customs and rituals, some Reform Jewish men have begun wearing a *kippah* during prayer.

In Israel today, a Jewish man's head covering serves to distinguish the Zionist Orthodox from the *haredi* or ultra-Orthodox. Indeed, the ultra-Orthodox are often called the "black hat" because of their head coverings. (A *haredi* man wears a *kippah* underneath his black hat.) The Zionist Orthodox man is also easily recognizable because of his small, knit *kippah*.

From the seventies onward, a number of American Jewish women have begun wearing a *kippah* during prayer.* Many women wear special *kippot* (plural of *kippah*) that they have made or purchased themselves. These "feminine" *kippot* often have more intricate color patterns than usual, are more lacy in appearance, or are larger than usual, midway between a standard *kippah* and a smallish hat. Because the *kippah* has a lesser status in Jewish law than either *tallit* or *tefillin*, a Jewish woman's decision to wear a *kippah* is not subject to the same obstacles as her decision to wear *tallit* or *tefillin*. The Torah does not command Jews to wear a *kippah*. Rather, wearing the *kippah* is a custom, based on the rabbis' practices in the Talmud. Nonetheless—as we see in today's equation of male head covering with Jewish religion—custom occupies an extremely important place in religious life, even acquiring the status of law after having been in effect for generations. The Babylonian Talmud, *Baba Metzia* 86b, teaches: "One should never break away from custom. When Moses ascended to Heaven [to receive the Torah at Mount Sinai], he refrained from food; when the ministering angels descended below [to visit Abraham], they partook of his meal."

by Claudia Chernov

---

* In general, American women who choose to wear a *kippah* are members of Conservative congregations. Head covering remains optional for both men and women in Reform congregations, and though it is more common than in the past, wearing a *kippah* is not standard practice. In Orthodox congregations, women who are married do cover their heads. Married women come to synagogue wearing a hat, a scarf, or a wig (or a wig covered by a hat or scarf). Unmarried women generally pray bareheaded. The reasoning behind Jewish married women's head covering differs from the reasoning behind Jewish men's and boys' head covering, and is discussed at length in Chapter 3.

HEAD COVERING IN JEWISH LITERATURE

Deuteronomy 22:5

In the introduction to Chapter 2, Hadassah Tropper noted that a woman who wears male-identified ritual garments may be in violation of the biblical prohibition against cross-dressing.

A woman shall not put on man's apparel, nor shall a man wear woman's clothing; for whoever does these things is abhorrent to the Lord your God.*

Mishnah, Nedarim 2.7

At the time of the compilation of the Mishnah (the first two centuries of the common era), Jewish men generally wore no head covering. This practice is deduced from a passage in Nedarim *(Vows), a tractate about the swearing of vows. For instance, Mishnah* Nedarim *discusses a person who vows to abstain from eating roasted meat, a person who vows not to wear wool, and a person who vows not to enter a particular town. In chapter 2, the Sages define some of the terms commonly used when vows are sworn. Here they speak of a man who has vowed never to profit from other men. Through the explanation of the term "black haired," modern scholars deduce the lack of head covering.*

If a man vowed to have no benefit from "the black haired," he is forbidden to benefit from the bald and the gray haired, but he may benefit from women and children, because only men are called black haired.

Babylonian Talmud, Nedarim 30b

In the talmudic period (200–500), male head covering was optional, as we deduce from the Talmud's analysis of the Mishnah passage: "If a man vowed to have no benefit from 'the black haired,' he is forbidden to benefit from the bald and the gray haired."

What is the reason? Because he did not say "from those who possess hair." [Bald and gray-haired men are included in the vow, since they were once black haired.]

"But he may benefit from women and children, because only men are called black haired." What is the reason? Men sometimes cover their heads and sometimes not, but women's hair is always covered, and children are always bare headed. [Rabbi Nissim ben Reuben of Gerondi, a

---

* In *The JPS Torah Commentary: Deuteronomy* (Philadelphia: Jewish Publication Society, 1996, page 200), Jeffrey H. Tigay writes that, according to current interpretation of Jewish law, "women may not wear armor or clothing, hairdos, or other adornments that are characteristic of men, nor may men wear what is characteristic of women (what is characteristic of each sex is defined by local practice)."

fourteenth-century scholar, explains that women would be referred to as "those of covered hair" and children as "the bareheaded."]

Babylonian Talmud, *Kiddushin* 31a

Though wearing a hat was optional, some of the talmudic Sages teaching in Babylonian academies covered their heads at all times.

Rabbi Huna the son of Rabbi Joshua would not walk four cubits [six or seven feet] bareheaded, saying, the *Shekhinah* [God's presence] is above my head.

Babylonian Talmud, *Shabbat* 156b

In a lengthy passage concerning planetary influence, the Sages of the Talmud tell of Rabbi Nahman ben Isaac's mother, and today's readers learn that head covering was considered conducive to piety.

From Rabbi Nahman ben Isaac too we learn that the people of Israel are free from planetary influence. For Rabbi Nahman ben Isaac's mother was told by astrologers, "Your son will be a thief." So she did not allow him to be bareheaded, saying to him, "Cover your head so that the fear of heaven may be upon you, and pray for mercy." Now, he did not know why she said that to him. One day he was sitting and studying under a palm tree when temptation overcame him. He climbed up and bit off a cluster of dates with his teeth [though the tree did not belong to him].

Louis Ginzberg (1873–1953)

Louis Ginzberg, a principal architect of the Conservative movement, taught Talmud at the Jewish Theological Seminary from 1903 until his death. Among his responsa (answers to Jewish legal problems) is this reply to a layman's question on head covering. No mention is made here of woman's head covering.

Question: Kindly advise a layman whether it is permitted to walk bareheaded, in the street or house. If it is permissible according to Jewish laws and traditions, kindly advise us as to the source.

Answer (by Irving H. Fisher): In response to your inquiry I beg to say that I have consulted Professor Louis Ginzberg, the Chairman of our Committee on the Interpretation of Jewish Law. He stated as follows: "It is against Jewish law and custom to pray, study religious works, or perform a religious ceremony while bareheaded. Some pious men refrain from having their heads uncovered at any time, and while this is, or at least was, a widespread custom, it never was considered binding."[1]

Rabbi Ovadiah Yosef, *Yehaveh Da'at,* part 5, paragraph 55 (1976)

As we will read in the section on tallit, *one ancient text does indeed forbid women to wear both* tallit *and* tefillin *because of the prohibition against cross-dressing. That text, however, is not considered legally binding, and Jewish scholars before the modern era generally based their objections to women wearing ritual garments on entirely different grounds. This is because the rabbis have usually interpreted the biblical prohibition against cross-dressing narrowly, as does Rabbi Ovadiah Yosef (born 1920), former Sephardi Chief Rabbi of Israel. According to such a narrow interpretation, the prohibition applies to a woman who wears male clothing to resemble a man, to sexually incite a man, or to indulge in obscene behavior.*

We find according to the Bayit Hadash* ... that the prohibition of "A woman shall not put on man's apparel" (Deuteronomy 22:5) is applicable only to an object that is meant for decorative and beautifying purposes. This is proven from the words of Maimonides (*Laws of Idolatry,* 12). And even in its applying to an object that is meant for decorative and beautifying purposes, the prohibition only applies to a woman who wears a man's clothing so that she will resemble a man. And so for a man who wears a woman's clothing so that he can resemble a woman. But if they wear it so as to protect themselves from the cold or heat, it is allowed... And this is definitely the law here, as the verse concludes, "for whoever does these things is abhorrent to the Lord your God," that the Torah only prohibited this act when the man is intending to do an abominable act, which is resembling a woman, and vice versa.

TALLIT

The word *tallit,* today translated as prayer shawl, in the rabbinic era meant coat or cloak. The fringes, *tzitzit,* are the essence of the *tallit*; they transform a piece of cloth into a prayer shawl. In ancient times, the *tzitzit* were attached to the hem of one's coat or outer garment, but as clothing styles changed, the fringes were attached to two ritual garments: the *tallit,* worn over one's clothing during morning prayer, and the *tallit katan* (literally, small prayer shawl), worn throughout the day underneath a man's or boy's shirt.**

by Claudia Chernov

---

* Rabbi Joel Sirkes (1561–1640) of Poland is known as Bayit Hadash (the New House), the title of his commentary on the *Shulhan Arukh.* The citation used by Rabbi Ovadiah Yosef is from the section *Yoreh De'ah.*

** *The Jewish Catalog* provides an excellent introduction to both the rituals concerning the prayer shawl and the symbolic meanings associated with its use. Refer to the chapter "Tallit" in *The First Jewish Catalog,* edited by Richard Siegel, Michael Strassfeld, and Sharon Strassfeld (Philadelphia: Jewish Publication Society, 1973), pages 51–57.

TZITZIT IN JEWISH LITERATURE

Numbers 15:37-41

The Book of Numbers commands the children of Israel to wear tzitzit, *translated below as fringes, and to look at the* tzitzit. *Because the* tzitzit *remind us of God's commandments, the* tallit—*the garment to which* tzitzit *are attached—is invested with holiness. The* tallit *itself has come to evoke the awe that a Jew may experience while praying.*

The Lord said to Moses as follows: Speak to the Israelite people and instruct them to make for themselves fringes on the corners of their garments throughout the ages; let them attach a cord of blue to the fringe at each corner.* That shall be your fringe; look at it and recall all the commandments of the Lord and observe them, so that you do not follow your heart and eyes in your lustful urge. Thus you shall be reminded to observe all My commandments and to be holy to your God. I the Lord am your God, who brought you out of the land of Egypt to be your God: I, the Lord your God.

Deuteronomy 22:12

The Book of Deuteronomy uses the Hebrew word gedilim, *translated as tassels. Today's* tallit *is rectangular or square because of the four corners specified in this verse.*

You shall make tassels on the four corners of the garment with which you cover yourself.

Mishnah, *Kiddushin* 1.7

The question of whether women must wear a tallit, *are permitted but not required to wear a* tallit, *or are forbidden to wear a* tallit, *hinges on the ruling in Kiddushin 1.7. Here the Sages exempt women from the obligatory performance of the affirmative precepts that depend on a precise time. Affirmative or positive precepts are commandments (mitzvot) that involve doing or acting ("thou shalt"), whereas negative commandments are those that prohibit an action ("thou shalt not"). In other words, women are not required to perform those positive commandments that must be done at a specific time of day or at a specific time of year.*

---

*During ancient times and even through to the Second Temple era, a blue thread was attached to the fringe at each corner of the garment. During the early years of the common era, when the proper blue dye had become prohibitively expensive, the Rabbis ruled that a fringe consisting only of white threads fulfilled the commandment (Mishnah *Menahot* 4.1; Midrash *Numbers Rabbah* 17:5). For more on *tzitzit*, refer to Jacob Milgrom, "Excursus 38: The Tassels 'Tsitsit'" in *The JPS Torah Commentary: Numbers* [Philadelphia: Jewish Publication Society, 1996], pages 410–414.

The observance of affirmative precepts dependent on time (*mitzvot aseih shehazeman grama*) is incumbent on men but not on women, and of affirmative precepts that do not depend on time is incumbent both on men and on women. The observance of all negative precepts, whether they depend on time or do not, is incumbent both on men and on women.

Sifrei Numbers (4th–5th century)

Sifrei Numbers is a Hebrew work of legal exegesis based on the Book of Numbers. The selection below comments on verses 37 and 38 of Numbers 15, "And the Lord said to Moses as follows: 'Speak to the Israelite people and instruct them to make for themselves fringes.'"

Even the women are implied. Rabbi Shimon exempts women from *tzitzit* because women are exempt from affirmative precepts dependent on time. This is the rule: Rabbi Shimon says, for all affirmative precepts dependent on time, women are exempt; these laws apply to men, not to women; to those fit [to observe the laws], not to those unfit [to observe the laws]. Rav Yehudah ben Bava says, specifically the Rabbis exempted the veil of a woman from fringes and only obligated a shawl (*tallit*) because there are times when her husband covers himself with it.

Babylonian Talmud, *Kiddushin* 33b–34a

The Sages of the Talmud elucidate the ruling in Mishnah Kiddushin 1.7.

"The observance of affirmative precepts dependent on time is incumbent on men but not on women, and of affirmative precepts that do not depend on time is incumbent both on men and on women." Our Rabbis taught: Which are affirmative precepts limited to time [from which women are exempt]? *Sukkah, lulav, shofar, tzitzit,* and *tefillin.** And what are affirmative precepts not limited to time [that women must perform]? *Mezuzah,* parapet, lost property, and releasing the nest.**

---

* Leviticus 23:42 commands us to dwell in a booth—*sukkah*—seven days every year. Leviticus 23:40 commands us to take up the *lulav*—the palm branch, together with the willows, myrtles, and citron—on the holiday of Sukkot. Leviticus 23:24 and Numbers 29:1 command us to hear the blowing of the ram's horn—*shofar*—on Rosh Hashanah. (The commandments of *tzitzit* and *tefillin* are discussed in this chapter.)

** Deuteronomy 6:9 commands us to affix the biblical words of the *Shema* on the *mezuzah* or doorpost of our house. Deuteronomy 22:8 commands us to build a parapet on the roof of our home to prevent falls. Exodus 23:4 and Deuteronomy 22:1–3 command us to return lost animals or other possessions to their owners. Release of the nest is commanded in Deuteronomy 22:6–7: "If, along the road, you chance upon a bird's nest, in any tree or on the ground, with fledglings or eggs, and the mother sitting over the fledglings or on the eggs, do not take the mother together with the young. Let the mother go, and take only the young, in order that you may fare well and have a long life."

Now, is this a general principle? But unleavened bread, rejoicing, and assembling* are affirmative precepts limited to time, and yet they are incumbent upon women. Furthermore, study of the Torah, procreation, and the redemption of the son,** are affirmative precepts not limited to time, and yet women are exempt. Rabbi Yoḥanan explained: "No inferences can be made from the generalization, even when certain other exceptions are already specified."

Babylonian Talmud, Menaḥot 43a

During talmudic times, certain Sages viewed tzitzit *as a precept that did not depend upon time. Consequently these Sages required women to wear* tzitzit. *Tractate* Menaḥot *records lengthy discussions about the rules of* tzitzit, *such as: Is the blessing recited when attaching fringes or when putting on the garment? Must fringes be placed on a garment that has less than or more than four corners? Does the garment require fringes if it remains folded in a drawer or only if it is worn?*

Rav Yehudah attached fringes to the aprons of [the women of] his household [for he held that both women and men are obligated to wear *tzitzit*]. Moreover, he used to say every morning the blessing "to wrap ourselves with fringes." But since he attached [fringes to women's garments], obviously he is of the opinion that it is a precept not dependent on time. [As Mishnah *Kiddushin* teaches, women must observe only those positive precepts that do not depend on time. Therefore, by imposing the precept of *tzitzit* upon women, Rav Yehudah obviously holds that night as well as day is the proper time for the fringes.]

Why then did he say the blessing every morning? [If the precept does not depend on time, the blessing should be said only once, when the garment is put on for the first time, rather than every morning.] He follows Rabbi's [Judah HaNasi's] view. For it was taught: Whenever a man puts on the *tefillin* he should make a blessing over them, says Rabbi. But if this is so, at any time [of the day, whenever he puts on the garment, he should say the blessing]? Rav Yehudah was a most decorous person and would not take off his cloak the whole day long. Then why [did he say the blessing] in the morning? [He should have recited the blessing even earlier than dawn, as soon as he rose.] The morning was when he changed from night clothes into day clothes.

---

* Exodus 12:18 commands us to eat unleavened bread on the first evening of Passover. Deuteronomy 16:14 commands us to rejoice during Sukkot. Deuteronomy 31:10–12 command us to assemble every seventh year on Sukkot to hear the public reading of the Torah.

** Women are exempt from the commandment to study Torah, Deuteronomy 5:1 and 11:9, from the commandment to procreate, Genesis 1:28, and from the commandment to redeem the first-born son from service in the priesthood, Exodus 13:13, 34:20, and Numbers 18:15.

Our Rabbis taught: All must observe the law of *tzitzit*, priests, Levites, and Israelites, proselytes, women, and slaves. Rabbi Shimon declares women exempt, since *tzitzit* is a positive precept dependent on time [and women are exempt from all positive precepts that depend on time].

The Master said, "All must observe the law of *tzitzit*, priests, Levites, and Israelites." Is not this obvious? For if priests and Levites and Israelites were exempt, then who would observe it? It was stated particularly on account of priests. For I might have argued, since it is written [in Deuteronomy 22:11], "You shalt not wear a mingled stuff, wool and linen together," and [it is followed by Deuteronomy 22:12] "You shall make tassels" that only those who are forbidden to wear mingled stuff must observe the law of *tzitzit*. And as priests are permitted to wear mingled stuff, they need not observe [the law of *tzitzit*]. We are therefore taught [that priests, too, must wear *tzitzit*], for although they may wear [mingled stuff] while performing the service [in the Temple], they certainly may not wear it when not performing the service.

"Rabbi Shimon declares women exempt." What is Rabbi Shimon's reason? It was taught [in Numbers 15:39]: "Look at it"; this teaching excludes a night garment. You say it excludes a night garment, but perhaps it is not so, but it excludes rather a blind man's garment? The verse [Deuteronomy 22:12], when it says, "with which you cover yourself," clearly includes a blind man's garment. How then must I explain the verse, "Look at it"? As excluding a night garment. And why do you choose to include a blind man's garment and to exclude a night garment? I include a blind man's garment since others look upon it, while I exclude a night garment since others cannot look upon it.

Babylonian Talmud, *Sukkah 11a*

In tractate Sukkah, *the Sages discuss whether cutting a living vine that has been trained over the roof of a* sukkah *meets the requirement for a proper* sukkah *covering. In the course of their discussion on cutting plants, they speak of another Sage who required women to wear* tzitzit.

In the case of Rabbi Amram the Pious who attached fringes to the aprons of the women of his house, he hung them before cutting off the ends of the threads. [He folded one thread four times and attached it. He would then cut through the folds to make the requisite eight threads.] When he came before Rabbi Ḥiyya ben Ashi [to ask whether hanging fringes before cutting was valid], the latter said to him, "This is said by Rav: 'In such a case the threads may be cut and they are valid.'"

Targum Yonatan ben Uziel (7th–8th centuries)

Targum Yonatan ben Uziel, also called Targum Yerushalmi, is an Aramaic translation of the Bible. Rather than a literal translation, the Targum includes explanations, supplements, and alterations, designed to impart an understanding of the Bible according to scholarship current at the time of its compilation. This excerpt comments on Deuteronomy 22:5: "A woman shall not put on man's apparel."

A woman should not array herself with *tefillin* or with *tzitzit*, as this would constitute wearing a man's apparel.

Maimonides (1135–1204), *Mishneh Torah, Hilkhot Tzitzit* 3:9

Maimonides, known as the Rambam, codifies the laws concerning tzitzit. *Here he discusses women's performance of precepts from which they are exempt. (Like later codifiers, the Rambam makes no mention of Targum Yonatan ben Uziel.)*

Women, servants, and minors are not required by the Torah to wear *tzitzit*. It is, however, a rabbinical obligation for every child who knows how to dress himself to wear *tzitzit* in order to educate him to fulfill the commandments. Women and slaves who wish to wrap themselves in *tzitzit* may do so without reciting a blessing [that thanks God for commanding them to wear *tzitzit*]. Similarly, regarding the other positive commandments that women are not required to fulfill, if they desire to fulfill them without reciting a blessing, they should not be prevented from doing so.

Ravad (Avraham ben David of Posquières, c. 1125–1198), on *Mishneh Torah, Hilkhot Tzitzit* 3:9

Ravad comments on the Rambam's ruling that even women and slaves, who are not commanded to wear tzitzit, *nonetheless may perform the commandment. Ravad differs from Maimonides, however, in permitting women to recite a blessing.*

There are those who disagree and say [that women may perform the positive, time-dependent commandments] even with a blessing, and they say that even the recitation of the blessing is voluntarily possible.[2]

Rabbeinu Tam (1096–1171), in *Tosafot to Babylonian Talmud, Rosh Hashanah* 33a

Rabbi Jacob ben Meir, known as Rabbeinu Tam, was the principal architect of the Tosafot (literally additions), commentaries to the Talmud written between the 12th and 14th centuries. Rabbeinu Tam affords women the opportunity to perform commandments from which they are exempt in both Rosh Hashanah 33a (below) *and* Eiruvin 96a.

Women are permitted to recite blessings on a positive, time-dependent commandment, even though they are exempt from that commandment, and they may occupy themselves with that commandment.[3]

Maharil (Yaakov Moellin, c. 1360–1427), New Responsa 7

The Maharil raises the issue of arrogance—yoharah in Hebrew—in discussing women and tzitzit.

Even though I have seen women wearing four-cornered garments with fringes, and still today, there is one woman in our neighborhood, it seems to me astonishing and is considered arrogant of them and they are called fools.[4]

Yosef Karo, *Shulhan Arukh, Orah Hayyim 17:2 (1564)*

The Shulhan Arukh concisely explains Jewish law.

Women and bondsmen are exempt from *tzitzit* because it is a positive precept dependent upon a set time.

Rema (Moshe Isserles), to *Shulhan Arukh, Orah Hayyim 17:2 (1569–1571)*

The Rema, one of the leading authorities on Jewish law for Ashkenazim, added supplementary notes to the entire Shulhan Arukh, *thereby making Yosef Karo's work the accepted legal guide throughout the Jewish world. Like earlier codifiers, the Rema permits women to perform commandments from which they are exempt, and, following Rabbeinu Tam, he even permits women to recite the blessing. However, he follows the Maharil in condemning the practice.*

Nevertheless, should they desire to wrap themselves [in a *tallit*] and recite the blessings they may do so, as is the case with other positive precepts dependent upon a set time. However, this would be a manifestation of arrogance. Women should not wear *tzitzit* since it is not an obligation on the person. That is, one is not obligated to purchase a *tallit* (four-cornered garment) in order to become subject to the precept of *tzitzit*.*

Rabbi Moshe Feinstein, *Igrot Moshe, Orah Hayyim 4:49 (1959)*

Rabbi Moshe Feinstein is one of the leading authorities of Orthodox Jewry in the twentieth century.

It is clear that every woman has the right to perform even those commandments that the Torah did not require of her, and they are fulfilling

---

* The Sages of the Talmud and later codifiers discuss whether the obligation for fringes is required of the person or of the garment. Legally, the obligation for *tzitzit* is upon the garment: A man is not obligated to purchase a four-cornered garment in order to attach *tzitzit*. If, however, he wears a four-cornered garment, *tzitzit* must be attached. This type of obligation differs from the obligation to wave the *lulav* branch during the holiday of Sukkot; in this case men are obligated to purchase a *lulav*. Nonetheless, in practice, men do purchase four-cornered garments specifically to fulfill the precept of *tzitzit*. Indeed some later codifiers classify *tzitzit* as an obligation of both the person and the garment.

a precept and receive a reward for doing it. Even according to the opinion of Tosafot, they are permitted to recite the blessing, and it is our custom that women observe the law of *shofar* and *lulav* and also say the blessing. Therefore, even *tzitzit* are allowed for a woman who wants to wear a garment that is distinguishable from men's clothing, yet has four corners on which she is able to attach fringes and fulfill the commandment…. However, clearly this only applies when the woman desires in her soul to observe the law although she was not commanded; yet, when it is not due to this intention, but rather stems from her resentment toward God and His Torah, then it is not a precept. On the contrary, it is a forbidden act of denial when she thinks there will be any change in the laws of Torah which she took on.[5]

TEFILLIN

The *tefillin* (phylacteries) are two leather boxes with leather straps attached; the two boxes contain parchment inscribed with verses from the Torah: Exodus 13:1–16, Deuteronomy 6:4–9 and 11:13–16. An individual wears one box on the forehead and one box on the hand. The leather straps keep the two boxes in their proper positions. The wearer winds the long strap of the hand *tefillin* three times around the fingers and seven times around the arm. The precise rituals for these procedures are fairly complex, and every aspect is rich in symbolism. The word *tefillin* is derived from the Hebrew word for prayer, *tefillah,* and the *tefillin* are worn every weekday morning during *shaḥarit* prayers.

by Claudia Chernov

TEFILLIN IN JEWISH LITERATURE

Exodus 13:9-10

Four different Torah verses command Jews to wear tefillin.

And this shall serve you as a sign on your hand and as a reminder between your eyes—in order that the teaching of the Lord may be in your mouth—that with a mighty hand the Lord freed you from Egypt. You shall keep this institution at its set time from year to year.

Exodus 13:16

And so it shall be as a sign upon your hand and as a symbol between your eyes that with a mighty hand the Lord freed us from Egypt.

Deuteronomy 6:4-9

Deuteronomy 6:8 (the verse beginning "bind them," which concerns tefillin*) is a part of the* Shema, *Judaism's fundamental declaration of faith. The* Shema *is recited twice daily in Jewish liturgy.*

Hear, O Israel! The Lord is our God, the Lord is one. You shall love the Lord your God with all your heart and with all your soul and with all your might. Take to heart these instructions with which I charge you this day. Impress them upon your children. Recite them when you stay at home and when you are away, when you lie down and when you get up. Bind them as a sign on your hand and let them serve as a symbol between your eyes. Inscribe them on the doorposts of your house and on your gates.

Deuteronomy 11:18

Therefore impress these My words upon your heart and your soul: Bind them as a sign on your hand and let them serve as a symbol between your eyes.

Mishnah, Berakhot 3.3

Mishnah Berakhot *specifically exempts women from the precept of* tefillin.

Women and slaves and minors are exempt from reciting the *Shema* and from wearing *tefillin*, but they are not exempt from reciting prayer, from the law of *mezuzah*, or from saying the benediction after meals.

Mekhilta on Parshat Bo, 17 (circa 400)

The Mekhilta *is a halakhic Midrash (Jewish legal and exegetical work, written in Hebrew in the land of Israel) based upon the Book of Exodus.*

"In order that the teaching of the Lord may be in your mouth" (Exodus 13:9). Why is this stated? Scripture states, "And this shall serve you as a sign," which may cause me to infer that women are also enjoined to wear *tefillin*. Moreover, logic would appear to dictate: Since *mezuzah* is a positive precept and *tefillin* is a positive precept, just as we have learned that *mezuzah* is obligatory upon women as well as men, so too should *tefillin* be obligatory upon women as well as men. Therefore, Scripture teaches, "in order that the teaching of the Lord may be in your mouth," implying that the obligation to wear *tefillin* is restricted to those who are obligated to study Torah. Thus, the Sages taught, "All are obligated to wear *tefillin* except women and slaves."

Babylonian Talmud, Kiddushin 34a

The Sages of the Talmud continue their elucidation of the ruling in Mishnah Kiddushin 1.7.

"The observance of affirmative precepts dependent on time is incumbent on men but not on women." Whence do we derive it? It is learned from *tefillin*: Just as women are exempt from *tefillin*, so they are exempt from all positive precepts dependent upon time. [Women's exemption from] *tefillin* is derived from the study of the Torah: Just as women are exempt from the study of the Torah, so they are exempt from *tefillin*.

Babylonian Talmud, *Eiruvin* 96a–96b

The Talmud describes Mikhal, the daughter of the Kushite. She is considered the daughter of King Saul.

For it was taught [by a Rabbi of the Mishnah]: Mikhal the daughter of the Kushite wore *tefillin* and the Sages did not prevent her, and the wife of Jonah attended the festival pilgrimage and the Sages did not prevent her. Now since the Sages did not prevent her it is clearly evident that they hold the view that it [*tefillin*] is a positive precept the performance of which is not limited to a particular time. But is not another possibility that the author of this teaching holds the same view as Rabbi Yose, who ruled: "It is optional for women to lay their hands on a sacrifice"? [That is, the author of this teaching holds the view that laying *tefillin* and attending the festival pilgrimage are optional for women.]

Tosafot to Babylonian Talmud, *Eiruvin* 96a (12th to 14th centuries)

In earlier legal works, women's exemption from tefillin *had been described as the chief paradigm of women's exemption from affirmative precepts dependent on time. The exemption from* tefillin *was special, however, because of the symbolic relationship between* tefillin *and Torah study. In medieval France and Germany, the Tosafists introduce a new factor specific to* tefillin. *The Tosafists themselves permit women both to perform positive time-dependent commandments and to recite the blessing upon them, however they note the opposite view and attempt to explain it.*

It would seem that the reason behind those who say that a woman does not have permission [to wear *tefillin*] is because *tefillin* require a clean body, and women are not scrupulous to be careful [in maintaining cleanliness].[6]

Yosef Karo, *Shulḥan Arukh, Oraḥ Ḥayyim* 38:3 (1564)

Prior to writing the Shulḥan Arukh, *a concise guide to Jewish law, Rabbi Yosef Karo wrote the* Beit Yosef, *an extensive exploration of legal decisions and their precedents. In the* Beit Yosef, *he notes the issue of cleanliness in relation to women laying* tefillin. *Nonetheless, in the* Shulḥan Arukh, *he does not place* tefillin *in any special category.*

Women and bondsmen are exempt from *tefillin* because it is a positive precept dependent upon time.

Rema (Moshe Isserles), to *Shulḥan Arukh*, *Oraḥ Ḥayyim* 38:3 (1569–1571)

Though the Tosafot raised the issue of cleanliness yet still permitted women to lay tefillin, *subsequent authorities have used women's lack of cleanliness to prohibit women from optional performance of the* mitzvah. *The Rema does not mention cleanliness, but in his ruling protesting women wearing* tefillin *he cites the 14th-century Kol Bo, who had objected to women wearing* tefillin *on the grounds of insufficient attention to cleanliness.*

If women choose to be strict upon themselves [and lay *tefillin*], we should object.

Yeḥiel Epstein, *Arukh HaShulḥan, Oraḥ Ḥayyim 38* (1903–1907)

Following the opinion of the Rema, nearly all subsequent legal authorities object to women wearing tefillin. *Rabbi Yeḥiel Epstein (1829–1908), known by the name of his major work,* Arukh HaShulḥan, *is one of the foremost decisors of the modern era, and his restriction barring women from wearing* tefillin *is severe.*

Tefillin is a positive precept dependent on a set time, since one is exempt on Sabbath and festivals. If women should choose to be stringent upon themselves, we pardon them [that is, women are exempted even if they choose otherwise]. *Tefillin* is unlike *sukkah* and *lulav* [precepts from which women are exempt, yet which women commonly fulfill with the recitation of blessings] because *tefillin* requires that the person be meticulously clean. Thus the Talmud (*Shabbat* 49a) states: "*Tefillin* demand a body as clean as that of Elisha the Possessor of Wings." Men who are obligated to wear them perforce must take care to maintain their cleanliness during the reciting of *Shema* and the *Amidah*; and this is why men do not wear *tefillin* all day. Thus women, who are exempt from the obligation, have no need to undertake so great a risk [of not being clean while wearing *tefillin*]. For women there is no difference between the occasions of reciting the *Shema* and the *Amidah*, and the remainder of the day; they are obligated at no time. Therefore, we do not allow women to wear *tefillin*. The statement in *Eiruvin* that Mikhal the daughter of Saul donned *tefillin* and the Sages did not object, does not constitute a precedent. It can be assumed that the Sages were aware of her exceptional virtue and of her ability to maintain rigorous and constant cleanliness.

Rabbi Eliezer Berkovits, *Jewish Women in Time and Torah* (1990)

Most Orthodox authorities continue to object to women wearing tefillin, *which is considered a special case among the affirmative precepts dependent on time. In recent years, though, a small number of Orthodox rabbis have ruled that women are permitted to lay* tefillin.

How then is the opinion regarding the lack of bodily hygiene to be understood? The Magein Avraham,* in his commentary, apparently seeks to resolve this problem, though he does not make explicit mention of it. Explaining the words of the Rema, he quotes the statement of the Tosafot that we have quoted above. However, he adds: "But if women were obligated by biblical law to fulfill the *tefillin* commandment, they would be more careful about their bodily cleanliness." The Magein Avraham wishes to say that the original talmudic conclusion that women are free from the commandment of donning *tefillin* has nothing to do with the question of how well they care for their bodies. For if they were commanded to do the *mitzvah*, they would be competent in matters of hygiene demanded by the *mitzvah* of the phylacteries....

In talmudic sources the question of bodily hygiene does not enter into consideration. On the contrary, according to the Babylonian Talmud, which has been accepted as the valid law, the daughter of King Saul did practice the *mitzvah* of *tefillin*, and so too may all women. The opinion that nevertheless women should not be allowed to put on *tefillin* because of their hygienic carelessness with their bodies is a later post-talmudic development. The authors who accepted this idea obviously were doing so on the basis of their own experience: such were the women they knew, the women of their time. Let us state unequivocally that nowadays such an evaluation of female behavior would be utterly unjustified.... In matters of bodily hygiene, women are at least as reliable as men. We may completely disregard the opinion of the Rema in this matter and follow such authorities as Rashi,** Rabbeinu Tam,§ Rambam,§§ and Rashba,∞

---

*Rabbi Abraham Gombiner (c. 1637–1683) of Poland is known as Magein Avraham (The Shield of Abraham), the title of his commentary on the *Orah Hayyim* section of the *Shulhan Arukh*. The citation by Rabbi Berkovits comments on *Orah Hayyim* 38:3.

**Rashi, Rabbi Solomon ben Isaac (1040–1105), is the foremost commentator on the Bible and on the Talmud. His brief comments are remarkable for their clarity. Rashi does not single out *tefillin* from the other affirmative precepts dependent on time. In discussing them, he rules that women may not recite the blessing. From this ruling, later authorities infer that he permitted women to perform all optional commandments.

§Rabbeinu Tam, Rabbi Jacob ben Meir (1096–1171), is Rashi's grandson. He is cited in the section on *tzitzit*. Rabbeinu Tam specifically permits women to lay *tefillin* and to recite the blessing (Tosafot to Babylonian Talmud, *Eiruvin* 96a and *Rosh Hashanah* 33a).

§§The Rambam (Rabbi Moshe ben Maimon, known as Maimonides, 1135–1204) also does not single out *tefillin* from the other affirmative precepts dependent on time. He is cited in the section on *tzitzit* as permitting women to optionally perform these precepts.

∞Rashba, Rabbi Solomon ben Abraham Adret (1235–1310), wrote more than ten thousand responsa (answers to legal questions) as well as extensive commentary to the Talmud. He permits women to lay *tefillin*, even interpreting the Talmud's phrase that who make no distinction between the commandment of *tefillin* and the other *mitzvot aseih shehazeman grama* [affirmative precepts dependent on time]. The *Haggahot Maimoniyot** (that is, the commentary on the work of Maimonides) quotes the *Sar* of Coucy** that women may make the *brakhah* on *lulav* and *tefillin* and all similar *mitzvot*. Women today may well be guided by these authorities.[7]

Questions for Discussion

1. If you have seen Jews praying with *tallit* and *tefillin*, describe your impressions. Is your description positive or negative? If you first observed prayer with *tallit* and *tefillin* as a teen or an adult, describe your initial reactions. Is your reaction different today? If you have never observed prayer with *tallit* and *tefillin*, describe your attitude toward the ritual garments.

2. Orthodox Jews accept women's exemption from positive time-dependent precepts as a matter of faith. Just as no human can adequately explain why Jews must follow the laws of *kashrut*, no human can completely explain the reasons behind women's exemptions. Nonetheless, many different explanations have been given over the ages. Perhaps the most common explanation has been women's domestic duties: A woman of antiquity was bound to obey her husband, hence her time was not her own. Such a woman occupied the same legal category as the slave. As woman's status changed in recent centuries, classifying her with the slave has become impossible. Yet even in the twentieth century, with slavery almost universally abolished, the average woman has child care responsibilities that the average man does not, thus—like the woman of an earlier era—her time is not her own. Consider the "women's work" explanation. How is this explanation satisfying? How is this explanation disturbing?

3. In the past two centuries, another common explanation for women's exemption from positive, time-dependent precepts has been that a woman is innately more spiritual and closer to God than a man. Because of her superior religious status, a woman needs fewer reminders of God's sovereignty. Rabbi Aharon Soloveitchik, a leading Orthodox spokesman,

---

the Sages did not protest Mikhal's wearing of *tefillin* to mean that Mikhal acted in accordance with the wishes of the Sages (*Teshuvot haRashba* [Jerusalem: Makhon Tiferet haTorah, 1989], responsum 123).

*Rabbi Meir HaKohein of Rothenburg, Germany (died 1298) wrote the *Haggahot Maimoniyot*, a commentary upon the Code of Maimonides. Rabbi Berkovits cites his comment on *Mishneh Torah, Hilkhot Tzitzit* 3:9.

** Rabbi Moses ben Jacob of France (circa 1200).

stated in 1969, "There is an abundance of energy (*kibbush*) in the male gender which, if not tempered and controlled properly, might be released in a very destructive manner. Almighty God in His infinite wisdom therefore imposed upon the male gender the obligatory *mitzvot* created by a time element and the obligation of constantly being engaged in the study of Torah so that man's psyche will always be preoccupied with spiritual and intellectual endeavors.... Man has to struggle in order to be good, compassionate, tolerant, and noble. A woman's personality was molded in such a way that she is naturally disposed toward compassion and consideration."[8] Discuss Rabbi Soloveitchik's opinion. Are women spiritually superior to men? If so, in what ways? Why? (In other words, do you agree that women are "naturally disposed toward compassion"? Are men "naturally disposed" toward violence and destruction?) Supposing that women are more compassionate and considerate than men, should possession of these traits result in fewer religious obligations? How do obligations to God serve to temper and control our energy?

4. Rabbi Moshe Isserles, known as the Rema, summarized earlier Ashkenazi legal writers and codified Jewish law for Ashkenazim. He stated that a woman who wraps herself in a *tallit* is manifesting *yoharah*—pride or arrogance. For Jewish legal writers, *yoharah* implies an excessive show of piety. According to the Maharil and the Rema, a woman who takes on a non-obligatory precept is in effect saying that she fulfills every obligatory precept and is so extremely devout that she must now go further and fulfill the non-obligatory precepts as well. Discuss arrogance in religious observance, and consider the Rema's opinion about the *tallit*. Do you feel that a woman who wears a *tallit* implies that she fulfills every other *mitzvah*? In other words, are women who wear ritual garments in some way boasting of their piety? Or are they boasting of their commitment to feminism? How does custom affect our judgment of an individual's religious arrogance? For instance, if most of the women in a given synagogue wear a *tallit*, do they give the appearance of excessive piety? What other religious actions do you consider excessively showy? Why do we condemn showy piety so strongly?

5. Consider the prohibition against cross-dressing and the wearing of Jewish ritual garments. The Targum Yonatan in fact forbids women to wear a *tallit* because of this prohibition, and Rabbi Moshe Feinstein permits a woman to attach fringes only to "a garment which is distinguishable from men's clothing." (Many of these are currently available in Judaica shops; they tend to have attractive designs and be made of light-colored, rather than white, fabrics.) However, outside of Orthodox Judaism, the prohibition against cross-dressing has little or no impact on women's clothing choices. Should a woman's *kippah* or *tallit* have a uniquely feminine design? Or should ritual garments be considered unisex articles, akin to mittens or flotation devices?

6. The Arukh HaShulḥan (Rabbi Yeḥiel Epstein) argues that bodily cleanliness is difficult to maintain, therefore only those who are biblically obligated to lay *tefillin* should do so. How did you react to this discussion of cleanliness? In the Talmud, cleanliness is interpreted to mean that one must not suffer from flatulence while wearing *tefillin* and one must not sleep while wearing *tefillin*. Discuss this definition and its impact on women's performance of the commandment.

7. Which of the three ritual garments—*kippah, tallit, tefillin*—are you most comfortable observing others wear? Why? Which garment appeals to you the most? Why? Are your answers valid for both men and women? Which garment do you (or would you) feel most comfortable wearing? Why? Do you feel that wearing *tallit* or *tefillin* enhances your awareness of God's commandments? Does wearing *tallit* or *tefillin* make you feel holier? Warmer? Protected?

8. When you imagine committed Jewish women thirty years from today, are they wearing *kippah, tallit, tefillin*? Will the numbers of Jewish women wearing ritual garments be greater than or lesser than the numbers wearing them today? Explain the reasons for your prediction.

Suggested Activities and Programs

1. Arrange for the women in your group to try on a *kippah* and *tallit*, and if you are comfortable with *tefillin*, have them try these as well. Discuss your reactions. How did wearing the actual garment affect group members' opinions about the texts cited above?

2. Ask for two volunteers to enact a skit. Assign one the role of a woman who has begun wearing *kippah, tallit,* or *tefillin*. Assign the other the role of her good friend who has just learned of the woman's new observances. Possible reactions include shock, offense, support, admiration. Have the volunteers act out their roles. Request two more volunteers to enact a second skit. Assign one the role of a woman who has begun wearing a *kippah, tallit,* or *tefillin*. Assign the other the role of her brother, who has just learned of his sister's new observances. Have the two new volunteers act out the second role-play. Follow the two skits with a group discussion.

---

1. *The Responsa of Professor Louis Ginzberg*, volume 16, ed. David Golinkin (New York: Jewish Theological Seminary, 1996), page 76. Irving H. Fisher was apparently connected with the United Synagogue.

2. Translated by Aviva Cayam, "Fringe Benefits: Women and Tzitzit," *Jewish Legal Writings by Women*, eds. Micah D. Halpern and Chana Safrai (Jerusalem: Urim, 1998), page 125.

3. Adapted from the translation of Rabbi David Golinkin, "May Women Wear Tefillin?" *Conservative Judaism* 50:1 (Fall 1997), page 7.

4. Translated by Aviva Cayam, "Fringe Benefits," page 130.

5. Translated by Aviva Cayam, "Fringe Benefits," page 136.

6. Adapted from the translation of Rabbi David Golinkin, "May Women Wear Tefillin?" page 8.

7. Eliezer Berkovits, *Jewish Women in Time and Torah* (Hoboken, NJ: Ktav, 1990), pages 73–74.

8. Rabbi Aharon Soloveitchik, "The Attitude of Judaism Toward the Woman," in *Major Addresses Delivered at Midcontinent Conclave and National Leadership Conference*, Union of Orthodox Jewish Congregations (November 27–30, 1969), pages 29–30, cited in Avi Weiss, *Women at Prayer* (Hoboken, NJ: Ktav, 1990), page 3.

MODESTY

If you've ever been to an ultra-Orthodox community, you are familiar with the woman's uniform: long-sleeved blouse, long skirt, and opaque tights (even on a scorching summer day). If the woman is married, she also wears a wig, scarf, or hat. (She may even wear a wig covered by a scarf or hat.) She wears this modest outfit, so out of step with contemporary fashion, to preclude men from appraising her body and hair. If she wears revealing clothes, traditional Jews believe, she will cause men to have lascivious thoughts—which might lead to sexual overtures. Women are entrusted with the responsibility, this thinking goes, of curbing men's inappropriate sexual desires. This code of modesty, in dress and behavior, is called *tzeniut*.

Sexuality isn't, in and of itself, a bad thing according to Jewish law. In fact, Judaism encourages sexual expression to a remarkable degree—within marriage. According to the Talmud, a husband must notice his wife's desire and fulfill it. It is a *mitzvah* (commandment) for a man to sexually satisfy his wife. Nahmanides, the great biblical and talmudic commentator (known as the Ramban, 1194–1270), advised: "Know that the sexual intercourse of a man with his wife is holy and pure.... No one should think that sexual intercourse is ugly and loathsome.... Proper sexual union can be a means of spiritual elevation when it is properly practiced."[1] No surprise, then, that lingerie shops featuring racy, lacy confections are a hit in even the most ultra-Orthodox communities in Brooklyn.*

---

* Jewish attitudes toward sexuality within marriage are mixed. Positive voices such as the Ramban's are prominent, yet negative voices do exist. For example, according to

However, the married couple cannot have sex whenever they want. For approximately twelve days each month—the five days that the wife menstruates, followed by seven additional days—the husband and wife must separate, according to the laws of *niddah* (menstruating woman). They may not touch each other, let alone engage in sexual activity. Observant couples sleep in separate beds during this period. On the night of the twelfth day, the wife immerses in the *mikvah* (ritual bath), after which she and her husband may resume physical contact. Thus, even within marriage, sexuality is regulated by Jewish ritual law.

All sexual expression is forbidden to men and women who are not married. An ultra-Orthodox man never shakes hands with a woman (except his mother or daughter), lest he become sexually tempted. Most of the time, however, the woman is entrusted with keeping male desires in check. Thus the *mehitzah,* the partition between women and men in Orthodox synagogues, is said to keep worshipping men from being distracted by women. (As Susan Weidman Schneider, editor of the feminist Jewish magazine *Lilith*, observes dryly: "It's never suggested that the women might be distracted by the men."[2])

For the same reason, observant married women cover their hair—a bedrock part of the code of modesty. The belief is that a woman's hair is sexually provocative and therefore must be hidden from everyone except her husband. Nearly all Orthodox women—and even many Conservative women—cover their hair in synagogue, but the right-of-center Orthodox woman covers her hair even when dashing to the supermarket. Orthodox Jews accept that the sensuality of a woman's hair, left publicly unrestrained, poses a threat to the family and social structure. That same sensuality, however, becomes an enriching and stabilizing force when properly channeled, and indeed affirms the sanctity of marriage.

Over the last twenty years, the Orthodox movement has moved slowly but visibly to the right. Married Orthodox women who a generation ago covered their hair only with a piece of lace in synagogue now wear a hat in synagogue; and those who wore a hat only in synagogue now wear a hat every day. Within modern Orthodox circles, women don longer skirts each year. Modesty—*tzeniut*—is popular, even chic. One young woman, Wendy Shalit, recently wrote a book titled *A Return to Modesty*.[3] In it she argues that female modesty is innate, and that if women dressed and behaved demurely, there would be less sexual harassment, date rape, and stalking.

The belief that women are responsible—and therefore to blame—for

---

the ultra-Orthodox understanding of Jewish law, couples should engage in sexual intercourse only at night and only in a dark room (how can the husband see the seductive lingerie?), and should use only the missionary position.

men's sexual sins and crimes seems downright sexist. Men should be able to control *themselves,* thank you very much, and shouldn't need to be "protected" from the sight of a woman's elbow or collarbone. Besides, in claiming responsibility for men's sexuality, women may be repressing their own erotic impulses. Yet many women who adhere to the modesty code defend it in terms that sound practically feminist. Gila Berkowitz, an Orthodox writer, states: "Women are advised not to treat themselves as male playthings. Wearing suggestive, teasing clothing is a desperate and doomed attempt to wheedle favors from those in power—who tend to be people thoroughly covered from neck to toe."[4]

Obviously revealing clothing does call attention to one's sexuality. But does that mean that one *lacks* power, as Berkowitz contends? Could it not mean that one feels utterly comfortable with oneself—possessing another kind of power altogether? And isn't covering up one's body and hair just a step or two away from covering up entirely in a burka, the shroud-like garment worn by women in Afghanistan? Yet many forward thinking and, yes, feminist Orthodox women say that *tzeniut* does not limit them. On the contrary, it makes them feel independent and secure.

Ultimately, dressing according to the Orthodox code may be a way of effectively and publicly proclaiming one's affiliation with the community. Just like wearing a *kippah* or black hat, wearing a wig and an ankle-length skirt says to like-minded Jews: "See, I'm one of you." And perhaps that is the purpose of Jewish law in general—to distinguish ourselves from the gentiles, to remind ourselves that we are "different" and live by a different moral code.

by Leora Tanenbaum

MODESTY IN RABBINIC AND MEDIEVAL JUDAISM

The concept of *tzeniut*—modesty—fuses together several Jewish ideals. One of these is humility, an ideal that both women and men should strive to attain. Legends abound in the Talmud and Midrash of the extraordinary meekness displayed by the ancient Rabbis. Connected to the ideal of humility is the ideal of personal privacy, that is, restraint and docility in action and in speech on one's own behalf. This ideal, like the ideal of humility, applies to both women and men, but is considered a particular virtue of women. Thus, women are especially encouraged to be shy and submissive, and their role is considered a private and domestic one while men are deemed to have a public role.

Yet a third ideal, the ideal of bodily privacy, is in our day the most common meaning of *tzeniut*. In the Talmud and Midrash, this concept applies to both men and women.

Two other Jewish legal concepts also bear upon the ideal of bodily privacy as it has come to be understood today, that is, modest dress for women. The first is the law of *ervah* (literally "nakedness") or of sexual provocation, which prohibits a man from looking at a woman if his intent is sexual stimulation. Even if his intent is otherwise, however, the same law prohibits him from looking at a woman's exposed arms and shoulders, and indeed any exposed body part if that part is generally clothed. Looking at these body parts might cause sexual stimulation even if the man's intention had been pure. The second law relating to women's modest dress is the law of *beged ish*, or the attire of a man, which prohibits women from wearing men's clothing and likewise prohibits men from wearing women's clothing.

by Claudia Chernov

MODESTY IN CLASSIC JEWISH LITERATURE

Micah 6:8

The Hebrew root tzadi-nun-ayin *of the word* tzeniut *(modesty) is used twice in the Bible. Here the prophet Micah tells of God's message, using the Hebrew word* vehatzenei'a.

> He has told you, O man, what is good,
> And what the Lord requires of you:
> Only to do justice
> And to love goodness
> And to walk modestly with your God.

Proverbs 11:2

The second use of the Hebrew root tzadi-nun-ayin *is in the Book of Proverbs, which describes rules of practical ethics and discusses moral philosophy. The Hebrew for "those who are modest" is* tzenu'im. *In both biblical uses, modest is synonymous with humble.*

> When arrogance appears, disgrace follows,
> But wisdom is with those who are modest.

Deuteronomy 22:5

The law which prohibits women from wearing men's clothing is based upon this biblical passage.

A woman shall not put on man's apparel, nor shall a man wear woman's clothing; for whoever does these things is abhorrent to the Lord your God.

Psalm 45:14-16

Verse 14 of Psalm 45 has been used since rabbinic times as proof text for woman's reticence and her place within the home, both literally inside and figuratively caring for a household.

> All glorious is the king's daughter within the palace;
> Her raiment is of chequer work inwrought with gold.
> She shall be led unto the king on richly woven stuff;
> The virgins her companions in her train being brought unto thee.
> They shall be led with gladness and rejoicing;
> They shall enter into the king's palace.*

Numbers 5:12-18

Chapter 5 of the Book of Numbers describes the ordeal that a wife suspected of infidelity must undergo. The first six verses introduce the ritual and spell out its initial steps. In the last sentence of the selection, we find the biblical support for married women covering their hair.

If any man's wife has gone astray and broken faith with him in that a man has had carnal relations with her unbeknown to her husband, and she keeps secret the fact that she has defiled herself without being forced, and there is no witness against her—but a fit of jealousy comes over him and he is wrought up about the wife who has defiled herself; or if a fit of jealousy comes over one and he is wrought up about his wife although she has not defiled herself—the man shall bring his wife to the priest. And he shall bring as an offering for her one-tenth of an *ephah* of barley flour. No oil shall be poured upon it and no frankincense shall be laid on it, for it is a meal offering of jealousy, a meal offering of remembrance which recalls wrongdoing.

The priest shall bring her forward and have her stand before the Lord. The priest shall take sacral water in an earthen vessel and, taking some of the earth that is on the floor of the Tabernacle, the priest shall put it into the water. After he has made the woman stand before the Lord, the priest shall bare the woman's head and place upon her hands the meal offering of remembrance.

---

* The translation is by the Jewish Publication Society in 1917. The Jewish Publication Society published a new translation of the Bible in 1985, and it interpreted Psalm 45:14–16 in a very different way: "The royal princess, her dress embroidered with golden mountings, is led inside to the king, / maidens in her train, her companions, are presented to you. They are led in with joy and gladness; / they enter the palace of the king." In 1978, Rabbi Moshe Meiselman, writing in defense of traditional or pre-feminist understanding of women's role in *Jewish Woman in Jewish Law* (New York: Ktav/Yeshivah University Press, 1978), offered yet another interpretation of Psalm 45:14: "The entire glory of the daughter of the king lies on the inside, more so than the one who is clothed in golden garments" (page 14).

Mishnah, *Ketubot 7.6*

The Rabbis of the Mishnah state that a wife who transgresses either the law of Moses or Jewish custom may be divorced without receiving financial support from her husband. The Rabbis then enumerate both the biblical rules (that is, the laws of Moses) and the customary rules that the wife must not break. In the Mishnah, hair covering is considered a customary rule, not a biblical commandment.

What conduct by a wife transgresses the law of Moses? If she gives her husband untithed food, or has intercourse with him during the period of menstruation, or does not set apart the dough offering, or utters a vow and does not fulfill it.* And what conduct by a wife transgresses Jewish custom? If she goes out with her hair unbound, or spins in the street, or speaks with any man. Abba Saul says: Also if she curses his parents in his presence. Rabbi Tarfon says: Also if she is a scolding woman. And who is deemed a scolding woman? Whosoever speaks inside her house so that her neighbors hear her voice.

Babylonian Talmud, *Ketubot 72a-72b*

The Talmud comments on the discussion in the Mishnah: "And what conduct by a wife transgresses Jewish custom? If she goes out with her hair unbound." The Rabbis discuss whether hair covering is, in fact, a law of Moses or whether it is a custom.

Is not the prohibition against going out with hair uncovered a biblical prohibition? For it is written, "the priest shall bare the woman's head" (Numbers 5:18), and this, it was taught at the school of Rabbi Ishmael, was a warning to the daughters of Israel that they should not go out with uncovered head. [If the prohibition is actually biblical, that is, a law of Moses, why is it described in the Mishnah as merely a Jewish custom?] According to the law of Moses, it is quite satisfactory if her head is covered by her work-basket; according to Jewish custom, however, she is forbidden to go out uncovered even with her basket on her head.

Rabbi Assi stated in the name of Rabbi Yoḥanan: With a basket on her head a woman is not guilty of going about with an uncovered head. In considering this statement, Rabbi Zera pointed out this difficulty: Where is the woman assumed to be [when her head is covered by the basket only]? If it be suggested "in the street," it may be objected that this is already forbidden by Jewish custom; but if she is in the courtyard

---

*Giving her husband untithed food transgresses Numbers 18:21; having intercourse with her husband during her menstrual period transgresses Leviticus 18:19; failing to set apart the dough offering (failing to take *hallah*) transgresses Numbers 15:18; and uttering a vow that she does not fulfill transgresses Deuteronomy 23:21.

the objection may be made that if that were so, you will not leave our father Abraham a single daughter who could remain with her husband! [Since all married women go about in their courtyards with uncovered heads.] Abbaye, or it might be said Rav Kahana, replied: The statement refers to one who walks from one courtyard into another by way of an alley.

Babylonian Talmud, *Berakhot 24a*

Berakhot *deals with prayer. Men must recite the* Shema *at fixed times, both morning and evening, and when they recite it they must concentrate on its meaning. If men look upon women who are clothed immodestly, they will be unable to focus on the recital of the* Shema. *The Rabbis' discussion digresses to include other aspects of women's influence on men.*

Rabbi Isaac said: A handsbreadth [exposed] in a woman constitutes sexual incitement [*ervah*, literally "nakedness"]. In which way? Shall I say, if one gazes [looks with sexual intent] at it? But has not Rav Sheshet said, why did Scripture enumerate the ornaments worn outside the clothes with those worn inside?* To tell you that if a man gazes at the little finger of a woman, it is as if he gazed at her secret place! No, it means in a man's own wife and when he recites the *Shema*. [Thus, a man must postpone reciting the *Shema* until his wife covers the exposed handsbreadth or until he is no longer in her presence.]

Rav Ḥisda said: A woman's leg is a sexual incitement, as it says, "Bare your leg, wade through the rivers" (Isaiah 47:2), and it says afterwards, "Your nakedness shall be uncovered, and your shame shall be exposed" (Isaiah 47:3).

Samuel said: A woman's voice is a sexual incitement, as it says, "Your voice is sweet, and your face is comely" (Song of Songs 2:14).

Rav Sheshet said, a woman's hair is a sexual incitement, as it says, "Your hair is like a flock of goats" (Song of Songs 4:1).

Babylonian Talmud, *Yoma 47a*

It is told of the high priest Ishmael the son of Kimhit that one day, while he was talking with an Arab king [who may have come to observe the rites of Yom Kippur], a spray of saliva spurted from the king's mouth on Ishmael's garments, making him ritually unclean [therefore he was unable to minister further as high priest]. So his brother Yeshavav entered and ministered in his stead. Thus, their mother saw both her sons high priests on the same day.

---

*Among the ornaments taken by the Israelites from the women of Midian (Numbers 31:50) was the *kumaz* (which some translate as girdle), which the Rabbis supposed to have been worn underneath the clothing, in addition to ornaments worn over clothing.

According to our masters, Kimhit had seven sons, and all of them served in the office of high priest. The sages asked her: What good deeds are there to your credit that you should be so honored in your sons? She replied: The ceiling beams of my house have never seen the hair of my head nor the seam of my petticoat. The sages responded: Others were equally careful, but it did not avail them.*

Babylonian Talmud, *Shabbat* 118b

The Talmud praises Rabbi Yose for his extremely modest clothing. His manner of speech also reveals his humility.

Rabbi Yose said: Never have I called my wife "my wife" or my ox "my ox"; rather, I called my wife "my house" and my ox "my field."

Rabbi Yose also said: Never have the beams of my house seen the seams of my shirt. [When he undressed, he did not turn the shirt inside out, but pulled it over his head while in bed. Out of modesty, he remained covered as much as possible.]

Babylonian Talmud, *Baba Batra* 123a and *Megillah* 13b

The Talmud praises Rachel for her modesty, that is, her willingness to give up her own interests in consideration of her sister.

In reward for the modesty displayed by Rachel, she was granted to number among her descendants Saul; and in reward for the modesty displayed by Saul, he was granted to number among his descendants Esther.

What was the modesty displayed by Rachel? It is written: "Jacob told Rachel that he was her father's brother, that he was Rebecca's son" (Genesis 29:12). Now was he her father's brother? Was he not the son of her father's sister? What it means is this: he said to her, "Will you marry me?"

She replied, "Yes, but father is a trickster, and you will not be able to hold your own against him."

"Wherein," he asked her, "does his trickery lie?"

"I have," she said, "a sister who is older than I, and he will not allow me to be married before her."

"I am his *brother*," he said to her, "in trickery."

"But," she said to him, "may the righteous indulge in trickery?"

"Yes," Jacob replied, "Scripture says: 'With the pure, You act in purity,

---

*Adapted from Midrash *Pesikta deRav Kahanah* 26:10 and Midrash *Leviticus Rabbah* 20:11 as well as Babylonian Talmud, *Yoma* 47a. The passages about Kimhit in the Midrash conclude differently from the passage in the Talmud: After Kimhit describes her modesty, "the sages said, 'Ordinary flours (*kimhaya*) are coarse flours, but the flour of Kimhit is fine flour' [a pun on Kimhit and *kimhaya*]. To Kimhit was applied the verse: 'All glorious is the king's daughter within'" (Psalm 45:14).

and with the crooked You are wily'" (II Samuel 22:27). Thereupon he entrusted Rachel with certain identification marks.

While Leah was being led into the bridal chamber, Rachel thought, "my sister will now be disgraced," and so she entrusted her with these very marks. And this accounts for the Scriptural text, "When morning came, she was Leah!" (Genesis 29:25), which seems to imply that until then she was not Leah! But this is the explanation: On account of the identifying marks which Jacob had entrusted to Rachel—who had then entrusted them to Leah—he knew not who she was until that moment.

Babylonian Talmud, *Baba Metzia 87a*

The Talmud praises Sarah for her modesty in remaining indoors.

Genesis 18:9 states, "And the angels said to Abraham: 'Where is Sarah your wife?' And he said: 'Behold, in the tent.'" This verse comes to teach us that Sarah our mother was exceedingly modest, for even when visitors arrived she did not leave her tent. Rav Yehudah said in the name of Rav (and some say it was Rabbi Yitzhak): The ministering angels knew very well that Sarah our mother was in the tent. So why did they inquire about her whereabouts, requiring Abraham to explain to them that Sarah was "inside the tent"? They did this in order to endear her to her husband. By reminding Abraham about his wife's unusual modesty, they hoped to make her even more beloved to him.

Babylonian Talmud, *Shabbat 140b*

Rabbi Hisda teaches his daughters modesty both in circumspect speech and in patient behavior.

Rabbi Hisda advised his daughters: Act modestly before your husbands. When someone calls at the door, do not say, "Who is he who wishes to enter?" Instead say, "Who is she who wishes to enter?" [This will indicate that the daughters do not associate with strange men.]

Rabbi Hisda used to take a jewel in one hand and a berry in the other. He showed them the jewel, but he did not show them the berry until they were distressed by their eagerness to know what was in the other hand. Only then did he show it to them. [He thus proved the folly of lacking in reserve.]

Babylonian Talmud, *Ketubot 65a*

After the sage Abbaye dies, his wife Homa—who had been married and widowed twice before—petitions the rabbinic court, headed by Rava, concerning her inheritance. Homa's immodest clothing upsets Rava.

Homa, Abbaye's wife, came to Rava and asked him, "Grant me an allowance for food" [from my husband's estate]. He granted it to her. "Grant me an allowance for wine."

"I know," Rava said to her, "that Naḥmani [my comforter, as Abbaye was called] did not drink wine."

"By your life, master, I swear," she replied, "that he gave me drink from beakers as long as this." And as she was exhibiting it, her arm was uncovered and its beauty lit up the court chamber. At once Rava rose and went home.

His wife, Rabbi Ḥisda's daughter, noticing that his appearance was greatly changed, asked, "Who was at court today?"

Rava replied, "Ḥoma, the wife of Abbaye."

Rava's wife immediately went after her, whipping her with leather scraps, until she chased her clean out of Maḥoza. "You have already killed three men," she kept saying to her, "and now you come flirting to kill another!"

Midrash, *Ruth Rabbah* 4:6 (500–640)

Ruth Rabbah is an exegetical and homiletic work on the biblical Book of Ruth. It praises Ruth's modesty, giving three examples.

"Boaz said to the servant who was in charge of the reapers, 'Whose girl is that?'" (Ruth 2:5). Did he then not recognize her? The meaning is that when he saw how attractive she was, and how modest her attitude, he began to inquire concerning her. All the other women bent down to gather ears of corn, but she sat down to gather them; all the other women hitched up their skirts, but she kept hers down; all the other women bantered with the reapers, but she was reserved—"she sat down beside the reapers" (Ruth 2:14), not in their midst. All the other women gathered from between the sheaves, while she gathered only what was already abandoned....

"The servant in charge of the reapers replied, 'She is a Moabite girl'" (Ruth 2:6), and yet you say that her conduct is praiseworthy and modest. Her mother-in-law has instructed her well.

Derekh Eretz Zuta 5 and 7 (600–1000)

Derekh Eretz means "The Way of the World" or "Proper Deportment." (Zuta means small, but Derekh Eretz Zuta is not particularly short.) Though compiled well after the completion of the Talmud, the book is considered a minor talmudic tractate, as it includes many portions that were compiled earlier. Derekh Eretz Zuta exhorts us to engage in self-examination and to strive for resignation, patience, decency, and temperance. Many of its statements are brief and cogent.

The adornment of a precept is modesty. [One should not boast of one's own piety.][5]

A disciple of the wise should be modest at eating, at drinking, at bathing, at anointing himself, at putting on his sandals; in his walking, in dress, in the sound of his voice, in the disposal of his spittle, even in his good deeds. A bride, while still in her father's house, acts so modestly that when she leaves it her very presence proclaims: "Whoever knows of anything to be testified against me, let him come and testify." Likewise, a disciple of the wise should be so modest in his actions that his ways proclaim what he is.[6]

Midrash, *Numbers Rabbah* 1.3 (circa 12th century)

Numbers Rabbah is an exegetical and homiletic work on the Book of Numbers. The passage depicts God seeking privacy and loving modesty. In addition, Moses himself is considered "the king's daughter within the palace" of Psalm 45.

Scripture states: "The Lord spoke to Moses in the wilderness of Sinai, in the Tent of Meeting" (Numbers 1:1). Before the Tent of Meeting was set up, God spoke with him from the bush, as it says, "God called to him out of the bush" (Exodus 3:4). Then, "The Lord spoke to Moses and Aaron in the land of Egypt" (Exodus 12:1). God also spoke to him in Midian, as it says, "The Lord said to Moses in Midian" (Exodus 4:19). At Sinai also God spoke to him, as it says, "The Lord spoke to Moses on Mount Sinai" (Leviticus 25:1). As soon, however, as the Tent of Meeting was set up, God thought, "How beautiful is modesty!" As it says, "Walk modestly with your God" (Micah 6:8), and so God thenceforth spoke to him in the Tent of Meeting.

David likewise said, "All glorious is the king's daughter within the palace; her raiment is of chequer work inwrought with gold" (Psalms 45:14). "The king's daughter" alludes to Moses, as is inferred from the following passages. It is said, "And I will place the Egyptians at the mercy of a harsh lord" (Isaiah 19:4); this applies to the plagues that came upon Egypt. "And a strong king [*melekh az*] shall rule over them" (Isaiah 19:4) applies to Moses who was master (literally "king") of the Torah, which is designated "strength"; as it is said, "The Lord will give strength [*az*] to his people" (Psalms 29:11). Therefore, "All glorious is the king's daughter within the palace."

"Her raiment is of chequer work inwrought with gold" [*mishbetzot zahav*] alludes to Aaron; as it says [giving instructions for the High Priest's garments], "Then make frames of gold" [*mishbetzot zahav*] (Exodus 28:13).

From here it has been inferred that a woman who conducts herself with becoming modesty deserves, though she be a lay Israelitess [not the daughter of a priest or Levite], to be married to a priest and to rear up High Priests; since it is said, "Her raiment is of chequer work inwrought with gold."

The Holy One, blessed be He, said, "In like manner, it befits My dignity that I should speak in private," as is implied in the text, "When Moses went into the Tent of Meeting that God might speak with him" (Numbers 7:89).

Maimonides, *Mishneh Torah, Laws of Forbidden Intercourse* 21:17 (1180)

Maimonides (1135–1204), known as the Rambam (because of the Hebrew initials for Rabbi Moses ben Maimon), wrote the law code Mishneh Torah. *His ruling on hair covering, however, did not become standard practice among Ashkenazim.*

Daughters of Israel should not walk in the market place bareheaded, regardless of whether they are married or unmarried.

Joseph Karo, *Shul<u>h</u>an Arukh, Ora<u>h</u> Hayyim* 75:1,2 (1564)

The Shulḥan Arukh concisely explains Jewish law. The rule concerning married women's head covering is discussed among the rules concerning men's recital of the Shema.

In the presence of a woman exposing a handsbreadth that she normally keeps covered, even one's own wife, one may not recite the *Shema*.

In the presence of a woman exposing her hair, which she normally keeps covered, one may not recite the *Shema*. But in the presence of virgins, who normally go out bareheaded, it is permitted.

Questions for Discussion

1. In the Talmud and Midrash, the Rabbis understand modesty to incorporate humility, reticence, and bodily privacy. For example, in *Ruth Rabbah* the Rabbis praise Ruth for her modest behavior, and they give illustrations of these three aspects of modesty: bodily privacy—rather than bending over to gather grain, Ruth gathers from a sitting position; reticence—Ruth sits to one side of the other reapers; and a humble attitude—Ruth gathers only the leftovers. Today, we tend to think of these three ideas as separate. Discuss the ways in which these concepts are connected in the excerpts from rabbinic literature above. In your own experience, how are they related?

2. The value of modesty as espoused in classic Jewish texts seems starkly opposed to the prevailing values of contemporary American society. Comment.

3. Consider the story about Rachel told in the Talmud (the same story is told in both *Baba Batra* and *Megillah*). According to the Talmud, Rachel acts modestly when she gives the identifying marks to her sister Leah. How would you define Rachel's act? Is it, for instance, an act of kindness, love for her sister, pity? In what way does your definition of Rachel's action conform to your definition of modesty?

4. The Rabbis of the talmudic era praise modesty in both men and women. Both Rabbi Yose and Kim<u>h</u>it are strikingly modest in their dress; both Saul and Rachel are rewarded for their selflessness; and the modest bride is considered a role model for the (male) disciple of the wise. Nonetheless, modesty—especially modesty in dress—is today

considered a particular virtue of women. Why has modesty's applicability narrowed?

5. Jewish law, developed over centuries and over continents, never adopts a specific and detailed dress code. Instead, contemporary usage (along with certain general prohibitions) is the rule: In any given place and time what is normally covered in that place and time should remain covered by Jewish women. Does this sort of dress code seem logical? How is the rule of contemporary usage developed in the rabbinic literature presented in this chapter?

MODESTY IN TWENTIETH-CENTURY JUDAISM

Today, when an American rabbi speaks of *tzeniut*, that rabbi is almost certain to be Orthodox. Though the value of humility—of putting others first and oneself last, of avoiding conceit and boastfulness—is upheld among all denominations of American Judaism, this type of modesty is generally not known as *tzeniut* in non-Orthodox settings. The value of demure clothing for women, by way of contrast, is upheld primarily among the Orthodox. Indeed, among today's Orthodox Jews, a woman's modest dress code has become almost synonymous with the word *tzeniut*. Nonetheless, Orthodox Jews do see a woman's modest clothing as symbolic of her commitment to the ideals of humility, decency, reticence, patience, and privacy.

Because Jewish law offers no detailed rules for women's dress, different Orthodox populations currently adopt slightly different codes. For instance, no observant Orthodox woman will expose her shoulders or thighs, but the modern Orthodox woman may well expose her elbows and most of her calves, while the most right-wing Orthodox woman will wear sleeves to her wrists and a skirt that reaches her ankles. And all the gradations between these two clothing styles indicate the degree of modernity or the lack thereof! Similarly, right-of-center Orthodoxy interprets the law of *beged ish* to forbid women from wearing trousers and even from wearing culottes and split skirts, while left-of-center Orthodoxy interprets the law to allow women to wear slacks (and culottes) that have been specifically designed and marketed for women—reasoning that these items are not "men's apparel."

Rabbi Moshe Feinstein (1895–1986), cited extensively, is perhaps the pre-eminent twentieth-century interpreter of Jewish law for American Orthodoxy. His reasoning is at one and the same time strikingly original and deeply traditional. His rigorous application of rabbinic law to the modern world, alongside his understanding and appreciation of modernity, ensures that his influence remains vital.

by Claudia Chernov

MODESTY IN RECENT JEWISH WRITINGS

Rabbi Moshe Feinstein, *Igrot Moshe, Yoreh De'ah*, 1:81 (1959)

As far as the clothing worn here in the United States, recent fashions which are downright promiscuous, even though among our sins Jewish women wear them as well, are considered as non-Jewish practice, due to its very promiscuity. Thus, quite apart from the obvious problem of their being promiscuous, such garments should be forbidden to Jewish women by virtue of "Do not follow their [the non-Jews'] practices" (Leviticus 18:3).

Rabbi Moshe Feinstein, *Igrot Moshe, Ora*h *Hayyim*, 1:42 (1959)

In response to a question about reciting the Shema *in the presence of women with uncovered heads, Rabbi Feinstein carefully differentiates between the issue of male erotic stimulation during prayer or Torah study and the issue of appropriate clothing for Jewish women.*

In our age, when amongst our many sins most women unfortunately go bareheaded despite the prohibition, *Arukh HaShulhan** wrote that we may be lenient about reciting the *Shema* in their presence. After all, they do not normally cover their hair, and what constitutes an erotic stimulus as far as the *Shema* and Torah study is determined by what normally is covered. Hence, the prohibition itself does not render hair a "covered part."

An important proof for his view is Rav Sheshet's need to demonstrate the erotic nature of hair from the verse, "Your hair is as a flock of goats" (Song of Songs 4:1), that is, from a verse praising her beauty. Why did he not quote the verse, "the priest shall bare the woman's head" (Numbers 5:18), from which we derive that it is forbidden to go bareheaded? Rather, a prohibition against going with hair uncovered is clearly not enough to redefine the hair as an erotic stimulus, hence a verse had to be brought praising her beauty.

Also, since it is not forbidden to recite the *Shema* in the presence of unmarried women, we see the verse's praise does not create any prohibition for those who normally go bareheaded. Therefore, nowadays, that even married women have become accustomed to going bareheaded despite the prohibition, their hair no longer constitutes an erotic stimulus regarding the *Shema* or Torah study. When there is no other choice this logic may be relied upon, although the God-fearing should be careful to

---

* Rabbi Yehiel Epstein (1829–1908) is known as the *Arukh HaShulhan*, the title of his commentary on the *Shulhan Arukh*.

turn their heads away from the women throughout the service, and if this is impossible, they should shut their eyes.

Rabbi Moshe Feinstein, *Igrot Moshe, Even HaEzer*, 2:12 (1961)

Since the nineteenth century, Orthodox Jewish women have covered their hair with wigs. Although most rabbis have permitted wigs as hair covering, certain stricter rabbis have forbidden them.

Although some sages refuse the use of wigs, most allow it, including our chief halakhic authorities. Since we find no prohibition in the Talmud, we cannot learn from other sources that forbid it because of *marit ayin*, suspicion on the part of others.

One can usually discern that a woman is wearing a wig, and even if a man cannot tell, in the vast majority of cases, a woman can. Those few instances in which women cannot tell provide the rabbis with insufficient cause to forbid it. Another main reason not to apply *marit ayin*: Everyone knows that a woman may be wearing a wig, and will assume her to be reputable.

You cannot halakhically prevent your esteemed *rebbetzin* [rabbi's wife] from wearing a wig. Even if you wish to be strict, you may not force your own strictures upon her, for this is exclusively her realm. She is behaving lawfully, following the majority view, the one that seems right, and you cannot be strict with her, even if she does not cover her wig at all.

Rabbi Jehiel Jacob Weinberg, *Seridei Eish* II, Paragraph 91 (1961-1966)

Rabbi Weinberg (1885-1966) was a popular teacher and prominent talmudic authority.

Now we can understand the topic better, when noting the words of Maimonides that he wrote in his *Book of the Commandments* (negative precepts 39, 40), and the following are his words: "that we are prohibited from following the ways of those who rebel against God in that the women wear men's clothing and adorn men's adornments because this violates 'A woman shall not put on man's apparel' (Deuteronomy 22:5), meaning that any woman who should adorn herself in a man's adornment that is well known in her time to be designated specifically for a man, should receive lashes [be penalized]."

... And note that the action that is prohibited is women adorning themselves with men's adornments, or the men adorning themselves in women's adornments, because these types of actions often cause people to be brought to illicit sexual behavior. Such behavior is well known among those who are debauched, and is often done among those heathens who worship idols.

Rabbi Ovadiah Yosef, *Yabia Omer VI, Yoreh De'ah 14,* letter 1 (1976)

Rabbi Ovadiah Yosef (born 1920), the former Sephardi Chief Rabbi of Israel, is the head of Israel's Shas party, a religious Sephardi political party. He is a renowned authority on religious law. Yabia Omer *is a multi-volume collection of his responsa.*

It is a great *mitzvah* [commandment] to rebuke those girls who wear short skirts, or at least those enrolled in schools that teach Torah observance. We must strive in earnest toward the improvement of our young women, guiding them in the modest ways of our saintly matriarchs.

Giti Bendheim (1984)

Giti Bendheim, an Orthodox Jewish woman living in New York, gives a personal view of hair covering.

Covering one's hair ... creates a constant personal awareness of a commitment to dressing according to criteria other than those dictated by vanity, fashion, politics, or mood. A commitment to hair covering pulls one back, if in only an emotional sense, into the bosom of the traditional community, where the values may differ from those of the marketplace....

I think that one of the more subtly significant aspects of hair covering is the controlling effect it has, not only over the behavior of others, but over other aspects of one's own behavior.... If I perceive my hat as a barrier between myself and the people around me—or if they perceive it in that way—maybe that in itself is a form of self-imposed modesty that would be otherwise unattainable.[7]

Susan Grossman and Rivka Haut, *Daughters of the King* (1992)

Susan Grossman, a Conservative rabbi, and Rivka Haut, an Orthodox activist, discuss the connection between the ideal of modesty and restrictions placed upon Jewish women's public activity.

"The king's daughter is all glorious within" (Psalm 45:14).*

This verse has been cited as proof that, according to tradition, women have divinely ordained roles that preclude any public activity. Rabbis throughout the ages, including our own, have cited this beautiful image to justify excluding women from public life, restricting their dress, and stressing that women's sole legitimate sphere of activity is *within* the home....

Psalm 45 is a beautiful hymn written in praise of an earthly king. It

---

* This is the King James translation.

describes the "kings' daughters" of other nations who have come to wait upon the Israelite king (Psalm 45:10)....

By the rabbinic period, this verse was already taken out of its original biblical context and endowed with completely different meanings.

An anecdote that appears several times in the Jerusalem Talmud and midrashic literature praises a woman named Kimḥit for her unusual modesty.... This oft-repeated anecdote is meant to encourage modesty by stressing its rewards. Kimḥit's reward is vicarious. Paradoxically, the more private Kimḥit is, the more public will be her son's position.[8]

Susan Starr Sered, "Modesty and Israeli Women's Bodies" (2000)

In What Makes Women Sick? Maternity, Modesty, and Militarism in Israeli Society* *Professor Sered explores the cultural background to the poor health status of Israeli women. The book addresses women's role in the military, public policies that shape women's reproductive lives, and religious rituals and discourses relevant to women's bodily experiences. The following excerpt is from chapter 5, "The Scrutinized Body: Under the Knife, in Front of the Camera, and in Back of the Bus." This chapter also discusses anorexia among young Israeli women, portrayals of women in the Israeli media, attitudes toward Women of the Wall, and other cases of conflict over women's bodily presence in the public sphere.*

Portrayals of women in the Israeli media frequently express concern with women's bodies: The message of newspapers, magazines, radio, and television is that women's bodies are interesting—women's *bodies* but not women's *issues*. In Israeli culture, scrutiny of women's bodies—with the possible exception of openly pornographic scrutiny—tends to be presented as a means to a legitimate and noble end. The most common expressions of corporeal scrutiny are linked to consumerism, fashion, advertising, and more generally Israel's increasingly capitalist ethos.

What is singularly Israeli is that the construction of the beautiful female consumer-consumable body co-exists with deeply embedded, Jewish religious discourses of female corporeality. The consumer-driven scrutiny of women's bodies is mirrored in a religion-driven scrutiny, the most commonly specified reasons for which are modesty and purity—attributes considered especially important, yet especially precarious, in women. Female bodies are thought to be complex, capricious, and contestable—and thus legitimate objects for on-going exercises in deciphering. In Jewish religious discourse, women seem to be defined as intrinsically immodest, a state that can be corrected only partially and

---

*The research for this book was conducted in 1998–99 while Susan Sered was Scholar-in-Residence at the Hadassah International Research Institute on Jewish Women, located at Brandeis University.

temporarily through strict dress codes, on-going supervision, and confinement to the domestic sphere. Because modesty and purity are understood to be precarious and impermanent states for women, new demands and friction are frequent. A great deal of the public discourse regarding women's bodies has to do with acts of covering and uncovering. As cultural symbols women's bodies are not understood to be static. Rather they are unpredictable and unreliable—in need of surveillance, investigation, and mending.

In an exceptionally insightful headline, the *Jerusalem Post* of August 9, 1996, declared, "The Ultra-Orthodox Attempt to Control Jerusalem Is Being Waged Over the Bodies of Local Women." The text of the article reported a series of verbal, spitting, and rock-throwing attacks on women Ministry of Education employees at a Ministry branch located on the seam between downtown Jerusalem and the ultra-Orthodox Mea She'arim neighborhood. Apparently, the clothing practices of the Ministry's employees did not meet ultra-Orthodox standards for women's modesty. During the six weeks preceding the newspaper report, *more than thirty women had been attacked* in the neighborhood of the Ministry, and Ministry women had staged at least one protest demonstration.

The press reported that an undercover policewoman sent to the neighborhood of the Education Ministry as a decoy (she was instructed to wear a sleeveless dress and walk around in the neighborhood) was violently assaulted. Upon leaving the car, "I heard a man shouting, 'Whore, get out of here.'" This kind of derogatory sexual language is typical in a wide range of situations of gender conflict, serving to reduce women from agents capable of ideological stances to female bodies immutably mired in sexuality. Two hours later when the policewoman returned to the car, another ultra-Orthodox man reiterated the same corporeal accusation, and then, "He picked up a large rock and threw it at me."

In a characteristic public reaction to conflicts of this sort, Deputy Mayor of Jerusalem Haim Miller (a representative of the ultra-Orthodox Yahadut HaTorah Party) demanded that the Ministry of Education instruct its employees to wear suitable clothing to work "and not like to the sea shore" (*HaAretz*, July 31, 1996). Miller's comments invoke two somewhat distinct issues. The first concerns *who* has the right to determine what women should wear, the second shifts the focus of the conversation away from who to *what*—what style of clothing is appropriate? In a culture accustomed to gazing at women's bodies, discussions of "what she was wearing" easily supersede the deeper question of who controls women's bodies.

As the conflict progressed, *HaAretz* reported, posters had gone up around the neighborhood of Mea She'arim demanding that the offices of the Ministry of Education be moved. The posters, invoking a language of purity, called on ultra-Orthodox residents to prepare themselves for a struggle. Mea She'arim men framed their objection to the "immodest" clothing of the Ministry women in culturally resonant terms: The women "pollute the eyes of our children" (*Ma'ariv*, September 30, 1996). This short sentence attributes cosmic, or at least symbolic, danger to women's bodies. The danger inherent in women's bodies, it seems, is specifically menacing to children; women's bodies in their "natural" state imperil the collectivity's future.[9]

Questions for Discussion

1. Rabbi Moshe Feinstein writes that wearing revealing clothing "here in the United States [is] considered as non-Jewish practice." Among Orthodox Jews, women's hair covering is a public symbol, similar to the *kippah*, proclaiming the wearer to be observant. In the introduction to this chapter, Leora Tanenbaum claimed that today's Orthodox clothing is a uniform: "a way of effectively and publicly proclaiming one's affiliation with the community" and a way to differentiate oneself from non-Jewish Americans. Do you agree? What are the advantages and disadvantages to this type of public proclamation? Discuss also the similarities and differences in men's and women's public proclamations.

2. Though Rabbi Feinstein does permit men to study Torah or recite the *Shema* in the presence of bareheaded women, this option should be exercised only "when there is no other choice." His recommendation is: "the God-fearing should be careful to turn their heads away from the women throughout the service, and if this is impossible, they should shut their eyes." Discuss Rabbi Feinstein's differentiation between behavior that Jewish law would permit and the ideal behavior that Jewish law would prefer.[10] (An aside: Should "the God-fearing" women turn their heads away from the men?)

3. Discuss Rabbi Feinstein's attitude toward wigs. What is the tone of his remarks? Why?

4. As Susan Grossman and Rivka Haut point out, women remaining indoors is a core notion in rabbinic literature. As we read, the Mishnah prohibited women from spinning in the street, and the Talmud praised Sarah for remaining in her tent. These two passages are just a sampling of the extensive literature written in praise of women remaining indoors. Grossman and Haut remark that this notion has been used to argue against women's participation in synagogue ritual and also to argue against women working outside of the home. Yet in American society, where even the most traditional wives are expected to shop for food and household supplies and also to transport children to and from piano lessons, scouts, religious school, sports team practices, and so on, any argument based on the notion of remaining indoors seems extremely remote. Can we claim this personal privacy or "indoors" aspect of

modesty in any way that makes sense both to our lives today and to the Rabbis' intent?

5. Giti Bendheim states: "There are certain limits that Judaism wants me to set, that I want to set for myself, and my consciousness of having deliberately thwarted my own vainer instincts in favor of a higher principle confirms and strengthens my higher expectations of myself."[11] The concrete act of covering her hair thus reinforces her sense of spiritual purpose. Compare Bendheim's attitude toward hair covering with your own experience of the spiritual value of other concrete ritual acts such as lighting Shabbat candles, eating kosher foods, etc.

6. Susan Grossman and Rivka Haut note that midrashic literature rewards a woman for her bodily privacy with the public acclaim of her sons. (*Numbers Rabbah* promises the modest woman the public acclaim of her husband.) Why are these rewards vicarious?

7. Discuss the modest dress worn by Orthodox women today. How does your own dress code conform to or reject the ideal of modesty?

8. Susan Starr Sered writes, "The message of [Israeli] newspapers, magazines, radio, and television is that women's bodies are interesting— women's *bodies* but not women's *issues*." To what extent is this also true in the United States? What accounts for Israelis' dismissive attitude toward women's issues?

9. Professor Sered shows how escalating demands for women's modest clothing reveal attitudes toward women's bodies as "unpredictable and unreliable—in need of surveillance, investigation, and mending." Discuss.

Suggested Activities and Programs

1. Ask one or more volunteers to read *What Makes Women Sick? Maternity, Modesty, and Militarism in Israeli Society* by Susan Starr Sered, and to report to your Rosh Hodesh group. Professor Sered masterfully analyzes relationships between culture (both secular and religious culture) and women's bodies, and she reaches a number of provocative conclusions. Have volunteers choose passages from Sered's work to read aloud and then have them lead a group discussion about the concepts.

2. Organize a debate on the value of modest clothing. Divide the group into two sides: those who will argue that modest clothing supports and reinforces the concept of women as innately worthy, and those who believe that modest clothing reinforces the concept of women as innately impure. Allow ten minutes for the two sides to discuss their rationale, then have each side appoint a spokeswoman to debate.

3. Organize an education day on women in Orthodox Judaism. Refer to pages 145–146 for a suggested schedule.

1. Taken from Morris J. Sugarman's translation of *Iggeret Hakodesh* (The Holy Letter) in *Ethical Literature, Teacher's Edition* (West Orange, NJ: Behrman House, 1987), pages 31–32. Reprinted in Carol Diament, ed., *Jewish Women Living the Challenge* (New York: Hadassah, 1997), page 71.

2. Susan Weidman Schneider, *Jewish and Female: Choices and Changes in Our Lives Today* (New York: Touchstone, 1985), page 66.

3. Wendy Shalit, *A Return to Modesty: Discovering the Lost Virtue* (New York: Free Press, 1999).

4. Cited in Susan Weidman Schneider, page 235.

5. Cited in *The Book of Legends, Sefer Ha-Aggadah: Legends from the Talmud and Midrash*, eds. Hayim Nahman Bialik and Yehoshua Hana Ravnitzky, trans. William G. Braude (New York: Schocken, 1992), page 462.

6. Cited in *The Book of Legends, Sefer Ha-Aggadah: Legends from the Talmud and Midrash*, pages 434–435.

7. Giti Bendheim, cited in Susan Weidman Schneider, pages 239–240. Bendheim wrote on hair covering specifically for Schneider's *Jewish and Female*.

8. Susan Grossman and Rivka Haut, Preface to *Daughters of the King: Women and the Synagogue* (Philadelphia: Jewish Publication Society, 1992), pages xxii–xxiii.

9. Susan Starr Sered, excerpt adapted from typescript of "The Scrutinized Body: Under the Knife, in Front of the Camera, and in Back of the Bus," in *What Makes Women Sick? Maternity, Modesty, and Militarism in Israeli Society* (Hanover, NH: University Press of New England, 2000).

10. We are indebted to Norma Baumel Joseph, who writes that Rabbi Feinstein's "decisions reveal a distinction between the preferred and the adequate" ("Hair Distractions: Women and Worship in the Responsa of Rabbi Moshe Feinstein" in *Jewish Legal Writings by Women*, Micah D. Halpern and Chana Safrai, eds. [Jerusalem: Urim, 1998], page 10).

11. Giti Bendheim, cited in Susan Weidman Schneider, page 240.

JEWISH SELF-HATRED

Being ashamed of one's Jewishness—and making jokes about being ashamed—seem to be staples of contemporary American Jewish culture. Think of Woody Allen's *Annie Hall*, in which Allen anxiously imagines that his WASP girlfriend's family sees him as a pasty-faced <u>H</u>asid with earlocks and long beard—not that he's wrong. Consider the 1996 "Too Jewish?" art exhibit, sponsored by New York's Jewish Museum, which featured the work of Jewish artists as they explored anti-Jewish stereotyping and its impact on self image.

American Jews, by and large, want to fit into mainstream American—that is, non-Jewish—culture. Many who have rejected Judaism, as well as many who try to balance its claims with the claims of American culture, feel embarrassed by association with anyone or anything considered "too Jewish." This sentiment is a mild manifestation of Jewish self-hatred, a psychological phenomenon first described in the early twentieth century. Jewish self-hatred can be defined as rejection and fear of one's own Jewish characteristics that leads to antipathy toward other Jews who display Jewish characteristics. Hatred of self because of real or imagined Jewish qualities is possible only when another cultural model exists, and hatred of self is *likely* only when the members of the other culture hate Jews. Thus, Jewish self-hatred, a recently defined psychological category, has roots stretching back thousands of years, with recognizable self-haters found in every era and every land where Jews have been a despised minority.*

---

*The definition and analysis of Jewish self-hatred are derived from Zionist theory:

In examining Jewish history, we identify the self-haters by their disproportionate hatred of other Jews, particularly by their hatred of Jews committed to Judaism. Yet even though Jews have hated other Jews since biblical times (witness Jacob's sons, who despise their brother Joseph only because of their jealousy), to meet the definition of self-hate, one's hatred of other Jews must be rooted in hatred of self. The closest ancient counterpart to Jewish self-hatred, therefore, can be found in the Hanukkah story. During the years of the Syrian Greek empire, very many Jews admired Greek culture. When Antiochus, governor of Judea, banned all Jewish religious observance, many of the wealthier, more intellectual, and more sophisticated Jews complied; they were willing to abandon Judaism in exchange for the lifestyle and religion of Greece. When the Maccabees battled the Syrian rulers, they were in essence fighting a civil war against their hellenized brothers and sisters. These Jews who sided with the Syrian Greeks are precursors to modern self-hating Jews.

Moving forward in time, the Middle Ages provide clear examples of Jewish self-hatred. In Europe, continual public humiliation of Jews, alongside unremitting pressure to convert to Christianity, led many Jews to forsake Judaism. Of the Jews who chose Christianity, many continued to secretly observe Jewish rituals, hoping one day to return to the faith of their ancestors. Others, though, despised the Jewish religion, and some went as far as to viciously persecute Jews who refused to convert. In the 13th century Pablo Christiani, a French man who had been born a Jew, became a fervent anti-Jewish polemicist. In 1263, he entered a disputation with the renowned Bible and Talmud commentator Rabbi Moses ben Naḥman (known as Naḥmanides) in the presence of King James I of Aragon. Such disputations, ostensibly public debates on the relative merits of Judaism and Christianity, were in fact Christian propaganda exhibitions, aimed at forcing the Jewish participants to admit the truth of the Christian faith. In 1269, Pablo Christiani, who had returned from Spain, persuaded Louis IX to require that all French Jews wear an identifying badge on their clothing.[1]

In 1391 the Spanish Jew Solomon HaLevi, a 40-year-old scholar who held an eminent diplomatic position, converted to Christianity. He took the name Paulus de Sancta Maria and traveled to Paris to study theology. When he returned to Aragon, he tried to persuade King John I to enact anti-Jewish legislation.

Jewish self-hatred arises in the diaspora. Jews who hate themselves in the State of Israel would be given a different label (perhaps psychotically depressed)—similar to Americans who hate themselves in the United States or Chinese who hate themselves in Taiwan. Israeli Jews who hate Judaism would be labeled anti-clerics—similar to British Anglicans who hate the Church of England.

Joshua Lorki, a Jewish physician and writer who had studied with Solomon HaLevi, converted to Christianity in 1412 and took the name Hieronymus de Sancta Fide. Hieronymus immediately arranged a disputation with the leading Jews of Aragon and Catalonia. The anti-pope, Benedict III, who was accepted in Spain as pope, presided. The Jewish scholars, who knew that winning the disputation—or even speaking freely—would not be permitted, participated against their will. During the disputation Hieronymus treated the Jews with contempt, and he openly threatened them with trial by Inquisition if they failed to agree with his conclusions. The disputation lasted nearly twenty months, and during that time the Jewish scholars, absent from their homes and livelihoods, became impoverished. Their communities, disheartened and persecuted, lost many members to Christianity. After the disputation ended, Hieronymus traveled widely, always attempting to convince Jews to turn to Christianity.[2]

What caused these and other apostates to persecute Jews? Why did they not simply live Christian lives, find spiritual sustenance in their new Catholic faith, and find contentment in the company of their new non-Jewish companions? Modern psychological theorists answer that the convert's shame and hatred of self led him to try to eradicate all that was Jewish, and in so doing eradicate his own connection to Judaism.

When we examine the modern period, we find ample documentation for the hatred of self felt by the Jews of Western and Central Europe. With the Enlightenment and the possibility of Jewish participation in Europe's civic life, antisemitism—and self-hatred—took a different, less theological form. Jewish self-hatred now expanded to become hatred of one's Jewish ethnic origins or of the "Jewish race"—encompassing not only religious customs, but Jewish physical features, speech, style of clothing, manners, cultural traditions, ancestry, and familial connections.

Several Jews seeking acceptance into European society wrote of their feelings of shame and humiliation over their Jewish origins. Heirs to the Enlightenment and the finest ideals of Western civilization, they described their inner torment when forced to acknowledge kinship to the impoverished residents of the Eastern European *shtetl*. In some Central European Jews, self-hatred took an extreme and psychotic form, leading even to suicide.[3] It is this type of self-hatred that gave rise to the term, coined in 1930 by the German philosopher Theodor Lessing (1872–1933).

In democratic countries, as the scholar Jacob Neusner observed, Jewish self-hatred appeared not "as an acute pathology" but "as a chronic malady of neurosis."[4] Jewish self-haters in early twentieth-century America often focused their anxiety on recently-arrived Eastern European Jews (as did Jews in Germany, England, and elsewhere). With growing acceptance of Jews after the birth of the State of Israel, succeeding generations of American Jews focused their antipathy on religious Jews, on Jews of different denominations, on recognizable Jews, on

Israeli Jews, and—perhaps most of all—on Jewish women through insults about Jewish mothers and Jewish American Princesses.

By the end of the century, however, even non-psychotic expressions of Jewish self-hatred had become relatively rare. The concept of self-hatred, though, had become so much a part of America's psychic turf that every minority group referred to it. For example, a *New York Times* reviewer criticized the 1999 film *Flawless* for reinforcing "every negative stereotype ascribed to gay men in drag," because the main character "is hysterical, masochistic, voracious, self-loathing, and ragingly 'on' every minute."[5] At the same time, within the Jewish community, calling a political or ideological adversary a self-hater had become so routine that it conveyed little more than a general sense of disapprobation.

by Claudia Chernov and Leora Tanenbaum

WRITINGS BY AND ABOUT THEODOR LESSING, 1872–1933

As a young man, Lessing converted from Judaism to Lutheran Christianity and became an impassioned antisemitic propagandist. Through exposure to Zionism, he gained an awareness of the motives behind his hatred of Jews. He describes his motivation, together with other case studies, in the 1930 book Der jüdischer Selbsthass (Jewish Self-Hatred), *the first comprehensive analysis of the phenomenon. Lessing was murdered by Nazis in 1933.*

Der jüdischer Selbsthass by Theodor Lessing (1930)

Lessing describes his recently-acquired Zionist outlook.

We were told: you are parasites on the land of others—and so we tore ourselves loose. We were told: you are the middlemen among the peoples—and so we raised our children to be farmers and peasants. We were told: you are decaying and becoming cowardly weaklings—and so we went into battles and produced the best soldiers. We were told: everywhere you are only tolerated—and we answered: our greatest longing is to be an object of tolerance no more. But when we insisted on maintaining ourselves as a distinct people, we were told: have you not yet learned that your preserving your distinctiveness is treason against all international, pan-human values? And so we replied by quietly disbanding the Jewish Legion, by giving up our self-defense, and by placing our just cause under the protection of the European conscience. And what is the result?—[Massacres in Palestine and agitation for pogroms in the diaspora. From nowhere can help be expected. Hereafter each Jew must plan his own salvation. He must grope his way to some kind of spiritual equanimity. He is most likely to find this equanimity by learning to love his fate, by learning to will what he must. Fate and necessity have made him part of a people—as strange as any, as heroic and as decadent as others on the present scene. Let him learn to love this people and to help in its resurgence. He is not only the son of some peddling tradesman and some insignificant woman, but also the offspring of Judas Maccabaeus and Queen Esther. He is a link in a chain that reaches back to Saul and David and Moses. By regenerating himself and by assuming his share of the suffering and struggle that fall to the lot of Jews, let him pave the way for a brighter heaven for his children and the children of his people.][6]

Memoir by Theodor Lessing (1935)

In a memoir published after his murder, Lessing told of his youth and his feelings about himself as a Jew. In the excerpt below, Lessing mentions a man wearing a caftan. This article of clothing symbolized the differences between immigrant and German-born Jewish men, who wore trousers. In fact, American as well as European Jews often derisively referred to Jews who had fled from Russia or Galicia as "caftan Jews."

Once, on the street, my mother pointed to a man in a caftan and said, "There goes a Jew." I then concluded that we were not really Jews.[7]

Profile of Theodor Lessing by Solomon Liptzin (1944)

Solomon Liptzin (1901–1995), a scholar of German and Yiddish literature, wrote brief biographies of Lessing and several other Jews in a book entitled Germany's Stepchildren.

[The Nazis found] in the early essays of Theodor Lessing ... a Jewish cultural historian who was [extremely] harsh in his condemnation of his co-religionists, especially of those whose habitat lay east of Berlin, Breslau, and Vienna.

Lessing, a disciple of Nietzsche and a contemporary of Spengler, was professor of philosophy at Hanover and a publicist of note, famed for his bold paradoxes, pungent anecdotes, and vitriolic satires. In his early years, when he strutted about as a German super-patriot ... he exercised his wit and scholarship in furthering anti-Jewish feeling. Later, when he underwent a complete change of heart and trumpeted forth his faith in the Jewish renaissance, he made a public confession that his former views resulted from self-hatred, a psychological phenomenon to which German Jews of assimilationist background easily fell a prey. It was self-hatred that led him to ridicule and defame the Eastern Jews after a tour of several weeks in Galicia. It was self-hatred that led him to pillory the literary and critical contributions of Jews in such unfair and extravagant language that Thomas Mann, a non-Jew, had to take him to task and had to castigate him for his antisemitic approach to intellectual problems. This extreme self-hatred, which he himself afterwards best described in his book *Der jüdischer Selbsthass*, changed under the impact of the First World War to an equally extreme overestimation of Judaism, so that by

1933 the Nazis rightfully saw in him a most violent champion of the non-Aryans and found it necessary to send assassins to Prague in order to put an end to his dangerous pen.

[In Lessing's later works] he saw [the Jews as] an Asiatic people hurled upon the European scene and hence foreordained to occupy an intermediate position between the two cultural continents. Transvaluating accepted values, he discovered the strength of the Jews in a direction which others failed to perceive, in a closeness to life's elemental roots, in a proximity to the warm bosom of nature, in a preservation of pagan, pre-Christian opposition to all logical and ethical obscurantism, in an awareness of the relative unimportance of the individual soul in comparison with the eternally immutable absolute, in a fearless facing of fate, and in a consciousness of the responsibility of each being toward every other being. Despite the strong earth-bound instincts with which fate endowed the Jews, a tragic history cut them off from all contact with the soil and subjected them, ever since the dim and distant past, to thousands of years of torture amidst artificial surroundings, until their divorce from nature was complete and until this people of peasants became over-spiritualized and decadent. To appreciate what happened to this group, Lessing compared it to a beautiful body subjected to tortures, infected with poisons, and then exhibited with all its sores and wounds to prove it contaminated and unworthy of brotherhood. Judaism was made a victim of the economy of exploitation during the centuries of Christianity and, in the end, it was held responsible for the exploitation practiced by those centuries. As the oldest and most closely knit group on this planet, the Jews could by now have supplied the world with its most ancient nobility, if it had been allowed a normal development.... A small minority—Lessing called them the elite of contemporary Jewry—found its way back to the horribly abused and exploited Asiatic soil and, beginning with the afforestation of the ruined Palestinian land, paved the way for others to follow. A people, dying and almost dead, started to trek back to its historic soil, which was also apparently beyond recovery; and in the union of this people with this particular land, both were being revived and restored to health....

This miracle of regeneration, which Lessing preached to others, he experienced in his own soul. The ultra-German philosopher of the early twentieth century, with his scorn of Jews and hatred of Judaism, ended as an ultra-Jewish patriot, atoning for his former aberration by his death in 1933 at the hands of Gestapo agents.[8]

Summary of Lessing's *Der jüdischer Selbsthass* by Jacob Neusner (1979)

The most important early analysis of the phenomenon [of self-hatred] among Jews appeared in Berlin in 1930, in Theodor Lessing's *Der jüdischer Selbsthass*. Lessing appears to have coined the phrase since he gives it in quotation marks and finds it necessary to define it. To the self-hating Jew, all misfortune derives from the fact that one is Jewish. The Jews, moreover, are held responsible for their own fate and therefore are "to blame for all their misfortunes." Clinical reports by Lessing include Jews who urge the Aryans to exterminate the Jews like vermin, and others who remained childless or even committed suicide so as "to remove the stain of Jewishness from mankind." Lessing therefore describes Jewish self-hatred as an acute pathology of psychosis.[9]

HATRED OF JEWS AND SELF-HATRED IN JEWISH WRITINGS

Babylonian Talmud, *Yoma 9b*

The Talmud recounts a legend about two Jewish men who hate each other. Though the Talmud never states that either man feels hatred of self, the men's names, Kamtza and Bar Kamtza, are suggestively similar. Their senseless feud eventually leads to the destruction of the Second Temple in Jerusalem.

Why was the First Temple destroyed? Because of three [evil] things which prevailed there: idolatry, immorality, bloodshed.... But why was the Second Temple destroyed, seeing that in its time they were occupying themselves with Torah, [observance of] precepts, and the practice of charity? Because therein prevailed hatred without cause. That teaches you that groundless hatred is considered as of even gravity with the three sins of idolatry, immorality, and bloodshed together.

Joshua Lorki, Letter to Paulus de Sancta Maria (1391)

About twenty years before his own conversion to Christianity, Joshua Lorki wrote to Paulus (born Solomon HaLevi), asking him why he had converted to Christianity. Joshua Lorki's own doubts are clear, and reveal an emerging Jewish self-hatred. Paulus never answered the letter.

Did you perchance lust after riches and honors? ... Or did the study of philosophy cause you to change so radically and to regard the proofs of faith as vanity and delusion, so that you therefore turned to things more apt to gratify the body and satisfy the intellect without fear and anxiety and apprehension? Or, when you beheld the doom of our homeland, the multitude of the afflictions that have recently befallen us, which ruined and destroyed us, the Lord having almost turned away His countenance from us and given us for food to the fowl of the air and the beasts of the field—did it then seem to you that the name of Israel would be remembered no more? Or perhaps the secrets of prophecy have been revealed to you and the principles of faith—matters not revealed to the great pillars of faith whom we had with us in all the ages of our Exile;

and you saw that our fathers had inherited falsehood, that they had but little comprehension of the intent of the Torah and the Prophecy, and you chose what is true and established?[10]

Rahel Varnhagen, Letter (1795)

Rahel Levin Varnhagen (1771–1833), hostess to one of the most prominent salons of early nineteenth-century Berlin, could be considered the first completely assimilated Jew in German history. Though she never cut herself off from her Jewish friends and relatives, she hated her Jewish origins—her "infamous birth."[11] In her forties she converted to Christianity and married a Prussian diplomat.

I have a strange fancy: it is as if some supramundane being, just as I was thrust into this world, plunged these words with a dagger into my heart: "Yes, have sensibility, see the world as few see it, be great and noble, nor can I take from you the faculty of eternally thinking. But I add one thing more: be a Jewess!" And now my life is a slow bleeding to death. By keeping still I can delay it. Every movement in an attempt to staunch it—new death; and immobility is possible for me only in death itself.... I can, if you will, derive every evil, every misfortune, every vexation from *that*.[12]

Dorothea Veit, Letter (1802)

Dorothea Veit was the daughter of Moses Mendelssohn, the Enlightenment philosopher and leader of German Jewry. Of Mendelssohn's six children, Dorothea and three siblings converted to Christianity.

According to my own feeling, Protestant Christianity [is] much purer and to be preferred to the Catholic one. Catholicism has for me too much similarity to the old Judaism, which I greatly despise. Protestantism, though, seems to me to be the total religion of Jesus and the religion of civilization.[13]

Moses Hess, *Rome and Jerusalem* (1862)

Moses Hess (1812–1875), a writer and political activist, was an early Zionist theorist. The brief volume Rome and Jerusalem *is an exhortation to Jewish nationalism.*

German Antisemitism and Jewish Assimilation: ... Because of the hatred that surrounds him on all sides, the German Jew is determined to cast off all signs of his Jewishness and to deny his race. No reform of the Jewish religion, however extreme, is radical enough for the educated German Jews. But even an act of conversion cannot relieve the Jew of the enormous pressure of German antisemitism. The Germans hate the religion of the Jews less than they hate their race—they hate the peculiar faith of the Jews less than their peculiar noses. Reform, conversion, education, and emancipation—none of these open the gates of society to the German Jew; hence his desire to deny his racial origin. (Moleschott, in his *Physiological Sketches*,[14] tells how the son of a converted Jew used to spend hours every morning at the looking glass, comb in hand, endeavoring to straighten his curly hair, so as to give it a more Teutonic appearance.) ...

The Reawakening of the Nations: As long as the Jew denies his nationality, as long as he lacks the character to acknowledge that he belongs to that unfortunate, persecuted, and maligned people, his false position must become ever more intolerable. What purpose does this deception serve? The nations of Europe have always regarded the existence of the Jews in their midst as an anomaly. We shall always remain strangers among the nations. They may even be moved by a sense of humanity and justice to emancipate us, but they will never *respect* us as long as we make *ubi bene ibi patria* [wherever it is good, that is the homeland] our guiding principle, indeed almost a religion, and place it above our own great national memories. Religious fanaticism may cease to cause hatred of the Jews in the more culturally advanced countries; but despite enlightenment and emancipation, the Jew in exile who denies his nationality will never earn the respect of the nations among whom he dwells. He may become a naturalized citizen, but he will never be able to convince the gentiles of his total separation from his own nationality.

The really dishonorable Jew is not the old-type, pious one, who would rather have his tongue cut out than utter a word in denial of his nationality, but the modern kind, who, like the German outcasts in foreign countries, is ashamed of his nationality because the hand of fate is pressing heavily upon his people. The beautiful phrases about humanity and enlightenment which he uses so freely to cloak his treason, his fear of being identified with his unfortunate brethren, will ultimately not protect him from the judgment of public opinion. These modern Jews hide in vain behind their geographical and philosophical alibis. You may mask yourself a thousand times over; you may change your name, religion, and character; you may travel through the world incognito, so that people may not recognize the Jew in you; yet every insult to the Jewish name will strike you even more than the honest man who admits his Jewish loyalties and who fights for the honor of the Jewish name.[15]

Friedrich Blach (1911)

With the enormous migrations of Jews from Eastern Europe to Western Europe and America in the late nineteenth and early twentieth centuries, assimilated Jews were forced, in a sense, to confront their own ghetto roots. Still subject to pervasive antisemitism and insecure about their status as citizens, many German Jews channeled their anxiety into disdain for the immigrants. Friedrich Blach, like many German Jews, zealously believed in assimilation into non-Jewish German culture, and he argued that Eastern European immigrants would spoil German Jews' progress.

We must finally end our involvement with our overseas *Glaubensgenossen* [co-religionists]. As long as they are in need, we will certainly help them. That is our human duty. But to ask them to make their homes in our country, that is against duty and reason. Duty toward Germany: We really cannot use these "East European" elements here.... Against reason: For over fifty years our most passionate goal has been the extinction of all traces of our centuries-old ghetto life and to efface all cultural distinctions between us and the majority....

Well, then, so be it, free and joyful suicide. For I no longer want to be the self that I was, I want to belong to that magnificent people in whose midst I was born. "Die at the right time: thus spoke Zarathustra." We have endured too long.[16]

Jakob Loewenberg (1914)

In an autobiographical novel, the German writer Jakob Loewenberg (1856–1929) remembers his childhood feelings about Eastern European Jewish immigrants.

We were a little ashamed in the presence of our Christian playmates that these dirty, shabbily dressed beggars were also Jews.[17]

Kurt Lewin (1946)

Kurt Lewin (1890–1947) was born in Germany, and immigrated to the United States in 1932. He was a pioneering psychologist in the study of group interactions, and a lifelong Zionist. Much of his work was devoted to the problems of Jewish self-acceptance as members of a minority.

[The self-hating Jew] will dislike everything specifically Jewish, for he will see in it that which keeps him away from the majority for which he is longing. He will show dislike for those Jews who are outspokenly so, and will frequently indulge in self-hatred....

Jewish self-hatred will die out only when actual equality of status with the non-Jew is achieved. Only then will the enmity against one's own group decrease to the relatively insignificant proportions characteristic of the majority groups. Sound self-criticism will replace it....

There is nothing so important as a clear and fully accepted belonging to a group whose fate has a positive meaning. A long-range view, which includes the past and the future of Jewish life, and links the solution of the minority problem with the problem of the welfare of all human beings, is one of these sources of strength. A strong feeling of being part and parcel of the group and having a positive attitude toward it is ... sufficient condition for the avoidance of attitudes based on self-hatred.[18]

Nathan W. Ackerman and Marie Jahoda,
"Jewish Antisemitism" (1950)

Psychoanalyst Nathan Ackerman (1908–1971), a founder of family therapy, and social scientist Marie Jahoda (born 1907) studied both non-Jewish antisemites and Jewish self-haters, whom they call Jewish antisemites.

Perhaps the most striking manifestation of the power of pervasive group pressures in shaping antisemitism is Jewish antisemitism. The intrapsychic determinants of Jewish and gentile antisemitism seem to be essentially identical. The same emotional predispositions occur in both: the central personality conflict is a deep-seated self-rejection. [One difference between Jewish and gentile antisemites, however, is that the Jew's antisemitism is] in flagrant contradiction of reality; his conflicted, confused concept of self permits him to pretend that he stands outside the Jewish group. Once this pretense is established he can project "bad" qualities onto Jews and conform to the dominant majority like gentile antisemites. This explains why Jewish antisemites must expend so much energy in dissimulating their group membership.

One violent antisemite [among Ackerman and Jahoda's patients] changed his Jewish-sounding name and adopted Christianity not because of religious conviction but in response to the desire to fortify the barrier between himself and the Jewish group. Several patients ... plan conversion to Catholicism, and one woman ... underwent a nose operation to alter her appearance so that she might pass as a Christian. To this end she also wears a cross. Although she wants very much to be married, this can never be with a Jew—"Who wants to be a 'Mrs. Cohen'?"

One patient had, as a boy, avoided all contact with the few Jewish children in his class, and as an adult he has carried through this pattern by living in an area where Jews are barred, trying to achieve his main ambition in life—to be "as good as a gentile." Other patients ... simply changed their Jewish-sounding names.

Two interesting differences between Jewish and gentile antisemitism emerge. First, in examining the content of the antisemitic projections of Jewish antisemites, the absence of "good" qualities is conspicuous. Here, there are no conscious claims that Jews are intelligent, powerful, successful, sexually potent, or ethical. The reason for this probably lies in the precarious illusion of not belonging to the Jewish group, the even greater ambivalence stemming from a dread of discovery, and even more, "conversion" to their Jewishness. Their antisemitism seems better fortified by denying the "good" elements of the cultural stereotype. Knowing deep down that they are Jews—and failures, to boot—they cannot reconcile the culturally favorable aspects of the Jewish stereotype with their own state of being.

Second, it appears that while most gentiles in our case material hate not only Jews but also other groups as well, the Jewish need for hatred is more exclusively directed against Jews. None of the Jewish patients and clients manifested significantly any other form of prejudice.[19]

Philip Roth, "Eli, the Fanatic" (1959)

Philip Roth, author of Portnoy's Complaint *and many other novels, has often been accused of Jewish self-hatred himself. In this short story excerpt, Eli Peck writes to the principal of a residential yeshivah that has recently opened with 18 students.*

Dear Mr. Tzuref:

Our meeting this evening seems to me inconclusive. I don't think there's any reason for us not to be able to come up with some sort of compromise that will satisfy the Jewish community of Woodenton and the Yeshivah and yourself. It seems to me that what most disturbs my neighbors are the visits to town by the gentleman in the black hat, suit, etc. Woodenton is a progressive suburban community whose members, both Jewish and gentile, are anxious that their families live in comfort and beauty and serenity. This is, after all, the twentieth century, and we do not think it too much to ask that the members of our community dress in a manner appropriate to the time and place.

Woodenton, as you may not know, has long been the home of well-to-do Protestants. It is only since the war that Jews have been able to buy property here, and for Jews and gentiles to live beside each other in amity. For this adjustment to be made, both Jews and gentiles alike have had to give up some of their more extreme practices in order not to threaten or offend the other. Certainly such amity is to be desired. Perhaps if such conditions had existed in prewar Europe, the persecution of the Jewish people, of which you and those 18 children have been victims, could not have been carried out with such success—in fact, might not have been carried out at all.

Therefore, Mr. Tzuref, will you accept the following conditions? If you can, we will see fit not to carry out legal action against the Yeshivah for failure to comply with township Zoning ordinances No. 18 and No. 23. The conditions are simply:

1. The religious, educational, and social activities of the Yeshivah of Woodenton will be confined to the Yeshivah grounds.

2. Yeshivah personnel are welcomed in the streets and stores of Woodenton provided they are attired in clothing usually associated with American life in the 20th century.

If these conditions are met, we see no reason why the Yeshivah of Woodenton cannot live peacefully and satisfactorily with the

Jews of Woodenton—as the Jews of Woodenton have come to live with the gentiles of Woodenton. I would appreciate an immediate reply.

Sincerely,

ELI PECK, Attorney[20]

Jay Y. Gonen, "Antisemitism and Zionism" (1975)

Gonen was born in Israel in 1934. He recently retired as professor of psychology from the University of Cincinnati.

One of the dire effects of antisemitism was the internalization by Jews of antisemitic notions. The tragic result has been Jewish self-hate....

Jewish self-hatred and acceptance of antisemitic judgments is a notorious phenomenon. I remember how as a boy in Israel I used to hear children make remarks about modes of prayer. Synagogues were "phooey" and consisted of *Yehudim miztofefim vetzorhim* (overcrowded Jews shouting). The blurted-out Jewish praying in crowded synagogues was unfavorably compared with the unhurried Christian singing in roomy churches where one could feel *hashra'ah* (inspiration).

The negative image that antisemitism imparted to Jews ... appears in a Jewish joke ... in which two Jews, by a miracle, find time to pause and reflect in front of a holy site, the Wailing Wall.... One of them notices that the other is weeping profusely over the destruction of the Second Temple. "Why are you crying so much?" he says. "True, the Temple has been destroyed, but the lot is still worth something!"

Among the Jews of the diaspora, self-hate often reached the proportions of self-negation....

Unlike diaspora Jews, Israeli Jews could adopt antisemitic notions with the illusion that it did not involve self-hate. The hate is allegedly directed only toward diaspora Jews who seem to be rotting in a stultifying state of affairs which Israeli Jews have successfully rid themselves of. A study of Israeli students between the ages of fifteen and twenty-two was conducted by Tamarin and Ben-Zwi [in 1965]. The students' stereotyped descriptions of diaspora Jews [revealed] "a caricatured conception of East-European ghetto-Jew of the turn of the century," and [Tamarin and Ben-Zwi] concluded that these stereotypes had been transmitted to the Israeli youth by their parents....

My own understanding of the phenomenon of Jewish self-hate is that in past generations it was largely nourished by the psychological mechanism of identification with the aggressor. Jews who felt victimized could identify with the aggressing *goyim* and in the process incorporate into their own psychological makeup a badly needed sense of mastery. Zionism served as an effective antidote to this traditional self-hate on the part of diaspora Jews. The basic remedy of Zionism was the psychological switch from passivity to activity and the founding of the Jewish

State. Currently, those Jews who are being oppressed by gentiles (as are many Russian Jews) need not turn to gentiles as they seek an example of mastery, statehood, self-reliance, and staunch nationalism. Now there is Israel with which to identify. As for American Jews, they are not subject to crude oppression or to the typical stress that diaspora Jews were subjected to for generations. Identification with the aggressor is a defense that is being called into operation to meet a felt stress. If there is no stress—that is, if there is no aggression along the old historical patterns of pogroms and legal restrictions—then there is no need for this defense. Things are therefore different for American Jewry. On the one hand, the current gentiles are significantly less oppressive. On the other hand ... by emulating Israelis rather than gentiles, Jews have succeeded in reducing substantially the hitherto stiff price of Jewish self-hate.

The current manifestations of self-hate in Israel are mostly of a different order. They are not a result of identification with others which boomerangs and inflicts wounds of self-hate. Rather, they are the results of identification with one's own ego-ideal. The background for this development is the deep crisis of historical continuity. The sharp break from centuries of "the Jewish way" produced intrapsychic conflicts and fluctuations of self-esteem....

In the past, self-hate and the resultant self-destruction were largely an individual matter, leading to assimilation or suicide. In today's Israel, self-hate is directed against the collective Jewish existence as such. In the past, the diaspora Jew could not blame the collective existence of Jews. There was no Jewish collective holding the reins of power and bearing sole responsibility for its way of life. But now there is one, and sometimes it can serve as a target for hate. Therefore, we now witness a new form of self-hate [such as]: "Everywhere in the world the Jews are the most successful businessmen, but not in Israel; everywhere else they are financial wizards, but not in Israel. You want to know why? Because here in Israel they can deal only with other Jews." ... The real "why," the truly stinging insinuation, is that in Israel there are too many Jews who have to deal with each other. Such needling remarks express an inheritance from antisemitism. On the whole, incorporation of antisemitic notions is not the major force behind Israeli self-hate, but it is there. After all, allusion to the idea of "too many Jews" is an old practice of antisemites....

It is an intriguing phenomenon that both Zionism and antisemitism, in directing their magnifying glass at the Jewish people, tended to focus their attention on the same issues, yet differed in their respective judgments of what they had seen.[21]

Rabbi Susan Schnur (1987)

In 1987, Rabbi Schnur taught a university course on "Contemporary Issues of Jewish Existence." Though her original plans did not include discussion of stereotyping of young Jewish women, her students forced her to examine this manifestation of antisemitism and its effect on Jewish self-image.

My students, as it turned out, were obsessed with JAPs. Week after week, in personal journals that they were keeping for me, they talked JAPs: the stereotypes, dating them, hating them, not *being* them....

The first, and most striking, ostinato in the students' journals was the dissociative one. As one Jewish student framed it, "There are so many JAPs in this class, it makes me sick." (An astonishing number of students were desperate to let me know this.) ...

One pre-law Jewish male in the class ... stated point-blank that he did not date Jewish women. I was shocked by the number of 20-year-old, seemingly fully-assimilated Jewish males who were right up there with Alexander Portnoy* on this subject.[22]

Richard Goldstein (1994)

Goldstein, executive editor of The Village Voice, *wrote in 1991 of the Crown Heights riots and their blatantly antisemitic character, which many left-leaning Jews failed to recognize during the violence itself. Not until well after the murder of Yankel Rosenbaum did major Jewish organizations denounce the riots. Goldstein questions whether this failure stemmed, in part, from hostile attitudes toward* Hasidim, *and he describes his own feelings as an example.*

As a child, I was intensely aware of the old men, stooped and scarred, wandering through the neighborhood with long beards and strange fringes spilling out of their pants. They frightened me—and I still recoil from hasidism. To me they are no different from Christian fundamentalists—just as nasty, narrow-minded, and contemptuous. I remember a group of Hasidim picketing in Greenwich Village during the early days of the AIDS epidemic. "A gay synagogue is like a whorehouse on Yom Kippur," their handout read. That night, I had a nightmare in which a Hasid wearing a long black coat strode into the hospital room where I lay in a stark white bed. He reached across me and turned the resuscitator off.

These days, when Hasidim cruising the Village in their Mitzvah Mobile ask me, "Are you Jewish?" I reply, "Not if you are." Yet I know my uneasiness in their presence is not just a matter of belief. Sitting across from a Hasid in the subway, I feel that old chill [the fear of antisemitism] in my shoulders. It's not so different from a closet case eyeing a drag queen. These people are *flaming*, and they remind me of my vulnerability. To the antisemite all Jews have horns.[23]

---

* Rabbi Schnur refers to Alexander Portnoy, a fictional creation of Philip Roth, who has entered the American lexicon as an exemplar of hatred and fear of Jewish women. Portnoy and his mother may rank as two of the most repellent characters ever written.

Aviva Cantor, "Matriphobia" (1995)

Jewish feminist theorist Aviva Cantor offers a detailed analysis of the Jewish mother stereotype. She refers to such classics of Jewish-mother hate as Philip Roth's Portnoy's Complaint, *Woody Allen's* Oedipus Wrecks, *and Dan Greenburg's* How To Be a Jewish Mother, *as well as to a host of lesser-known works.*

The Jewish mother "jokes" were a phenomenon of men who were making it into the middle class who felt that their mothers had impeded their assimilation by the behavior they had imparted. These men were also embarrassed by the vestiges of anti-assimilationist behavior in the women, another variation of the anti-*Ostjuden* [anti-Eastern European Jews] syndrome....

A final note here: not only have no men of other ethnic groups insulted their mothers publicly, but never before in history have Jewish men publicly proclaimed hostility toward the women who made so many sacrifices to enable them to "make something of themselves."[24]

Questions for Discussion

1. How can "groundless hatred" possibly be worse than idolatry, immorality, and bloodshed?

2. Joshua Lorki asks Paulus de Sancta Maria why he decided to convert to Christianity, and posits four possible reasons. List these reasons and discuss which, if any, would have provided a strong motivation for conversion in medieval Europe.

3. Theodor Lessing concluded that he was not "really" Jewish. The Jewish students in Rabbi Schnur's class asserted that they were not really JAPs. Discuss.

4. Why did Friedrich Blach fear the presence of Eastern European Jews in Germany? How would their presence have affected the native German Jewish population?

5. Why was Jakob Loewenberg ashamed in the presence of his *Christian* playmates?

6. Why do the Jews of Woodenton in Philip Roth's story oppose the new yeshivah? Eli Peck says, "both Jews and gentiles alike have had to give up some of their more extreme practices in order not to threaten or offend the other." Which extreme practices, if any, do Jews give up? Which extreme practices, if any, do gentiles give up?

7. Rabbi Susan Schnur reports that one of the Jewish students in her class wondered why he felt that "every JAP on campus somehow implicates me," and whether this feeling was a "minority culture reflex." Do you feel that other Jews' behavior or appearance implicate you? How? Is this feeling typical of other minorities as well as Jews?

8. Jay Gonen states: "It is an intriguing phenomenon that both Zionism and antisemitism, in directing their magnifying glass at the Jewish people, tended to focus their attention on the same issues yet differed in their respective judgments of what they had seen." Review the selections from Moses Hess and from Theodor Lessing, and explain.

9. In both Israel and America, Jewish self-hatred has frequently found its outlet in attacks upon Judaism and religious Jews. Review the selections by Joshua Lorki, Dorothea Veit, Philip Roth, Jay Gonen, and Richard Goldstein. How is antipathy toward Judaism expressed by the self-hater? Which of these selections describe hatred of religious practice and Jewish rituals? Which describe antipathy toward Jewish beliefs? How have negative attitudes toward religion affected Jewish life in the United States? In Israel?

10. Richard Goldstein says that he recoils from <u>Hasidim</u>. What is your reaction when you see <u>Hasidim</u>? Do you think of what you share or of how you differ? If you too recoil, consider your reactions to non-Jewish sects, for instance, the Amish or Mennonites.

11. Even though anti-women stereotypes are common in non-Jewish society, Aviva Cantor notes that only Jewish men have "insulted their mothers publicly." What might account for this? To what extent does anti-woman antisemitism indicate Jewish self-hatred? To what extent does it indicate other forces? Are Jewish mother and JAP stereotypes part of a backlash against feminist? Why or why not?

Suggested Activities and Programs

1. In Anzia Yezierska's 1920 short story, "The Fat of the Land," the mother realizes that she is not invited to the Broadway performance of her son's play, which the President will attend. She sobs with rejection. It turns out that her daughter Fanny, the playwright's sister, is responsible. Fanny's brother had asked her to invite their mother, but Fanny deliberately did not. Request a volunteer to read the following excerpt aloud:

> "Well, I don't care," snapped Fanny. "I can't appear with mother in a box at the theater.... You know mother. She'll spill the beans that we come from Delancey Street the minute we introduce her anywhere. Must I always have the black shadow of my past trailing after me? ... I've tried harder than all of you to do my duty. I've *lived* with her." She turned angrily upon [her brothers]. "I've borne the shame of mother while you bought her off with a present and a treat here and there. God knows how hard I tried to civilize her so as not to have to blush with shame when I take her anywhere. I dressed her in the most stylish Paris models, but Delancey Street sticks out from every inch of her. Whenever she opens her mouth, I'm done for. You fellows had your chance to rise in the world because a man is free to go up as high as he can reach up

to; but I, with all my style and pep, can't get a man my equal because a girl is always judged by her mother."[25]

Consider the shame that Fanny and other immigrant children felt because of their parents, and consider also the relationship between rejection of one's parents and Jewish self-hatred. Based on group members' own family stories as well as their knowledge of history, list the many ways in which the children of Jewish immigrants' related to their parents. To what extent, if any, does rejection of parents also involve rejection of Judaism? Is Fanny's relationship with her mother typical or aberrant? Ask group members to describe how they cope with feelings of shame for their parents (or their children or other relatives).

2. Go around the room and ask each Rosh Hodesh group member to write out and tell a Jewish mother joke or JAP joke. Are any of the jokes funny? If yes, what distinguishes the funny jokes from the rest? Ask the group: Have you ever protested a Jewish mother or JAP joke? Have you ever laughed along? Have you ever remained silent? Discuss the combination of anti-Jewish and anti-women hatred that these jokes encapsulate. Also ask the group: Who usually tells the jokes—men or women? Jews or non-Jews? How does your reaction vary depending on the sex, ethnic identity, and religion of the joke teller?

3. Have participants write one-page letters responding to Eli Peck in "Eli, the Fanatic." Direct them to think about Eli's demands and his inflammatory statement that cultural assimilation in prewar Europe might have averted the Holocaust. Participants can either work alone or in groups, whichever is preferred. Ask participants to read their letters aloud, and discuss together.

4. The 65-minute video *The Disputation: A Theological Debate Between Christians and Jews* recreates the disputation of 1263 between Father Pablo Christiani and Rabbi Moses ben Nahman. Rent the video, and discuss. Order online at www.films.com or telephone 1-800-257-5126.

---

1. Refer to "Christiani, Pablo," *Encyclopaedia Judaica* 5, page 505; and to *Masterpieces of Hebrew Literature*, ed. Curt Leviant (New York: Ktav, 1969), pages 415–416.

2. Refer to "Lorki, Joshua," *Encyclopaedia Judaica* 11, pages 494–495; "Pablo de Santa Maria," *Encyclopaedia Judaica* 13, pages 3–4; "Tortosa, Disputation of," *Encyclopaedia Judaica* 15, pages 1270–1272; and Yitzhak Baer, *A History of the Jews in Christian Spain, Volume II: From the Fourteenth Century to the Expulsion* (Philadelphia: Jewish Publication Society, 1966), pages 139–144; 170–211.

3. Steven E. Aschheim, in *Brothers and Strangers: The East European Jew in German and German Jewish Consciousness, 1800–1923* (Madison: University of Wisconsin Press, 1982) mentions Otto Weininger, whose suicide "had its roots in radical Jewish self-hatred." Aschheim also describes the 1898 novel *Werther der Jude* in which a young Jewish man commits suicide because of shame and despair over his Jewish origins (page 55).

4. Jacob Neusner, "Self-Hatred, Jewish" *Encyclopaedia Judaica Yearbook 1977/8* (Jerusalem: Keter, 1979), page 352.

5. Stephen Holden, "Drag Queen Rescues a Disabled Cop," *New York Times*, November 24, 1999, page E5.

6. Theodor Lessing, *Der jüdischer Selbsthass* (Berlin, 1930), page 11; cited in Solomon Liptzin, "Theodor Lessing," *Germany's Stepchildren* (Philadelphia: Jewish Publication Society, 1944), page 168. The lengthy paraphrase of Lessing's *Der jüdischer Selbsthass* is by Solomon Liptzin, pages 168–169.

7. Theodor Lessing, *Einmal und nie wieder* (Gutersloh, 1969), page 112, originally published 1935; cited in Aschheim, *Brothers and Strangers*, page 47.

8. Solomon Liptzin, "Theodor Lessing," *Germany's Stepchildren* (Philadelphia: Jewish Publication Society, 1944), pages 165–169.

9. Jacob Neusner, "Self-Hatred, Jewish" *Encyclopaedia Judaica Yearbook 1977/8* (Jerusalem: Keter, 1979), page 352.

10. Cited in Yitzhak Baer, *A History of the Jews in Christian Spain*, pages 143–144.

11. Cited in Hannah Arendt, *Rahel Varnhagen: The Life of a Jewess, First Complete Edition*, ed. Liliane Weissberg, trans. Richard and Clara Winston (Baltimore: Johns Hopkins University Press, 1997), page 89. Varnhagen regrets her "infamous birth" in a letter of 1806.

Hannah Arendt first wrote her study of Rahel Varnhagen in 1933. It was nearly complete when Arendt was imprisoned by the Nazis. Shortly afterward she escaped with the manuscript to France. On the eve of the German occupation of Paris, she escaped to America. After the war, a copy of the manuscript was found with a relative in Jerusalem, but its publication was delayed for years, and an English-language translation was not published until the late fifties. By this time, Arendt was well known as the author of *The Origins of Totalitarianism*. In the early sixties, Arendt covered the trial of Adolf Eichmann for *The New Yorker*, and her 1963 book *Eichmann in Jerusalem: A Report on the Banality of Evil* spurred enormous controversy in which Arendt herself was frequently accused of Jewish self-hatred.

12. Cited in Hannah Arendt, *Rahel Varnhagen*, page 88.

13. Cited in Haim Hillel Ben-Sasson, "Assimilation," *Encyclopaedia Judaica*, volume 3, page 773.

14. Jacob Moleschott (1822–1893) published *Physiological Sketches* in 1861; Hess cites page 257.

15. Moses Hess, "Rome and Jerusalem," trans. Arthur Hertzberg, based on an earlier translation by Mayer Waxman, in *The Zionist Idea: A Historical Analysis and Reader*, ed. Arthur Hertzberg (Garden City, NY: Doubleday/Herzl Press), pages 120–122. *Rom und Jerusalem* was first published in 1862.

16. Friedrich Blach, *Die Juden in Deutschland* (Berlin, 1911), pages 20–21, 42, cited in Aschheim, *Brothers and Strangers*, page 49.

17. Jakob Loewenberg, *Aus Zwei Quellen* (Berlin, 1914), cited in Aschheim, page 51.

18. Kurt Lewin, *Resolving Social Conflicts: Selected Papers on Group Dynamics [1935–1946]* (New York: Harper, 1948), pages 159–168, 186–200. Cited in Jacob Neusner, "Self-Hatred, Jewish" *Encyclopaedia Judaica Yearbook 1977/8* (Jerusalem: Keter, 1979), page 352.

19. Nathan W. Ackerman and Marie Jahoda, *Anti-Semitism and Emotional Disorder: A Psychoanalytic Interpretation* (New York: Harper, 1950), pages 79–80.

20. Philip Roth, "Eli, The Fanatic," in *Goodbye Columbus and Five Short Stories* (New York: Vintage, 1987), pages 261–262. Originally published in 1959.

21. Jay Y. Gonen, Ph. D., *A Psychohistory of Zionism* (New York: Mason/Charter, 1975), pages 270–275.

22. Susan Schnur, "Blazes of Truth: When Is a JAP Not a Yuppie?" *Lilith* 17 (Fall 1987), pages 10–11.

23. Richard Goldstein, "The New Anti-Semitism—A *Geshrei*" in *Blacks and Jews: Alliances and Arguments*, ed. Paul Berman (New York: Delacorte, 1994), page 207. Adapted from an essay printed in *The Village Voice*, October 1, 1991.

24. Aviva Cantor, *Jewish Women/Jewish Men: The Legacy of Patriarchy in Jewish Life* (San Francisco: HarperSanFrancisco, 1995), page 229.

25. Anzia Yezierska, "The Fat of the Land," in *How I Found America* (New York: Persea, 1991), page 20. Originally published in 1920.

5

Shevat

MEDICAL ETHICS

As the new millennium begins, we prepare for future technological advances by examining and perhaps altering our values to acclimate to a new way of life.

Over the past century, medicine has been an extraordinary and exciting field. Because of inoculations and antibiotics, deadly bacterial infections of centuries past are now almost always curable. Because of the heart-lung machine, children with heart defects live normally for a full life span, and adults with cardiovascular disease prolong their lives for years, even decades. Some cancers are now curable; many other cancer patients remain disease-free for years after treatment. We believe that progress in the cure and treatment of disease will continue into the twenty-first century.

In this chapter we explore Jewish views on some of today's major debates in medical ethics. In addition to citing Jewish literature, we include interviews with two experts in Jewish medical ethics.

by Claudia Chernov and Hadassah Tropper

FERTILITY DRUGS

A basic Jewish commandment is to bear children, but many Jewish couples face infertility. Jewish women attend college and graduate school in numbers exceeding the national norm, and as a consequence many delay childbearing until their late thirties or early forties. Because female infertility increases with age, Jews may be particularly vulnerable. Many turn to new methods of conceiving, including the use of fertility drugs. Judaism regards such medical intervention as necessary.* Indeed, in the Bible, God intervenes to help Sarah, Rebecca, Rachel, and Hannah conceive.

Fertility drugs and other types of medically-assisted reproduction, however, often result in multiple births—twins, triplets, quadruplets, and more. The Centers for Disease Control and Prevention report that approximately 38 percent of deliveries involving assisted reproductive techniques produce multiple births, compared to 3 percent of all deliveries.[1] The lives of mothers and babies are jeopardized in multiple births, leading fertility specialists to suggest aborting some of the fetuses, a procedure called selective reduction.

by Leora Tanenbaum and Claudia Chernov

Interview with Rabbi David M. Feldman

Rabbi David M. Feldman, MD, is spiritual leader of the Teaneck Jewish Center, a synagogue affiliated with Conservative Judaism. He is the author of Birth Control in Jewish Law; The Jewish Family Relationship; *and* Health and Medicine in Jewish Tradition, *and he is editor of the* Compendium on Medical Ethics. *He has served as an editorial advisor and writer for the* Encyclopedia of Bioethics, *and he has written for the* Encyclopaedia Judaica. *He has served as chairman of the Committee on Medical Ethics of the UJA/Federation, and he is a founding fellow of the Hastings Institute of Society, Ethics, and Life Sciences. He also serves on the Bioethics Review Board of the Hackensack Medical Center and on the board of trustees of the New York Society for the Deaf.*

Hadassah Tropper: Would you advocate the use of fertility drugs by barren Jewish women over adopting a child?

Rabbi Feldman: Yes, for a few reasons. First, by adopting, one does not fulfill the commandment of *pru urvu* [procreation], which one could fulfill with fertility drugs. Second, as much as adoption is an ongoing kindness to a needy child, one avoids the religious problems of adoption by successful use of fertility drugs. The problem of inadvertent incest by

---

*Orthodox Judaism, along with Conservative and Reform Judaism, endorses medical interventions that enable an infertile Jewish woman to conceive. Conservative and Reform Judaism, however, also endorse medical interventions that enable an infertile Jewish man to produce offspring. At present some Orthodox rabbis do not allow medical intervention for infertile men, making exceptions only in rare cases. This is because testing for male infertility involves scientific examination of seminal fluid, and Orthodox religious law prohibits ejaculation without sexual intercourse.

children of the same father is why Rabbi Moshe Feinstein* daringly stated that couples using artificial insemination should either seek a non-Jewish sperm donor or should adopt a non-Jewish baby and convert the child to Judaism. Many Jews were distressed by his statement, but I think that it was a logical preventive to the real problems of not knowing who one's blood relatives are.

Tropper: Many women who take fertility drugs become pregnant with five or six babies. Should a woman take this risk? Or should it prevent a woman from taking the drugs?

Feldman: Fertility drugs have risks, but I believe the risks should not deter a woman from taking them.

Tropper: If the health of the mother is at risk because of multiple births, should she abort one or more of the fetuses?

Feldman: Yes. But only if the risk is to the mother's health or to the viability of some of the fetuses. She should not abort for purposes of convenience or gender selection, nor for financial constraints.

Tropper: Do you have any final comments?

Feldman: Yes. Judaism is pro-natalist. Having a child is a great blessing. From a Jewish standpoint, not having a child is equal to not having one's health. So we try to bring it about for everyone—no matter what. On the other hand, the commandment of *pru urvu* means that you do your best. You do not *have* to take fertility drugs. Jewish law does not require going beyond what is naturally possible. If a woman wants to take fertility drugs, she may certainly do so.

FERTILITY, THE DUTY TO PROCREATE, AND ADOPTION IN JEWISH LITERATURE

Genesis 1:27-28

And God created man in His image, in the image of God He created him; male and female He created them. God blessed them and God said to them, "Be fertile and increase, fill the earth and master it; and rule the fish of the sea, the birds of the sky, and all the living things that creep on earth."

---

*Rabbi Moshe Feinstein was one of the most prominent Jewish scholars of the twentieth century. (Refer to page 49 for more.)

Genesis 9:1-7

God blessed Noah and his sons, and said to them, "Be fertile and increase, and fill the earth. The fear and the dread of you shall be upon all the beasts of the earth and upon all the birds of the sky—everything with which the earth is astir—and upon all the fish of the sea; they are given into your hand. Every creature that lives shall be yours to eat; as with the green grasses, I give you all these. You must not, however, eat flesh with its life-blood in it. But for your own life-blood I will require a reckoning. I will require it of every beast; of man, too, will I require a reckoning for human life, of every man for that of his fellow man!

> Who ever sheds the blood of man,
> By man shall his blood be shed;
> For in His image
> Did God make man.

Be fertile and increase; abound on the earth and increase on it."

Mishnah, *Yevamot* 6.6

No man may abstain from keeping the law "Be fertile and increase," unless he already has children. According to the school of Shammai, two sons; according to the school of Hillel, a son and a daughter, for it is written, "male and female He created them." ... The duty to be fertile and increase falls on the man and not on the woman.

Babylonian Talmud, *Yevamot* 63b

The Rabbis of the Talmud comment on Genesis 9.

Rabbi Eliezer stated: He who does not engage in propagation of the race is as though he sheds blood; for it is said, "Who ever sheds the blood of man, by man shall his blood be shed" and this is immediately followed by "Be fertile and increase; abound on the earth and increase on it."

Rabbi Jacob said: [He who does not engage in propagation of the race is] as though he diminishes the divine image; since it is said, "For in His image did God make man" and this is immediately followed by "Be fertile and increase; abound on the earth and increase on it."

Ben Azzai said: [He who does not engage in propagation of the race is] as though he sheds blood *and* diminishes the divine image.

Babylonian Talmud, *Megillah* 13a

If anyone brings up an orphan boy or girl in his house, the Scripture accounts it as if he had begotten the child.

Rashi (1040-1105) on Genesis 1:28

Rashi, Rabbi Solomon ben Isaac, is the foremost commentator on the Bible and on the Talmud. Here he analyzes the passage in which God blesses the first man and first woman and says, "Be fertile and increase, fill the earth and master it."

"Master it." The word is written defectively so that it could be read as singular, "and [you singular] master it"; this teaches that the command to procreate (be fertile and increase) was addressed only to man whose function it is to master, but not to woman.

Rashi (1040-1105) on Genesis 9:7

Rashi comments on God's words to Noah and his sons, "Be fertile and increase; abound on the earth and increase on it."

"Be fertile and increase." The plain meaning suggests that when the words were addressed to Adam they were intended to be a blessing; but here they are a positive command to populate the earth.

Rashbam (circa 1080-85 to circa 1174) on Genesis 30:14

Rabbi Samuel ben Meir, known as Rashbam, was a leading commentator on the Bible and the Talmud. His comment here concerns an aspect of the story of Rachel and Leah: "Once, at the time of the wheat harvest, Reuven came upon some mandrakes in the field and brought them to his mother Leah."

"Mandrakes." They were herbs that promoted conception.

Rabbi Marc Gellman (1987)

Marc Gellman, rabbi of the Reform Beth Torah Synagogue in New York, has served as the chairman of the Medical Ethics Committee of UJA/Federation. In an essay that strongly criticizes surrogate motherhood, Rabbi Gellman argues on behalf of adoption.

If adoption was not just difficult (which it surely is) but impossible (which it surely is not), then a case might be made for surrogate motherhood. But not in this world. The need of unwanted babies to be wanted is of greater moral moment than the egotistical need of a person to see his chromosomes live on.[2]

Questions for Discussion

1. Rabbi David Feldman asserts that using fertility drugs is preferable to adopting a child. First, when a woman uses these drugs and becomes pregnant, she enables her husband to fulfill the commandment of procreation. Second, whenever a child is the genetic offspring of the couple who raise him or her, the child can avoid future incestuous relationships. (An adopted child, however, might grow up to unwittingly marry a biological relative.) Do these reasons override the importance of adopting an unwanted child, or would you agree with Rabbi Marc Gellman that they do not? How does your knowledge of infertile couples or your experience of infertility influence your position?

2. Rabbi Feldman believes that using assisted reproduction techniques is worth the risk of multiple births. At the same time, Rabbi Feldman would argue against selective abortions to limit the number of fetuses, unless the multiple births would seriously impair the mother's health or affect the fetuses' viability.* A grave danger in multiple births, though, is impairment of the children's health. Discuss.

3. Consider Judaism's "pro-natalist" position. As Rabbi Feldman notes, Judaism strongly supports and encourages childbearing, even though religious law does not *require* an infertile woman to use fertility drugs or to take any extreme measures. First, how has this pro-natalist position affected your life or the lives of those close to you? Second, in our age, when new and more extreme measures for treating infertility are continually being developed, should Jewish medical ethicists ever back away from pro-natalism? If so, when? If not, why?

SURROGATE MOTHERHOOD

Surrogate motherhood has caused passionate controversy throughout America. A surrogate, as generally defined, is a woman who bears a child for another couple. In some cases, the couple's fertilized egg** is implanted into the surrogate's uterus. In other cases, the surrogate donates an egg cell that is fertilized outside of her body by the father's sperm. And in yet other cases, the surrogate's egg cell is fertilized inside her body through the use of artificial insemination. Regardless of how the embryo is conceived and how it arrives in the womb, the surrogate mother carries the fetus to term and gives birth. The couple who has entered into the surrogacy agreement then legally adopt the infant.

by Claudia Chernov

Interview with Rabbi David Feldman

Hadassah Tropper: What position do Jewish legal scholars take on surrogate motherhood?

---

* The majority of Orthodox rabbis oppose abortion unless the threat to the mother's health is one of life or death. Conservative rabbis tend to interpret possible threats to the mother's health more leniently. Reform rabbis believe each person must make his or her own choice, guided by Jewish tradition.

** The fertilized egg (the embryo) may be removed from the genetic mother's reproductive system, or the genetic mother's egg may be fertilized in a laboratory using the techniques of *in vitro* fertilization.

Rabbi David Feldman: The first principle is that surrogacy is only permissible when there is no alternative, in other words when the natural process of conception is unavailable to the couple.

Tropper: Some Jews argue that surrogate motherhood should be prohibited. The Bible commands us to guard our lives carefully, that is, to protect our health. Accordingly, we should risk our health only to fulfill a commandment. Though pregnancy is a health risk, bearing a child does fulfill the commandment of *pru urvu*—"be fertile and increase." But no woman is obligated to increase another's family, so she is putting herself at risk for no *mitzvah* (precept, commandment) at all.* Do you agree with this view?

Feldman: I believe that helping somebody else build a family is a *mitzvah*. You know that *mitzvah* means both *ḥiyuv*, an obligation, and *ḥesed*, a kindness.

Tropper: Would you call the biblical characters Hagar, Bilhah, and Zilpah surrogate mothers?

Feldman: Only in a limited sense. The difference is that in essence they were additional wives, living in the same household with the rest of the family. Hence, one danger of today's surrogate motherhood did not exist back then. Today, a surrogate mother may want to change her mind and decide that because she has bonded with the baby she carried for nine months, it belongs to her, and she wants to keep it. In the polygamous society of biblical times, the additional wives could keep their babies without removing them from the household.

Tropper: Some opponents of surrogate motherhood argue that it is a form of prostitution, in that the biological mother, motivated by financial gain, is using her body as a tool. What is your opinion?

Feldman: This situation does not really exist. Even in the conventional method of adopting a child, American law makes clear that the adoptive family is not *paying* for the child. No human being can be bought or sold. Similarly, one cannot pay the surrogate mother for the baby. Of course she will require money for her medical costs, for the time that she must miss from work, and for the necessary discomforts during pregnancy. But she does not do this for profit.

Tropper: Does *halakhah*—Jewish law—distinguish between a surrogate mother who carries the couple's fertilized egg and a surrogate mother who uses her own egg and carries only the man's sperm?

---

* Rabbi Marc Gellman argues this position. Refer to pages 87–88.

Feldman: It raises an interesting question about the religion of the child. If the surrogate mother uses her own egg, and she is not Jewish, then the child will not be Jewish and must be converted.

Tropper: Some worry that using the surrogate mother's egg together with the man's sperm constitutes a form of adultery.

Feldman: There is no adultery here. When artificial insemination first became a possibility, rabbinic authorities decided that adultery is not a result of laboratory procedures, but is a result of a violation of vows of intimacy and fidelity.

Tropper: The only way to commit adultery is through an actual sexual act?

Feldman: Exactly.

SURROGATES AND CONCUBINES IN JEWISH LITERATURE

Genesis 16:1–4

Sarai, Abram's wife, had borne him no children. She had an Egyptian maidservant whose name was Hagar. And Sarai said to Abram, "Look, the Lord has kept me from bearing. Consort with my maid; perhaps I shall have a son through her." And Abram heeded Sarai's request. So Sarai, Abram's wife, took her maid, Hagar the Egyptian—after Abram had dwelt in the land of Canaan ten years—and gave her to her husband Abram as concubine. He cohabited with Hagar and she conceived; and when she saw that she had conceived, her mistress was lowered in her esteem.

Genesis 30:1–24

As chapter 30 of the Book of Genesis begins, Leah, whom Jacob was tricked into marrying, has given birth to four sons: Reuven, Shimon, Levi, and Judah. Rachel, Jacob's true love, has no children.

When Rachel saw that she had borne Jacob no children, she became envious of her sister; and Rachel said to Jacob, "Give me children, or I shall die." Jacob was incensed at Rachel, and said, "Can I take the place of God, who has denied you fruit of the womb?" She said, "Here is my maid Bilhah. Consort with her, that she may bear on my knees and that through her I too may have children." So she gave him her maid Bilhah as concubine, and Jacob cohabited with her. Bilhah conceived and bore Jacob a son. And Rachel said, "God has vindicated me; indeed, He has heeded my plea and given me a son." Therefore she named him Dan. Rachel's maid Bilhah conceived again and bore Jacob a second son. And Rachel said, "A fateful contest I waged with my sister; yes, and I have prevailed." So she named him Naphtali.

When Leah saw that she had stopped bearing, she took her maid Zilpah and gave her to Jacob as concubine. And when Leah's maid Zilpah bore Jacob a son, Leah said, "What luck!" So she named him Gad. When Leah's maid Zilpah bore Jacob a second son, Leah declared, "What fortune!" meaning, "Women will deem me fortunate." So she named him Asher.

Once, at the time of the wheat harvest, Reuven came upon some mandrakes in the field and brought them to his mother Leah. Rachel said to Leah, "Please give me some of your son's mandrakes." But she said to her, "Was it not enough for you to take away my husband, that you would also take my son's mandrakes?" Rachel replied, "I promise, he shall lie with you tonight, in return for your son's mandrakes." When Jacob came home from the field in the evening, Leah went out to meet him and said, "You are to sleep with me, for I have hired you with my son's mandrakes." And he lay with her that night. God heeded Leah, and she conceived and bore him a fifth son. And Leah said, "God has given me my reward for having given my maid to my husband." So she named him Issakhar. When Leah conceived again and bore Jacob a sixth son, Leah said, "God has given me a choice gift; this time my husband will exalt me, for I have borne him six sons." So she named him Zevulun. Last, she bore him a daughter, and named her Dinah.

Now God remembered Rachel; God heeded her and opened her womb. She conceived and bore a son, and said, "God has taken away my disgrace." So she named him Joseph, which is to say, "May the Lord add another son for me."

Office of the Chief Rabbi, Dr. Immanuel Jakobovits, London (1970)

Rabbi Immanuel Jakobovits (1921–1999) was the previous Chief Rabbi of the British Commonwealth and a renowned expert in bioethics.

To use another person as an "incubator" and then take from her the child she carried and delivered for a fee is a revolting degradation of maternity and an affront to human dignity.[3]

Rabbi Marc Gellman, "The Ethics of Surrogate Motherhood" (1987)

Surrogate motherhood exposes the contracted mother to the risks of pregnancy without justifying those risks. The Jewish prohibition against risk taking is derived from the fourth chapter of Deuteronomy, *venishmartem me'od lenafshoteikhem*, "guard your lives carefully." The rabbinic elaboration of this biblical law basically prohibits risking your health or life if there is no *mitzvah* which justifies the risk.* Pregnancy,

---

*Rabbi Gellman cites Maimonides, *Mishneh Torah*, *Hilkhot Rotzei'ah* 11:4–5 and the Rema (Rabbi Moshe Isserles) to the *Shulḥan Arukh*, *Yoreh De'ah* 116:5.

no matter how routine, presents real risk to the pregnant woman, risks which are justified if she is bearing her own child and thus helping her husband to fulfill the *mitzvah* of *pru urvu*, "be fruitful and multiply." But [the surrogate mother] is under no *ḥiyuv*, no obligation, to fulfill the commandment of procreation for the [couple who will raise the child] and thus she has put herself at risk for no good reason.[4]

Questions for Discussion

1. Rabbi Gellman asserts that a woman who bears a child for another couple violates the precept of guarding her life carefully. Rabbi Feldman disagrees, because he maintains that helping others to build a family also fulfills a Jewish imperative, one that can override the precept of guarding one's health. Do you agree with Rabbi Gellman or with Rabbi Feldman? Why?

2. In what way does bearing a child for another family differ from bearing a child for one's own family? For instance, is bearing another's child more giving, more selfless than bearing one's own? Is it more calculated, more mercenary? Discuss.

3. Rabbi Feldman points out that the biblical servants, Hagar, Bilhah, and Zilpah, who bore children on their mistresses' behalf, were part of the mistresses' household. Therefore, they could not withhold the baby from the future parents. In contrast, women today who bear children on another's behalf generally live in an entirely separate household, and the surrogate mother could certainly decide to withhold the baby, as in the much publicized Baby M case. While hiring a maid to serve as a surrogate mother is today morally repugnant (and keeping a second wife or a concubine is illegal), do the biblical examples suggest any contemporary solutions? How can one lessen the chances of a surrogate mother withholding the child?

4. In chapter 30 of Genesis, we hear Rachel's and Leah's voices and understand something of their motivations. Compare their experiences of childlessness with your own or with those of your relatives or friends. Neither Zilpah nor Bilhah speak in the Bible, but Hagar, who bears a child for Sarah and Abraham, comes to look down on Sarah. Discuss Hagar's reaction and the possible emotions and motivations of the other biblical maidservants.

5. Rabbi Immanuel Jakobovits states that using a woman as a paid incubator is "a revolting degradation of maternity and an affront to human dignity." Is the objection here to payment for the surrogate mother, or is it to surrogate motherhood entirely, whether paid or unpaid? Assuming that Rabbi Jakobovits objects to payment, how can we reconcile his objection with Rabbi Feldman's statement that the future parents must pay the surrogate mother for medical expenses, for the time she must miss from work, and for "the necessary discomforts during

pregnancy"? What level of payment is low enough to prevent women from "degradation" yet high enough to cover their costs in bearing a child? How should the fee be determined—government regulation, market forces, etc.?

CLONING

In 1996, Scottish scientists cloned Dolly, probably the most widely publicized sheep in history. Dolly was cloned from a cell of an adult sheep's body. Since then, ethicists and scientists have been arguing about the ways cloning techniques can be used and whether cloning techniques *should* be used.

Clones are genetically identical individuals, a phenomenon that occurs naturally with identical twins. In general, cloning refers to creating a baby using genes from an adult cell. However, cloning techniques were first developed using embryonic cells. Scientists at George Washington University Medical Center cloned a human embryo in 1993 as part of an effort to enable infertile couples to conceive using *in vitro* fertilization. In the laboratory, the embryo is divided into separate clusters of cells. Each cluster develops into a separate embryo—or clone of the original embryo—which can then be implanted in the womb. The implantation of additional embryos leads to higher rates of success for *in vitro* fertilization.

Cloning embryonic cells and cloning differentiated adult cells are quite different, but progress has occurred with astonishing rapidity. Planning for the future is essential, and the United States government has organized medical and ethical panels to present opinions and make recommendations. President Clinton has spoken in support of legislation banning the cloning of humans, and several states have already signed legislation prohibiting human cloning.

by Claudia Chernov and Leora Tanenbaum

Interview with Rabbi Barry Freundel

Rabbi Barry Freundel is the rabbi of the Orthodox Kesher Israel synagogue in Washington, DC. He was ordained by the Rabbi Isaac Elchanan Theological Seminary in 1976. He has served as Vice President of the Rabbinical Council of America since 1995 and Chair of the Ethics Committee of the Rabbinical Council since 1993. He has written many publications on medical ethics and lectures throughout the United States.

Tropper: Does the concept of cloning interfere with Judaism's concepts of human individuality and equality? One could argue that cloning threatens the intrinsic uniqueness of each human.

Freundel: I do not think cloning touches upon these issues at all, at least with the current available technology. A clone created in a laboratory is theoretically no different from a twin created *in utero*. Having the same genetic content does not mean that you are the same person. When you clone someone you end up with a baby. Then life experiences take over. The clone will by definition become unique and have unique life experiences.

Tropper: Is cloning a problem on a theological level because humans are tampering with creating life—an activity viewed as belonging in God's domain alone?

Freundel: I do not know of any Jewish source that says that creating life is God's domain. Every source says instead "be fertile and increase." We are obligated to be a partner with God in creation.

Tropper: How about the verse in Genesis* that states that God breathed life into Adam's body?

Freundel: Yes, that verse talks about the first human being. But once he is created, what is the first thing that Adam is told? Go forth and multiply! *Pru urvu!* It doesn't say *how* you do it! Now, there are indeed issues with cloning. But the issue of tampering with God's domain is not our issue.

Tropper: Is there a distinction between cloning for the purposes of treating infertility and for other purposes?

Freundel: Yes. Judaism never bans the technology. Instead it asks: How is the technology being used? There are uses that would be perfectly fine, even meritorious! And there are uses that would be terrible and exploitative. As a fertility mechanism, I believe cloning is no worse than other fertility mechanisms that are permitted under Jewish law. In fact, if you imagine a couple who decides to have two children, one a clone of the father, one a clone of the mother, many issues that would have come up with other fertility mechanisms are mitigated.

Tropper: Then cloning is acceptable to treat infertility, but not for any other purposes?

Freundel: That depends on the other purposes. Let's say someone wants to produce a clone to have the necessary tissue match for a bone marrow transplant. Let's also assume that the child so produced would be loved

---

* The Lord God formed man from the dust of the earth. He blew into his nostrils the breath of life, and man became a living being (Genesis 2:7).

and cared for and accepted as a part of the family, and that the *mitzvah* of procreation had been fulfilled already. I am not sure that cloning in such a case would be prohibited under Jewish law. One would have to examine the circumstances very carefully.

Tropper: And what about the psychological consequences that the clone would suffer, knowing that his or her purpose was to provide bone marrow for a family member?

Freundel: That is why I emphasized first that the child would have to be loved and treated equally. Understand that a "clone" does not exist in Jewish law. The person created through cloning is a full-fledged human being—with all of the rights and associations thereto. From the way that cloning has been discussed in other circles, one of my concerns is that clones might be treated as second-class citizens. Now, a clone will show up one day. The technology is here. If we create an atmosphere in which the clones are second-class citizens, we create a huge problem.

Tropper: What other religious problems arise with cloning?

Freundel: One problem is, who is the mother*? With our present technology, to clone someone involves the child growing inside the mother, and most authorities agree that this defines who the mother is. In adoption cases, if the mother is not Jewish, the child must convert. This is relatively simple, but the child must know that his or her origins were not Jewish. Many more complex issues arise when donated eggs or sperm are used for *in vitro* fertilization: Who is the father, who is the mother, and who are the child's relatives? Some of these issues are resolved by cloning, but some remain. The technology itself, however, is not a problem.

---

* The individual created through cloning shares the same genes as the donor of the somatic cell (a cell that is neither an egg nor a sperm) that was cloned. Thus, the individual created through cloning shares the same genetic mother and genetic father as the donor of the somatic cell. The genetic mother may also give birth to the cloned baby; this will occur when a woman clones one of her existing children (the new baby will be the genetic twin of the existing—and older—child). In many cases, though, the genetic mother will not be the same as the mother who gives birth to the baby. For instance, if a woman clones a cell from her own body and then gives birth to the child so created, the child's genetic mother is also the child's grandmother—that is, the mother of the woman who gave birth to the child.

CREATION OF LIFE IN JEWISH LITERATURE

Babylonian Talmud, *Sanhedrin 65b*

Rava said: "If the righteous desired it, they could be creators, for it is written, 'But your iniquities have distinguished between you and Your God' (Isaiah 59:2)." Rava created a man, and sent him to Rabbi Zera. Rabbi Zera spoke to the man but received no answer. Thereupon he said to him: "Thou art a creature of the magicians. Return to thy dust."

Rabbi Ḥanina and Rabbi Oshaia spent every Sabbath eve studying the *Book of Creation*, by means of which they created a third-grown calf and ate it.

Babylonian Talmud, *Sanhedrin 67b*

Abbaye said, "The laws of the sorcerers are like those of the Sabbath: Certain actions are punished by stoning, some actions are exempt from punishment yet forbidden, while other actions are entirely permitted." Thus if one actually performs magic he is stoned; if he merely creates an illusion, he is exempt, yet it is forbidden. And what is entirely permitted? Such as was performed by Rabbi Ḥanina and Rabbi Oshaia.

Office of the Chief Rabbi, Dr. Immanuel Jakobovits, London (1970)

Genetic engineering may open a wonderful chapter in the history of healing. But without prior agreement on restraints and the strictest limitations, such mechanization of human life may also herald irretrievable disaster resulting from man's encroachment upon nature's preserves....

Man, as the delicately balanced fusion of body, mind, and soul, can never be the mere product of laboratory conditions and scientific ingenuity. To fulfill his destiny in the image of his Creator, he must be generated and reared out of the intimate love joining husband and wife together, out of identifiable parents who care for the development of their offspring, and out of a home which provides affectionate warmth and compassion.[5]

Questions for Discussion

1. Hadassah Tropper states: "One could argue that cloning threatens the idea of the intrinsic uniqueness of the human." Rabbi Freundel replies that a clone is no different, in theory, from an identical twin,*

---

*Although the clone is theoretically the same as an identical twin, no human clone has been created, so the differences between a clone and a twin may actually be significant. Twins share an intrauterine environment, whereas clones do not. Furthermore, the processes used in inducing somatic cells to become embryonic may affect the cloned individual's health throughout life.

and though twins share the same genetic material, each one is unique. Moreover, a clone will have different life experiences and thus his or her character will differ from the character of the person who provided cells for cloning. Do you agree that cloning is troubling because it threatens each person's uniqueness? Why or why not? (Are identical twins somewhat troubling also? Why or why not?) Consider Rabbi Freundel's reply and discuss.

2. Rabbi Freundel states that creating a clone so that one can obtain a bone marrow transplant would be ethically acceptable; however, the individual so created must be loved and treated as an equal by the members of his or her family. First, would the family members be capable of such love and equal treatment? Second, how would the cloned child be affected once old enough to understand that he or she had been created to donate bone marrow?

3. Hadassah Tropper believes that cloning might raise theological problems, "because humans are tampering with creating life—an activity viewed as belonging in God's domain alone." She, like many others, worries that cloning may lead humankind to overstep its boundaries, to play God. Rabbi Freundel, however, views the creation of human life as a religious commandment—regardless of the method used to do so. He claims that "Judaism never bans the technology" of cloning, "instead it asks, how is the technology being used?" He clearly states that for religious Jews, "the issue of tampering with God's domain is not our issue." Discuss these divergent beliefs. What accounts for the difference between currently popular beliefs and the beliefs of Jewish theologians? (Consider that Mary Shelley's novel *Frankenstein* focused on the pain felt by a spurned and despised creature. Hollywood's *Frankenstein* movies, however, focused on the arrogance of Dr. Frankenstein, who usurped God's role in bringing the creature to life—an issue neglected by Mary Shelley.)

4. Rabbi Freundel maintains that "cloning is no worse than other fertility mechanisms that are permitted under Jewish law." This is hardly a ringing endorsement. Should some fertility mechanisms be prohibited? If so, which ones? If not, why?

5. Rabbi Freundel fears that human beings created through cloning techniques "might be treated as second-class citizens," and he points out that Jewish law regards each person, no matter how that individual is created, as "a full-fledged human being—with all of the rights and associations thereto." Discuss the Jewish ethical principles involved. (Here also consider Mary Shelley's concern for the creature brought to life by Dr. Frankenstein.)

6. Are you surprised to find the Rabbis of the Talmud creating a person and a calf through magic or sorcery? How do you interpret these stories?

7. Rabbi Immanuel Jakobovits states that each person "must be generated

and reared out of the intimate love joining husband and wife together, out of identifiable parents who care for the development of their offspring, and out of a home which provides affectionate warmth and compassion." Can his position be reconciled with Rabbi Freundel's? If so, how? If not, with whom would you agree?

AUTOPSIES

Jewish law mandates respectful treatment of the dead body, and it prohibits desecration of the dead. Autopsy, which necessarily involves cutting the dead body, is forbidden under Orthodox interpretation of the prohibition against desecration of the dead, unless exceptional circumstances make an autopsy imperative. Orthodox scholars, however, vary somewhat in defining such exceptions.*

by Claudia Chernov

Interview with Rabbi Barry Freundel

Hadassah Tropper: Until the modern era, the prohibition against *nivul hameit,* desecration of a dead body, had caused religious Jews to abstain from performing autopsies. Today, however, most Orthodox authorities permit an autopsy when a particular patient is in dire need of an organ or when the information obtained from an autopsy will save a particular patient's life. These are the only cases in which most Orthodox rabbis today permit autopsies. Autopsies in other cases, though, increase medical knowledge and consequently have the potential to save lives in the future. Can you explain?

Rabbi Barry Freundel: *Halakhah*—Jewish law—says you can not perform the autopsy unless you know with certainty and conviction that the autopsy will help. In general, you don't know *whether* an autopsy will help. The idea that *maybe* we will gain information that *might* some day be helpful is not strong enough to overcome the prohibition against desecration of the dead. Thus Jewish law prohibits autopsies under general circumstances.

Tropper: In 1944 the Chief Rabbinate in Jerusalem allowed autopsy under certain conditions: to determine the cause of death, to save a life, or to advise surviving family members when an individual dies of hereditary illness. Are there other cases in which autopsy is appropriate?

---

* Both Conservative and Reform Judaism permit autopsies in a broader variety of situations than Orthodox Judaism.

Freundel: Yes. If we are in the midst of an unidentified epidemic and if we believe that a particular deceased person can provide us with the information that will enable us to work on stopping the epidemic, an autopsy would be allowed.

Tropper: Recently an Orthodox family lost a son. The boy had died suddenly, and it was evident that either he had been killed or he had committed suicide. The family decided not to allow an autopsy because of the prohibition against desecrating the body. But what if they had wanted to know the cause of the boy's death? What would the religious law have been? I feel that the family's peace of mind is important. Would that have any bearing?

Freundel: It would have to be a case in which the lack of peace of mind led to real psychological danger. Even then you have to weigh the question: How much psychological damage would occur? And would the knowledge gained bring peace of mind? At times people want information and believe that it will help them, but when they get the information, they do not feel any better. Many variables come into play, but Jewish law cannot be violated simply because people *think* something will make them feel better. The question, again, is of certainty versus uncertainty. The more uncertainty, the less you can overcome any religious barriers. There must be a clear and present reason: saving a life or preventing a serious illness or preventing serious mental consequences. Only then can you mitigate the prohibition.

AUTOPSY AND RESPECT FOR THE DEAD BODY IN JEWISH LITERATURE

Deuteronomy 21:22-23

If a man is guilty of a capital offense and is put to death, and you hang him on a tree, you must not let his corpse remain on the tree overnight, but you must bury him the same day. For a hanging body is an affront to God. You shall not defile the land that the Lord your God is giving you to possess.

Mishnah, *Sanhedrin* 6.5

Rabbi Meir said, when man suffers [because he has sinned], what expression does the *Shekhinah* [Divine Presence] use? "My head is too heavy for me, my arm is too heavy for me." And if God is so grieved over the blood of the wicked that is shed, how much more over the blood of the righteous! And not only of this one [a convicted criminal] did the sages say it [that a corpse must not be left hanging overnight], but whoever lets his dead lie overnight transgresses a negative commandment. If [however] he [the relative of the deceased] kept him overnight for the sake of his honor, to procure for him a coffin or a shroud, he does not transgress thereby.

Babylonian Talmud, *Sanhedrin 47a*

The Talmud explains the statement in the Mishnah, "If he kept him overnight for the sake of his honor" because the "his" is ambiguous.

Now surely that [his honor] means, for the honor of the dead?

No, for the honor of the living.

And for the sake of the honor of the living the dead is to be kept overnight?

Yes. When did the Merciful One say, "You must not let his corpse remain on the tree overnight"? Only in a case similar to the hanged, where it [delaying the burial of the corpse] involves disgrace. But here, where there is no disgrace, it does not apply. [The delay here is not caused by neglect of the corpse, but by the needs of the living.]

Come and hear [the words of a Sage of the Mishnah]! If he [the relative] kept him overnight for his own honor, so as to inform the [neighboring] towns of his death, or to bring professional women mourners for him, or to procure for him a coffin or a shroud, he does not transgress thereby, for all that he does is only for the honor of the deceased! What he [the Sage] means is this: Nothing that is done for the honor of the living involves dishonor to the dead.

Babylonian Talmud, *Ḥullin* 11b

The Sages discuss how the principle of following the majority's ruling has been deduced, and offer numerous cases that would lead one to deduce this principle. One such case applies to the desecration of a corpse.

Rabbi Kahana said, It [the principle of following the majority] is derived from the case of a murderer for whom the divine law prescribes death. Now why do we not fear that the victim may have been afflicted with a fatal disease? [In such a case, the killer cannot be convicted of murder.] Is it not because we follow the majority? [In the majority of murder cases the victim has no fatal disease.] And should you say, we can examine the body? This is not allowed because it would thereby be mutilated! And should you say, since a man's life is at stake, we should mutilate the body? [We should check to see if the person who was killed suffered from a fatal disease, because if so, his killer would not be punished with death.] Surely there is always the possibility that there was a hole in the victim in the place where he was struck by the sword! [The murderer may have killed the victim by striking him in the exact location of the organic lesion, thus removing all traces of disease. In such a case no postmortem examination would show that the victim was suffering from a fatal disease.]

Rashi (1040-1105) on Deuteronomy 21:23

"For he that is hanged is a reproach unto God." The degradation of human body is an affront to God in Whose image he is made.

Nahmanides (1194-1270) on Deuteronomy 21:23

Rabbi Moses ben Nahman was a leading biblical and talmudic commentator.

"His body shall not remain all night upon the tree." According to the Rabbis, this rule was extended also to the body of a person who died a natural death. A corpse should not be left overnight unburied.

Rabbi Ezekiel Landau (1713-1793), *Noda Beyehudah, Yoreh De'ah, 210*

By the eighteenth century, autopsy had become a crucial tool in the detection, understanding, and prevention of disease. A petitioner from London wrote to Rabbi Ezekiel Landau of Prague asking whether the autopsy of a Jew might be permitted in order to understand the cause of death and thereby find a cure for others who suffered from the same disease. Rabbi Landau's answer is the first clear, written example of permission for autopsy, and his responsum (answer to an inquiry on Jewish law) is cited by all subsequent authorities. However, permission for autopsy is limited only to situations where a specific life will definitely be saved through the knowledge gained (the position explained by Rabbi Freundel). Rabbi Landau's response begins by arguing that saving the life of a specific person who is ill would override the prohibition against desecration of the dead.

I wrote all of this according to the words of he who considered autopsy permissible in situations where one could definitely save a life. But I wonder if autopsy should be permitted even in situations when it is not certain that a life will be saved as a result? If so, why go through all of these discussions [to prove life-or-death situations]? For it is a known law that any deed that could even *possibly* save a life would defer the laws of the Sabbath, which are much more serious [than the laws of defiling the dead]. And a Mishnah in tractate *Yoma* states that all cases involving even a potential to save a life defer the laws of the Sabbath.

But all of this refers to cases of lives in danger that are present before us, for example, a sick person we know of at the time. And in tractate *Hullin*, in the case of the murderer, the potential to save life is definitely before us. And even in the case of an autopsy performed for financial reasons in tractate *Bava Batra*, the damage is before us.

The prohibition exists only when there is no sick person involved, but when they want to learn general knowledge, working on the assumption that in the future another will become ill and need the information that we have learned. In this case we do *not* perform an autopsy. Because this is a weak assumption, and we do not violate any biblical or even rabbinic laws for a weak assumption. For if you would call every weak assumption a life-or-death situation then it follows that doctors should not stop preparing every possible medicine and medical instrument on the Sabbath ever, because someone may get sick and need them. And it becomes hard to distinguish between a suspicion that a sick person will need something sooner or much later. And one should never permit this.[6]

Rabbi Ben-Zion Uziel, *Mishpetei Uziel* (1935)

With the opening of Hebrew University's medical school in the early twentieth century, the rift between religious precepts and modern medicine deepened. In the years before Statehood, Rabbi Abraham Isaac Kook (1865–1935), Israel's Ashkenazi Chief Rabbi, following Rabbi Landau, forbade the use of Jewish corpses for medical research unless the information would immediately save another's life. Rabbi Ben-Zion Uziel (1880–1953), the Sephardi Chief Rabbi of Israel from 1939 until 1953, interpreted previous rulings somewhat differently, however, and wrote two responsa permitting autopsy under less restrictive conditions.

The essence of the prohibition of *nivul hameit* is that it refers specifically to cases where there is a deliberate intention to desecrate a body or to treat it with disrespect without any advantage to others. Whenever others can benefit, however, and most certainly when there is a possibility of thereby saving life, the prohibition does not apply. Anyone with a knowledge of the development and progress of medicine will not for a moment doubt the benefits which accrue from autopsies and dissections. Autopsies are of inestimable value in establishing the cause of the ailment and its effect upon other organs of the body. In addition, where the preservation of life and the interests of the living are concerned, there is neither *nivul hameit* nor desecration of the body.[7]

Chief Rabbinate in Jerusalem and Hadassah Hospital, Agreement Concerning Autopsies (1944)

In 1944, Rabbi Isaac Herzog (1888–1959), Rabbi Kook's successor as Ashkenazi Chief Rabbi of Israel, along with the Rabbi Zvi Pesah Frank (1873–1960), Chief Rabbi of Jerusalem, entered into an agreement with Hadassah Hospital permitting autopsies under four different conditions. In 1953, Israel's legislature passed the Law of Anatomy and Pathology based on this agreement between the Chief Rabbinate and Hadassah Hospital.

The Chief Rabbinate will not hinder autopsies in the following four categories:

a) Autopsies required by law.

b) Cases in which, for lack of knowledge, the doctor cannot, without an autopsy, specify any disease as the cause of death. The permit to perform such an autopsy is given on condition that there shall be a certificate of evidence that there is no way of determining the cause of death without an autopsy. This certificate will be issued and signed by the following three doctors after consultation between them: the physician of the department in which the patient died, the head of the Institute of Anatomy and Pathologic Histology, and the director of the hospital.

c) Autopsies needed to save a life.

d) Cases of hereditary illness, when it is imperative to give the family precautionary advice.

Rabbi Isaac Arieli (1964)

A number of Orthodox rabbis allow exceptions to the prohibition against autopsy when medical knowledge is certain to be valuable in saving lives, especially in cases of heart disease and cancer, where new treatments are constantly being tested.

As it is the duty of the rabbi to prevent autopsies where no *pikuah nefesh* [saving of a life] is involved, so is his duty to insist on it where there is the slightest possibility of it being a benefit.[8]

Questions for Discussion

1. Deuteronomy admonishes against leaving a dead body unburied, because doing so would "defile the land that the Lord your God is giving you to possess." Why does the Bible connect desecration of the dead with defilement of the land?

2. Rashi asserts that leaving the body unburied "is an affront to God in Whose image [the human] is made." What is the connection between respect for the body and creation of humankind in the image of God?

3. Rabbi Barry Freundel states that the prohibition against desecration of the corpse can be overruled only by "a clear and present reason: saving a life or preventing a serious illness." He asserts that if the potential benefit is uncertain, autopsy is forbidden. Rabbi Isaac Arieli, in contrast, stated that he would "insist on" autopsy even when "there is the slightest possibility of it being a benefit." Discuss these different viewpoints, and the two sides' different interpretations of the commandment on saving a life—*pikuah nefesh*.

Suggested Activities and Programs

1. Jewish classic writings and the commentaries of pre-modern rabbis can be interpreted in a multitude of ways. Choose one of the topics discussed in this unit—fertility drugs, surrogate motherhood, cloning, or autopsy—and carefully review together the texts provided. Do these excerpts indicate a "pro" or "con" point of view? Or could certain excerpts be read to support either side? Have participants list those excerpts that

obviously support one side, those that obviously support the opposite side, and those that are subject to varying interpretation. Compare lists and discuss: How do the classic texts shed light on the norms and values of today? How do we examine modern circumstances through the lens of ancient or pre-modern writings?

2. Provide participants with photocopies of Genesis 16:1–16 and 18:1–15, about Sarah's infertility and her relationship with Hagar, and ask everyone to read. Assign one participant to read "Sarah Was a Woman" aloud, and then discuss reactions to the biblical story and to the poem using the questions that follow as a guide.

Sarah Was a Woman
by Edna Aphek

1
Sarah was
a woman
soft and pliant
like a furrowed field
and he with
Hagar.

2
Sarah was
soft and pliant
quiet and kind
a woman
and he with
Hagar.

3
Sarah was
a woman
quiet and kind
crushed and cruel
and he with
Hagar.

4
Sarah was
crushed and cruel
a woman
when her womb
was soft with son
call her the
laughing one.

a) Why is Sarah transformed from "soft and pliant" and "quiet and kind" to "crushed and cruel"? Was the transformation natural and expected in the circumstances or excessive and potentially avoidable? To what extent does Sarah's infertility account for the transformation?

b) Note where the words "a woman" occur in each stanza of the poem. What is the significance of each?

c) In Genesis, chapter 18, why did Sarah laugh? In Edna Aphek's poem, why is she called "the laughing one"?

d) Think about occasions when you have felt envious of another. What prompted your envy? In the poem, what causes Sarah's envy—Hagar's fertility or Hagar's sexual relations with Abraham? Does infertility still lead to envy today? If so, what do modern infertile women do about feelings of envy?

3. Religious feminists have recently written stories, poems, and commentary on infertility and its effects upon Sarah, Rebecca, Rachel, and Hannah, as well as stories, poems, and commentary on Hagar, Bilhah, and Zilpah. Assign one or more participants to research these modern *midrashim*, and present samples to the Rosh Hodesh group.

4. Organize an education day on infertility and Jewish medical ethics. Use the following schedule as a guide.

Judaism, Fertility, and Assisted Reproductive Technologies

9:15   **Registration**

10:15   **Infertility and Surrogate Motherhood in the Bible**
        Analyze and discuss these biblical passages:
        Genesis 16, 17, 21:1–20—Sarah and Hagar
        Genesis 29:16–35; 30:1–24—Rachel, Leah, Bilhah, and Zilpah
        Samuel I 1, 2:1–10—Hannah and Peninah

        Consider the relationships between the wives and maidservants—who are, in a limited sense, "surrogate mothers"—as well as between the fertile and infertile wives. Also discuss why God caused infertility among the matriarchs: did the infertility serve a purpose? What lessons can we learn from these passages?

12:00   **Lunch**

1:00   **Jewish Approaches to Assisted Reproductive Technologies**
        A panel discussion, consisting of (1) a physician or other medical expert who is involved in the treatment of infertility; (2) a rabbi or Jewish scholar with expertise in medical

ethics; (3) a Jewish parent of a child conceived through the use of assisted reproductive technology; and (4) a moderator.

The first three speakers are each allotted 10 to 15 minutes. The medical expert provides an overview of assisted reproductive technologies, why they are needed, how they are performed, medical risks, and so on. The rabbi or Jewish scholar presents the ethical and the religious implications of the use of assisted reproduction. The parent offers a personal view. The moderator introduces the speakers, and facilitates a question-and-answer session following the speakers' prepared presentations.

2:15   **Fulfilling the Commandment of Procreation—How Far Must We Go?**

What does the commandment *pru urvu*—"be fertile and increase" entail? To what lengths must the infertile man or woman go, according to Jewish law, to fulfill the imperative? In light of this commandment, what are the pros and cons of adoption and of assisted reproductive technologies?

4:00   **Conclusion**

---

1. Jennifer E. Mabry, "More Fertility Options Cause Ethical Concern," *USA Today* Internet edition, May 27, 1999.

2. Marc Gellman, "The Ethics of Surrogate Motherhood," *Sh'ma*, May 15, 1987, page 106.

3. Cited in Rabbi Dr. Immanuel Jakobovits, *Jewish Medical Ethics: A Comparative and Historical Study of the Jewish Religious Attitude to Medicine and its Practice* (New York: Bloch, 1975), page 265.

4. Marc Gellman, "The Ethics of Surrogate Motherhood," *Sh'ma*, May 15, 1987, page 106.

5. Cited in Rabbi Dr. Immanuel Jakobovits, *Jewish Medical Ethics*, page 266.

6. *Noda Beyehudah* #210 translated by Hadassah Tropper.

7. Rabbi Ben-Zion Uziel, *Mishpetei Uziel* (Jerusalem: Mosad Ha-Rav Kook, 1935), 1:28 and 29, cited in "Autopsies and Dissection," *Encyclopaedia Judaica* volume 3, page 933.

8. Rabbi Isaac Arieli in *Torah Shebe'al Peh: Proceedings from the Sixth Annual Conference on Oral Law* (1964), page 66, cited in "Autopsies and Dissection," *Encyclopaedia Judaica* volume 3, page 933.

CLAIMING A JEWISH FEMINIST HERITAGE

What is Jewish feminism? What qualities must a Jewish feminist have? Does being a Jewish feminist necessarily mean not observing the commandments to the letter of the law? In many Orthodox circles, the word "feminism" is taboo because of this notion. I myself, having been brought up in the Orthodox community, am afraid to label myself a feminist because of the many negative associations. Yet "feminism" is described in the Third Edition of the American Heritage dictionary as "belief in the social, political, and economic equality of the sexes." Are actions based on the belief in equality of the sexes to be viewed negatively? Are they to be shunned even as the new millennium begins?

In Chapter 6, we study four different women. We first explore Miriam the prophetess, sister of Moses, who helped to lead the exodus from Egyptian slavery. We next explore the biblical Queen Vashti of the Purim story. From the Talmud, we study Beruriah the scholar. We then leap into the twentieth century to read the words of Letty Cottin Pogrebin, who writes clearly and movingly on feminism and its place in Jewish women's lives. Learning about each of these four women will give us a richer and deeper perspective from which to examine our own lives and our society. Our path has been illuminated by our predecessors. Today's task is to ensure that the torch continues to burn brightly.

by Hadassah Tropper

MIRIAM THE PROPHETESS

"Here comes Miriam dancing with her timbrel, Miriam and the women dance the whole night long!" This is the refrain of a beautiful song composed by Debbie Friedman, perhaps the most influential songwriter dealing with American Jewish issues today. This song's melody, rhythm, and lyrics are all inspiring, bringing to mind the night when God split the Red Sea and the people of Israel passed through the walls of water, leaving their days as slaves in Egypt behind. In the Bible, we read that Miriam led the Hebrew women in dancing and singing as they reached the opposite shore, thanking God for the glorious miracle.

by Hadassah Tropper

MIRIAM IN JEWISH LITERATURE

Exodus 1:22–2:10

The first mention of Miriam in the Bible does not identify her by name. She here is called simply the sister of Moses, and she acts with intelligence and courage to preserve her baby brother's life.

Then Pharaoh charged all his people, saying, "Every [Hebrew] boy that is born you shall throw into the Nile, but let every [Hebrew] girl live."

A certain man of the house of Levi went and married a Levite woman. The woman conceived and bore a son; and when she saw how beautiful he was, she hid him for three months. When she could hide him no longer, she got a wicker basket for him and caulked it with bitumen and pitch. She put the child into it and placed it among the reeds by the bank of the Nile. And his sister stationed herself at a distance, to learn what would befall him.

The daughter of Pharaoh came down to bathe in the Nile, while her maidens walked along the Nile. She spied the basket among the reeds and sent her slave girl to fetch it. When she opened it, she saw that it was a child, a boy crying. She took pity on it and said, "This must be a Hebrew child." Then his sister said to Pharaoh's daughter, "Shall I go and get you a Hebrew nurse to suckle the child for you?" And Pharaoh's daughter answered, "Yes." So the girl went and called the child's mother. And Pharaoh's daughter said to her, "Take this child and nurse it for me, and I will pay your wages." So the woman took the child and nursed it. When the child grew up, she brought him to Pharaoh's daughter, who made him her son. She named him Moses, explaining, "I drew him out of the water."

Exodus 15:20-21

When the Hebrew nation leaves Egypt, embarking on its 40-year journey to the promised land, Miriam, identified by her name, assumes a leadership position along with her brothers, Moses and Aaron. Miriam initiates the women's rejoicing after the miracle of the Red Sea, and the Bible mentions for the first time that she is a prophetess.

Then Miriam the prophetess, Aaron's sister, took a timbrel in her hand, and all the women went out after her in dance with timbrels. And Miriam chanted for them:

> Sing to the Lord, for He has triumphed gloriously;
> Horse and driver He has hurled into the sea.

Numbers 12:1-16

Miriam, though she is a prophetess and leader of the Jewish people, nonetheless errs, and she is severely punished.

When they were in Hazeroth, Miriam and Aaron spoke against Moses because of the Cushite woman he had married: "He married a Cushite woman!"

They said, "Has the Lord spoken only through Moses? Has He not spoken through us as well?" The Lord heard it. Now Moses was a very humble man, more so than any other man on earth. Suddenly the Lord called to Moses, Aaron, and Miriam, "Come out, you three, to the Tent of Meeting." So the three of them went out. The Lord came down in a pillar of cloud, stopped at the entrance of the Tent, and called out, "Aaron and Miriam!" The two of them came forward; and He said, "Hear these My words: When a prophet of the Lord arises among you, I make Myself known to him in a vision, I speak with him in a dream. Not so with My servant Moses; he is trusted throughout My household. With him I speak mouth to mouth, plainly and not in riddles, and he beholds the likeness of the Lord. How then did you not shrink from speaking against My servant Moses!" Still incensed with them, the Lord departed.

As the cloud withdrew from the tent, there was Miriam stricken with snow-white scales! When Aaron turned toward Miriam, he saw that she was stricken with scales. And Aaron said to Moses, "O my lord, account not to us the sin which we committed in our folly. Let her not be as one dead, who emerges from his mother's womb with half his flesh eaten away." So Moses cried out to the Lord, saying, "O God, pray heal her!"

But the Lord said to Moses, "If her father spat in her face, would she not bear her shame for seven days? Let her be shut out of camp for seven days, and then let her be readmitted." So Miriam was shut out of camp seven days; and the people did not march on until Miriam was readmitted.

Numbers 20:1-2

The Israelites arrived in a body at the wilderness of Zin on the first new moon, and the people stayed at Kadesh. Miriam died there and was buried there. The community was without water, and they joined against Moses and Aaron.

Numbers 26:59

Numbers, the fourth Book of the Bible, clarifies the names of every member of Moses' family.

The name of Amram's wife was Yokheved daughter of Levi, who was born to Levi in Egypt; she bore to Amram, Aaron and Moses and their sister Miriam.

Babylonian Talmud, *Sotah* 9b

In the Book of Numbers, we read that Miriam is punished with disease and must withdraw from the encampment for seven days. The Rabbis explain that the Israelites waited for her because of her goodness.

Samson went after the desire of his eyes; therefore the Philistines put out his eyes, as it is said, "And the Philistines laid hold on him and put out his eyes" (Judges 16:21). Absalom gloried in his hair, therefore he was hanged by his hair. And because he cohabited with the ten concubines of his father, therefore he was stabbed with the ten lances, as it is said, "And ten young men that bore Joab's armor compassed about and slew Absalom" (II Samuel 18:15). [The principle of measure for measure] is the same in connection with the good. Miriam waited a short while for Moses, as it is said, "And his sister stationed herself at a distance," therefore Israel was delayed for her seven days in the wilderness, as it is said, "And the people did not march on until Miriam was readmitted."

Babylonian Talmud, *Sotah* 11b

Miriam's courage in guarding the baby Moses leads the Rabbis of the Talmud to attribute another act of bravery to her. The first passage that follows, from the Book of Exodus, tells of two Hebrew midwives who act in astonishing defiance of the Pharaoh. The next excerpt, from tractate Sotah of the Talmud, interprets Exodus 1:15.

Exodus 1:15–17: The king of Egypt spoke to the Hebrew midwives, one of whom was named Shifrah and the other Puah, saying, "When you deliver the Hebrew women, look at the birth stool: if it is a boy, kill him; if it is a girl, let her live." The midwives, fearing God, did not do as the king of Egypt had told them; they let the boys live.

Sotah 11b: Rab and Samuel [differ in their interpretations of Exodus 1:15]; one said [the two midwives] were mother and daughter, and the other said they were daughter-in-law and mother in-law. According to him who declared they were mother and daughter, they were Yokheved and Miriam [practicing midwifery under the names Shifrah and Puah]; and according to him who declared they were daughter-in-law and mother-in-law, they were Yokheved and Elisheva [Aaron's wife].

Babylonian Talmud, *Sotah 12a*

Recounting another legend about Miriam, the Rabbis of the Talmud also attribute to her wisdom and excellent reasoning skills. This legend was the teaching of a Tanna, that is, a Rabbi of the first two centuries of the common era, one of the sages whose deliberations are recorded in the Mishnah. The talmudic excerpt below begins by interpreting Exodus 2:1, "A certain man of the house of Levi went."

Where did he go? Rabbi Judah ben Zebina said that he went in the counsel of his daughter. A Tanna taught: Amram was the greatest man of his generation; when he saw that the wicked Pharaoh had decreed, "Every boy that is born you shall throw into the Nile," he said, "In vain do we labor." He arose and divorced his wife. All of the Israelites thereupon arose and divorced their wives. His daughter said to him, "Father, your decree is more severe than Pharaoh's, because Pharaoh decreed only against the males, whereas you decreed against the males and the females. Pharaoh decreed only concerning this world, whereas you decreed concerning this world and the world to come. And in the case of the wicked Pharaoh there is a doubt whether his decree will be fulfilled or not, whereas in your case, though you are righteous, it is certain that your decree will be fulfilled, as it is said, 'You will decree and it will be fulfilled'" (Job 22:28). He arose and took his wife back; and they all arose and took their wives back.

Babylonian Talmud, *Sotah 12b–13a*

Although the Bible does not elaborate on Miriam's prophecy, the Rabbis teach that her prophetic gift was apparent even as a young girl.

[Why does Exodus 15:20 say] "Miriam the prophetess, Aaron's sister" and not Moses' sister? Rav Amram said in the name of Rab, and according to others it was Rav Naḥman who said in the name of Rab: It teaches that she prophesied while she yet was the sister of Aaron only, and she said, "My mother will bear a son who will be the savior of Israel." When Moses was born, the whole house was filled with light; and her father arose and kissed her upon the head, saying, "My daughter, your prophecy has been fulfilled." But when they cast him into the river, her father arose and smacked her upon her head, saying, "Where now is your prophecy?" That is what is written, "And his sister stationed herself at a distance, to learn what would befall him" (Exodus 2:4)— what would be the fate of her prophecy.

Babylonian Talmud, *Ta'anit 9a*

Verse 1 of chapter 20 of the Book of Numbers tells of Miriam's death and burial. Verse 2 reveals that the Israelites lacked water. As Rabbi Yose teaches, this juxtaposition teaches us that Miriam provided water.

Rabbi Yose the son of Rabbi Judah says: Three good leaders had arisen for Israel, namely Moses, Aaron, and Miriam, and for their sake three good things were conferred upon Israel, namely, the well, the pillar of cloud, and the manna. The well for the merit of Miriam; the pillar of cloud for the merit of Aaron; and the manna for the merit of Moses. When Miriam died, the well disappeared, as it is said, "Miriam died there." And immediately after that verse it is written: "The community was without water." Hence we learn that all forty years they had the well because of the merits of Miriam.

Babylonian Talmud, *Pesaḥim 54a*

Our Rabbis taught: Ten things were created on the eve of the Sabbath at twilight, and these are they—the well, manna, the rainbow, writing, the writing instruments, the Tables, the sepulcher of Moses, and the cave in which Moses and Elijah stood, the opening of the ass's mouth, and the opening of the earth's mouth to swallow up the wicked.*

Midrash, *Numbers Rabbah 1:2*

The well was due to the merit of Miriam. For what does Scripture say? "Miriam died there and was buried there." And what is written after that? "The community was without water." How was the well constructed? It was rock-shaped like a kind of beehive, and wherever they journeyed it rolled along and came with them. When the standards [under which the tribes journeyed] halted and the tabernacle was set up, that same rock would come and settle down in the court of the Tent of Meeting and the princes would come and stand upon it and say, "Rise up, O well" (Numbers 21:17), and it would rise.

---

* Manna was the food eaten by the Israelites during their forty years in the desert; it appeared each morning on the ground, and had to be gathered and eaten each day (Exodus 16:11–35). The rainbow appeared after the flood, and symbolized the covenant between God and Noah (Genesis (9:13–16). Writing refers to the shapes of the Hebrew letters, believed to be holy. The writing instruments and the Tables refer to the Ten Commandments that God gave to Moses (Exodus 24:12, 32:16). The sepulcher of Moses was made by God (Exodus 34:6). The cave is at Ḥoreb, and it is here that God was revealed to Moses and later to Elijah (Exodus 33:22 and I Kings 19:8–13). The ass refers to the miraculous speech of Balaam's ass (Numbers 22:21–30). The opening of the earth's mouth refers to the story of Koraḥ and his followers, who rebelled against Moses and were swallowed up (Numbers 16:28–33).

Rashi (1040–1105) on Exodus 15:20

Rashi, Rabbi Solomon ben Isaac of France, is the foremost commentator on the Bible and on the Talmud. Here he comments on the verse about the Hebrew women following the crossing of the Red Sea: "All the women went out after her [Miriam] in dance with timbrels."

The righteous women of that generation trusted that God would do miracles for them, so they brought timbrels from Egypt.

Rashi (1040–1105) on Numbers 12:1

Numbers 12:1 states: "And Miriam and Aaron spoke against Moses." Yet only Miriam is stricken with disease. Rashi explains.

She began speaking first; therefore the Scripture places her first.... Now if Miriam, who did not intend to put him to shame, was punished thus, how much more one who tells of the shame of his fellow man?

Zohar III:163a (circa 1300)

The Zohar *reveals Miriam to be an inspired teacher, as was her brother Moses. Traditionally Moses is called Moshe Rabbeinu, Moses Our Teacher, and just as Moses instructed the men, Miriam instructed the women.*

All the righteous women of that generation come to Miriam.... The women on the eves of Sabbaths and festivals all come to Miriam to gain knowledge of the Sovereign of the universe. Happy is that generation above all other generations.

Rabbi Samson Raphael Hirsch (1808–1888) on Numbers 20:1–2

Rabbi Samson Raphael Hirsch was the foremost proponent of Orthodox Judaism in nineteenth-century Germany, and he is considered one of the founders of modern Orthodoxy. He discusses the verses "Miriam died there and was buried there. The community was without water."

During Israel's long wanderings, filled with so many sad experiences, it was the women who did the most to preserve serene trust and persevering devotion to God. This, according to Midrash *Numbers Rabbah* 27:1, was the reason why the women were not included in the decree under which the entire old generation had to die out before the nation could enter the promised land. As a result, the women, as grandmothers and mothers, were able to go with the new generation when it entered the promised land ... and to bring with them into that new future their personal recollections of their past in Egypt and of the momentous events they had witnessed in the wilderness under the protection and guidance of God. Thus they were given the opportunity to inspire their grandchildren and great-grandchildren.... That these Jewish women were so deeply and thoroughly imbued with the Jewish spirit may be ascribed in no small part to Miriam, who set them a shining example as a prophetess....

What Miriam's unobtrusive activities had meant for the moral future of the nation, and what a great loss her death was to the nation as a whole, can be seen from the fact that the well of Horeb dried up immediately after her passing.[1]

Questions for Discussion

1. In *Sotah*, Miriam tells her father to marry again and procreate, because having children is important—even if only the female infants survive. Jewish scholars frequently recount this legend as an example of Miriam's ardor to preserve Jewish lives and Judaism itself. Legends such as this are often constructed not as accurate historical records, but as pedagogical devices to relay an ethical message or to shed light on a biblical character or event. Keeping this in mind, what are the Rabbis who recount the legends about Miriam trying to teach us?

2. In the Book of Numbers, God punishes Miriam for speaking of Moses and his wife. The Torah does not make clear exactly what Miriam and Aaron have said, and Rashi points out that she may not have spoken disparagingly of Moses at all. Nonetheless, he continues, gossiping about another person is always a mistake. Rashi tries to lessen Miriam's offense. Although the Bible frequently describes the wrongdoing of our ancestors (for example, King David arranges for the death of an innocent man), the Rabbis of the Talmud and later scholars often find ways to mitigate these failings. Is mitigation of Miriam's offense Rashi's main purpose here? If so, why? If not, what is his purpose?

3. In the Book of Exodus, chapter 15 opens with Moses and the Israelites singing a song to praise God. Afterwards the Bible states that the women sang and danced with Miriam. Rashi explains that Miriam led the women in song while Moses led the men in song. If Rashi's interpretation makes sense to you, why does a separation occur here? Why do the women praise God separately? Why are the women singled out?

4. Miriam's well has become a symbol of significance for Jewish women today. Why is the well a women's or a feminist symbol? Why is water a women's symbol? Why is Miriam's legacy connected to water?

Suggested Activity

1. Miriam's character is complex and beautiful, and she could be portrayed artistically in many creative ways (painting, sculpture, dance, song, story, and so on). The images of Miriam watching the infant Moses drift down the river, her confrontation with the pharaoh's daughter, Miriam leading the women in song and dance—all are striking. Discuss different ways to represent aspects of her character artistically. Then ask

for volunteers to create such a representation, and present it at your next session.

VASHTI

All of my third grade teachers were talking about the exciting Purim story. I came home from school, elated at having decided on my Purim costume. "Mom," I said as I stepped off the school bus, "I'm going to be Queen Esther! I'll wear my long dress and you can put makeup on me and make my hair fancy with gold and silver ribbons. I'm so excited. Everyone is dressing up as Queen Esther, and I'll be the prettiest!"

I will never forget my mother's response. As she smiled down at me she said, "I have another idea. You can still dress up in your best dress, wear lots of makeup, and fix your hair with the gold and silver ribbons if you dress up as Queen Vashti!"

I grimaced. "No way! Vashti was bad and she was killed. She's not a big deal at all!"

My mother raised her eyebrows. "I think," she said, "that Vashti is a big hero."

Although I did not truly understand my mother at that age—nor in the next few years—I grew accustomed to being powdered and painted and decorated in flashy costume jewelry, wearing my best dress with a Miss America pageant strip slung across my shoulder, reading "Queen Vashti." I was a proud Queen Vashti, happy to be different from the dozens of Esther's scurrying about the synagogue. When stopped by children or adults who questioned my choice of costume, I would echo the infallible voice of my mother, "Vashti was a big hero, too!"

As I matured, I came to understand the significance of my mother's statement. Although the Rabbis of the Talmud condemn Vashti, in the biblical Book of Esther itself, Vashti's only negative act is to assert herself and maintain her pride and dignity.

The Persian queen Vashti provides a dramatic opening to the story of Esther. By refusing the king's wishes, Vashti paves the way for Esther's ascent to the throne and for Esther and Mordecai's subsequent salvation of the Jews of Persia. Until the past few decades nearly every Jewish man and woman viewed Vashti as wicked. Today, that view has begun to change.

by Hadassah Tropper

VASHTI IN JEWISH LITERATURE

Esther 1:1–2:1

It happened in the days of Ahasuerus—that Ahasuerus who reigned over a hundred and twenty-seven provinces from India to Nubia. In those days, when King Ahasuerus occupied the royal throne in the fortress Shushan, in the third year of his reign, he gave a banquet for all the officials and courtiers—the administration of Persia and Media, the nobles and the governors of the provinces in his service. For no fewer than a hundred and eighty days he displayed the vast riches of his kingdom and the splendid glory of his majesty. At the end of this period, the king gave a banquet for seven days in the court of the king's palace garden for all the people who lived in the fortress Shushan, high and low alike. There were hangings of white cotton and blue wool, caught up by cords of fine linen and purple wool to silver rods and alabaster columns; and there were couches of gold and silver on a pavement of marble, alabaster, mother-of-pearl, and mosaics. Royal wine was served in abundance, as befits a king, in golden beakers, beakers of varied design. And the rule for the drinking was, "No restrictions!" For the king had given orders to every palace steward to comply with each man's wishes. In addition, Queen Vashti gave a banquet for women, in the royal palace of King Ahasuerus.

On the seventh day, when the king was merry with wine, he ordered Mehuman, Bizzetha, Harbona, Bigtha, Abagtha, Zethar, and Carcas, the seven eunuchs in attendance on King Ahasuerus, to bring Queen Vashti before the king wearing a royal diadem, to display her beauty to the peoples and the officials; for she was a beautiful woman. But Queen Vashti refused to come at the king's command conveyed by the eunuchs. The king was greatly incensed, and his fury burned within him.

Then the king consulted the sages learned in procedure. (For it was the royal practice to turn to all who were versed in law and precedent. His closest advisors were Carshena, Shethar, Admatha, Tarshish, Meres, Marsena, and Memucan, the seven ministers of Persia and Media who had access to the royal presence and occupied the first place in the kingdom.) "What," he asked, "shall be done, according to law, to Queen Vashti for failing to obey the command of King Ahasuerus conveyed by the eunuchs?"

Thereupon Memucan declared in the presence of the king and the ministers: "Queen Vashti has committed an offense, not only against Your Majesty, but also against all the officials and against all the peoples in all the provinces of King Ahasuerus. For the queen's behavior will make all wives despise their husbands, as they reflect that King Ahasuerus himself ordered Queen Vashti to be brought before him, but she would not come. This very day the ladies of Persia and Media, who have heard of the queen's behavior, will cite it to all Your Majesty's officials, and there will be no end of scorn and provocation!

"If it please Your Majesty, let a royal edict be issued by you, and let it be written into the laws of Persia and Media, so that it cannot be abrogated, that Vashti shall never enter the presence of King Ahasuerus. And let Your Majesty bestow her royal state upon another who is more worthy than she. Then will the judgment executed by Your Majesty resound throughout the realm, vast though it is; and all wives will treat their husbands with respect, high and low alike."

The proposal was approved by the king and the ministers, and the king did as Memucan proposed. Dispatches were sent to all the provinces of the king, to every province in its own script and to every nation in its own language, that every man should wield authority in his home and speak the language of his own people.

Some time afterward, when the anger of King Ahasuerus subsided, he thought of Vashti and what she had done and what had been decreed against her.

Babylonian Talmud, Megillah 12a–12b

"Queen Vashti gave a banquet for women, in the royal palace of Ahasuerus." Should it have said, "in the women's royal palace"? Rava said, both of them [Ahasuerus and Vashti] had an immoral purpose. This bears out the popular saying, "He with large pumpkins and his wife with small pumpkins."

"On the seventh day, when the king was merry with wine." Was he not merry with wine until then? Rava said, the seventh day was Sabbath, when the people of Israel eat and drink. They begin with discourse on the Torah and with words of thanksgiving to God. But the nations of the world, the idolaters, when they eat and drink, only begin with words of frivolity.

And so it was at the feast of that wicked one. Some said, "The Medean women are the most beautiful," and others said, "The Persian women are the most beautiful."

Said Ahasuerus to them, "The vessel that I see is neither Median nor Persian, but Chaldean. Would you like to see her?"

They said, "Yes, but it must be naked."

(For man receives measure for measure. This remark teaches you that the wicked Vashti used to take the daughters of Israel and strip them naked and make them work on Sabbath. So it is written: "Some time afterward, when the anger of King Ahasuerus subsided, he thought of Vashti and what she had done and what had been decreed against her." As she had done, so it was decreed against her.)

"But Queen Vashti refused." Let us see. She was immodest, as the Master said above that both of them had an immoral purpose. Why then would she not come? Rabbi Yose ben Ḥanina said: "This teaches that leprosy broke out on her." In a *baraitha** it was taught that Gabriel came and fixed a tail on her.

"The king was greatly incensed." Why was he so enraged? Rava said, she sent him back the answer: "You son of my father's steward, my father drank wine in the presence of a thousand, and did not get drunk, and that man has become senseless with his wine." Straight away, "his fury burned within him."

Midrash, *Esther Rabbah* 5:1 (400–500)

According to rabbinic legend, Vashti was executed for her failure to appear before the king. Esther Rabbah *discusses the wine served at the king's banquet, making numerous connections between the Book of* Esther *and Proverbs 23:32–33: "Do not ogle that red wine as it lends color to the cup, as it flows on smoothly; in the end, it bites like a snake; it spits like a basilisk."*

Another explanation of "It spits like a basilisk": Just as the basilisk by its bite draws away from life to death, so wine drew away Ahasuerus from Vashti who was put to death, as it says, "On the seventh day, when the king was merry with wine" (Esther 1:10), the result of which was that he was enraged with her and put her to death.

Me'am Lo'ez on verse 19 (1864)

Written in Judeo-Spanish, the Me'am Lo'ez *is a multi-volume work of Bible commentary, weaving together ethics, homilies, anecdotes, historical narrative, legends, folklore, and detailed prescriptions for following Jewish law.*

"Upon another who is more worthy than she." Memucan told Ahasuerus that his second wife would most certainly be more obedient than her predecessor, having made note of the manner in which Vashti was killed, and having read the stern decree proclaimed throughout the land. His second wife would realize that if the king could not find it in his heart to forgive his first love for having disobeyed him, she, as his second choice, would have to tread very carefully.

Vilna Gaon (1720–1797) on verse 20

Elijah ben Solomon Zalman, known as the Vilna Gaon or Elijah Gaon, wrote books and commentaries on virtually every aspect of Jewish knowledge.

"All wives will treat their husbands with respect." All this was written in such detail to teach us how the Almighty weaves a web of intrigue

---

*A *baraitha* is a teaching or tradition of the sages of the first two centuries of the common era, that was excluded from the Mishnah (completed in 200).

and paradox to accomplish miracles for Israel. Ahasuerus issued a decree to accommodate the wishes of even his lowliest subjects; yet he did not hesitate to make the outrageous and humiliating demand on his own wife—his queen, daughter of royalty—to appear in public against her will. His caprice resulted in her death and paved the way for Esther, and the ultimate miracle.

Mary Gendler, "The Restoration of Vashti" (1973)

Mary Gendler was one of the first Jewish women to apply a feminist analysis to a female biblical character, and her essay on Vashti is now a classic. Reclaiming our foremothers began with the feminists of the nineteenth century, but became a prominent feature of Jewish life only with the second wave of feminism in the sixties and seventies.

Ahasuerus, a typical Near Eastern autocratic king, holds absolute power of life and death over everyone in his kingdom, men and women alike. Open defiance like Vashti's is simply not tolerated from anyone.... The reasoning for punishing Vashti's refusal [is that male] authority and power over women will be seriously undermined if Vashti is allowed to get away with her defiance. There is an interesting comparison with Mordecai here. When Mordecai refuses to bow down to Haman,* Haman is furious because Mordecai's refusal undermines his authority and piques his vanity. He seeks to have not only Mordecai but all the Jews punished in retribution. So, as with Vashti, there is generalization to a broader group of people. But note that it is not Vashti's "people" who are to be punished, but rather all females who are to be kept in line....

It is very clear that in no way was Vashti's refusal to debase herself seen by succeeding Jews as noble or courageous. Quite the contrary. The Rabbis must have found themselves in somewhat of a bind initially. On the one hand, they couldn't possibly approve of the demand Ahasuerus makes on Vashti. On the other hand, to support her would be to invite female disobedience in other situations, an idea they apparently could not tolerate. They solve this by condemning Ahasuerus as foolish and by creating legends whereby Vashti is shown as getting exactly what she deserves. If, then, in addition to decrees on obedience ... you reinforce this by vixenizing a woman who shows characteristics you want to obliterate, you have a much better chance of ensuring that other women will not follow her example.

[Rabbinic attitudes toward Esther and Vashti contrast with Rabbinic attitudes toward] Mordecai, who reacts with open defiance to Haman's

---

* Mordecai refuses to bow down before Haman, because he acknowledges no lord but God. In rabbinic literature, Mordecai is praised for heroism and moral strength.

arrogant demands, a reaction which we would expect to see from any red-blooded male. His direct challenge to authority, his refusal to debase himself as a person and as a Jew, is seen in all the succeeding commentaries as highly admirable. It is true that historically there is no comparison between the power held by Haman and that held by Ahasuerus, so at that level the comparison is unfair. What I am interested in here, however, is pointing up typical male and female models of behavior and, at that level, it is clear that society rewards men for being direct and aggressive while it condemns women, like Vashti, for equivalent behavior....

If women would begin to identify with Vashti, as I am proposing we do, we could discover our own sources of dignity, pride, and independence. When and under what circumstances do we say no?[2]

Questions for Discussion

1. The Talmud offers two explanations for Vashti's refusal to appear before the king: Yose ben Hanina said that leprosy afflicted her, and a rabbinic teaching said that Vashti had grown a tail. Clearly the Rabbis are not arguing that Vashti is obedient to her husband; instead they assert that her wickedness is so great that appearing naked before a multitude would cause her no deep embarrassment. What is the agenda of the Rabbis? Do you agree with Mary Gendler that the Rabbis are "creating legends whereby Vashti is shown as getting exactly what she deserves"?

2. The Purim story as told in the Book of Esther is dramatic and fast-paced. The Talmud goes on to add a sexually titillating element: Vashti strips Jewish maidens naked and forces them to work on the Sabbath. And in this context, the king's order to bring "Queen Vashti before the king wearing a royal diadem" means "bring Queen Vashti before the king wearing *nothing but* a royal diadem." Why do the Rabbis add this element?

3. To what extent has American Jewry heeded Mary Gendler and "restored" Vashti? Discuss changes that have occurred in your community since 1973. To what extent is Vashti now a heroine in Purim plays? How many mothers today tell their daughters, as did Hadassah Tropper's mother, that "Vashti is a big hero"?

4. Mary Gendler suggests that Vashti be a role model when we confront the question: "When and under what circumstances do we say no?" Discuss "saying no" in your own life. To what extent do your own role models resemble Vashti?

5. Discuss possible alternative actions that Vashti could have taken when asked to appear before the King. Would any of them have enabled her to remain Queen? If a similar situation occurred today, how would the results differ? Do you know of any similar situations in our era?

Suggested Activities and Programs

1. Write a poem or song about Vashti's actions and her fate. Refer to the rabbinic legends that Vashti was ordered to appear naked, that she was licentious, leprous, or had grown a tail. Be as humorous or as serious as you wish, but also make the point that the Bible itself provides no evidence that Vashti was evil or deserved to be executed.

2. Work together with your Hadassah chapter's *Al Galgalim* teacher to produce and enact a Purim play for *Al Galgalim* families. Incorporate Mary Gendler's advice, and make your Vashti the model for when and how to say "no." Use puppets or act out the roles!

BERURIAH

Beruriah lived during the worst of times. In the second century, the Roman emperor Hadrian had converted Jerusalem into the Roman city of Aelia Capitolina. After putting down a Jewish revolt, Hadrian's troops killed half a million Jewish men and sold thousands more into slavery. Hadrian prohibited the observance of all religious practices, including the Sabbath, and also prohibited all study of Torah. Roman spies and informers were everywhere, keeping a close watch on the Jews to ensure that the decrees were obeyed.

Beruriah was born in the land of Israel to the famous Rabbi Haninah ben Teradyon, and was educated from her early youth in Torah studies. Rabbi Haninah ben Teradyon, an outstanding scholar, became one of the ten martyrs; the Romans caught him teaching Torah, and for this crime he was tortured and killed.

The accounts of Beruriah's life are limited, yet the Talmud reveals her to possess exceptional intelligence, feisty wit, and a compassionate character. Because of Beruriah's brilliance, she achieved recognition as an authority among the *tanna'im* (Rabbis of the Mishnah). She was expert in all types of learning, from Jewish law to biblical exegesis. During her lifetime, other scholars often sought her opinion. She is cited several times in the Talmud, and later scholars nearly always follow her rulings.

Beruriah is unique in the Talmud as the only woman whose legal opinions set important precedents. Women of Beruriah's time rarely received any education at all, and no other woman of the Talmud is accorded the respect that Beruriah commands. Nonetheless, the presence of even one such remarkable woman in the Talmud indicates that the Rabbis could—at least in a rare instance—acknowledge women's learning. It also indicates that women, if given the opportunity, could excel in talmudic scholarship.

Later scholars, however, seem to turn against Beruriah. Although the Talmud speaks only of Beruriah's piety and intellectual eminence, Rashi recounts a legend of Beruriah committing adultery and killing herself in shame.* Post-talmudic rabbis perhaps recognized Beruriah's subversive power, and assigned her a bad end. Nevertheless, the tragic legend makes Beruriah an even more fascinating figure. She becomes something of a doomed heroine, one who ultimately could not be sustained in a world that did not accept her.

by Hadassah Tropper and Claudia Chernov

BERURIAH IN JEWISH LITERATURE

Tosefta, *Kelim* 1:3 (circa 400)

The Tosefta serves as a supplement to the Mishnah. Written in Hebrew, it was compiled at least two centuries after completion of the Mishnah.

Beruriah said that a door bolt may be drawn off one door and hung on another on the Sabbath [without violating the prohibition against work on the Sabbath]. Rabbi Joshua said: Beruriah ruled correctly.

Babylonian Talmud, *Pesahim* 62b

Rabbi Simlai came before Rabbi Jonathan and requested him, "Let the master teach me the Book of Genealogies" [a commentary on the Book of Chronicles]. Said he to him, "Whence are you?" He replied, "From Lod" [in the land of Israel]. "And where is your dwelling?" "In Nahardea" [in Babylon]. Said he to him, "We do not discuss it either with the Lodians or with the Nahardeans, and how much more so with you who are from Lod and live in Nahardea!" But Rabbi Simlai urged him and he consented. "Let us learn it in three months," Rabbi Simlai proposed. Thereupon Rabbi Jonathan took a clod and threw it at him, saying, "If Beruriah, wife of Rabbi Meir and daughter of Rabbi Haninah ben Teradyon, who studied three hundred laws from three hundred teachers in one day, nevertheless could not do her duty in three years, yet you propose to do it in three months?!"

Babylonian Talmud, *Eiruvin* 53b-54a

Rabbi Yose the Galilean was once on a journey when he met Beruriah. "By what road," he asked her, "do we go to Lydda?" "Foolish

---

*According to Rabbi Burton Visotsky, Rashi (who lived in the eleventh century) generally tells of legends that were first recorded in the late sixth or the seventh centuries. The source for this legend of Beruriah's seduction and suicide has not survived. Rashi's recounting of the legend is the earliest existing version.

Galilean," she replied, "did not the sages say this: 'Engage not in much talk with women' (*Pirkei Avot* 1:5). You should have asked: 'By which to Lydda?'"

Beruriah once discovered a student who was learning in an undertone. Rebuking him, she exclaimed, "Is it not written, 'Ordered in all things and sure' (II Samuel 23:5)? If it is 'ordered' in your two hundred and forty-eight limbs, it will be 'sure,' otherwise it will not be sure."

Babylonian Talmud, *Berakhot* 10a

There were certain highwaymen in the neighborhood of Rabbi Meir who caused him a good deal of trouble. Rabbi Meir accordingly prayed that they should die. His wife Beruriah said to him: "How do you make out [that such a prayer is permitted]?" "Because it is written, 'May sinners disappear from the earth'" (Psalms 104:35). "Is it written *hotim* [meaning, sinners]? It is written *hata'im* [meaning, sins]! Further, look at the end of the verse, 'and let the wicked be no more.' Since the sins will cease, there will be no more wicked men! Rather pray for them that they should repent, and there will be no more wicked men." He did pray for them, and they repented.

A certain heretic said to Beruriah, "It is written, 'Shout, O barren one, you who bore no child! Shout aloud for joy' (Isaiah 54:1). Because she did not bear, is she to shout aloud for joy?" She replied to him, "Fool! Look at the end of the verse, where it is written, 'For the children of the one forlorn shall outnumber those of the espoused—said the Lord.' But what then is the meaning of 'barren one, you who bore no child'? Shout for joy, O community of Israel, who resembles a barren woman, for not having born children like you destined for Gehenna [hell]."

Babylonian Talmud, *Avodah Zarah* 18a-b

Beruriah's father, Rabbi Haninah ben Teradyon, had been martyred by the Romans for teaching Torah. As further punishment, the Romans killed his wife, Beruriah's mother, and placed Beruriah's youngest sister in a brothel in Rome.

Beruriah, the wife of Rabbi Meir, was a daughter of Rabbi Haninah ben Teradyon. Said she to her husband, "I am ashamed to have my sister placed in a brothel."

So he took a *tarkab*-full of *dinarii* [an approximate measure of money] and set out. If, thought he, she has not been subjected to anything wrong, a miracle will be wrought for her, but if she has committed anything wrong, no miracle will happen to her. Disguised as a knight, he came to her and said, "Prepare yourself for me."

She replied, "The manner of women is upon me."

"I am prepared to wait," he said.

"But," said she, "there are here many, many prettier than I am."

He said to himself, that proves that she has not committed any wrong; she no doubt says this to every comer.

He then went to her warder and said, "Hand her over to me."

He replied, "I am afraid of the government."

"Take the *tarkab* of *dinarii*," he said, "one half distribute as a bribe, the other half shall be for yourself."

"And what shall I do when these are exhausted?" he asked.

"Then," he replied, "say, 'O God of Meir answer me!' and you will be saved."

"But," said he, "who can assure me that will be the case?"

Rabbi Meir replied, "You will see now." There were some dogs who bit anyone who incited them. He took a stone and threw it at them, and when they were about to bite him he exclaimed, "O God of Meir answer me!" and they let him alone.

The warder then handed her over to him.

At the end, the matter became known to the government, and the warder, on being brought for judgment, was taken up to the gallows, when he exclaimed, "O God of Meir answer me!" They took him down and asked him what that meant, and he told them the incident that had happened. Then they engraved Rabbi Meir's likeness on the gates of Rome and proclaimed that anyone seeing a person resembling it should bring him there.

One day some Romans saw him and ran after him, so he ran away from them and entered a harlot's house [so as to avoid being identified, because no rabbi would enter a harlot's house]. Others say he happened just then to see food cooked by heathens and he dipped in one finger and then sucked the other [and tricked them into believing he had eaten non-kosher food, and so was not a rabbi]. Others again say that Elijah the Prophet appeared to them as a harlot who embraced him. God forbid, said they, were this Rabbi Meir, he would not have acted thus, and they left him. He then arose and ran away and came to Babylon. Some say it was because of that incident that he ran to Babylon; others say because of the incident about Beruriah.

Midrash on Proverbs 31:1 (640-900)

When two of their sons died on a Sabbath, Beruriah did not inform Meir of their children's death upon his return from the academy, in order not to grieve him on the Sabbath. Only after the *havdalah* prayer did she broach the matter, saying, "Some time ago a certain man came and left something in my trust; now he has called for it. Shall I return it to him or not?" Naturally, Meir replied in the affirmative, whereupon Beruriah showed him their dead sons. When Meir began to weep, she asked: "Did you not tell me that we must give back what is given on trust? 'The Lord gave and the Lord has taken away; blessed be the name of the Lord' (Job 1:21)."[3]

Rashi (1040-1105) on *Avodah Zarah* 18b

Rashi, Rabbi Solomon ben Isaac of France, comments on the Talmud passage, "Others say because of the incident about Beruriah."

One time she scoffed at the saying of the sages, "Women are light-headed" (*Kiddushin* 80b), and Rabbi Meir said, "By your life! Your own end may yet testify to the truth of their words." And he commanded one of his disciples to endeavor [to seduce] her, to incite her to sin. After he tried many times to persuade her, she yielded. When she realized what she had done, she hanged herself. Rabbi Meir fled like a storm from his home.

Rabbi Samuel Edels (1555-1631) on *Eiruvin* 54a

Rabbi Edels, a great talmudic scholar known as the Maharsha, comments on Beruriah's advice to the student: "If it is 'ordered' in your two hundred and forty-eight limbs, it will be 'sure,' otherwise it will not be sure."

Therefore one should always study in a loud voice, because that stimulates movements in all the limbs of one's body, involving them all in the learning process, and that ensures that one's learning will not be forgotten.

Questions for Discussion

1. Opinions differ on Beruriah's remarks to Rabbi Yose the Galilean. Some say that she speaks resentfully of the passage from *Pirkei Avot*: "Engage not in much talk with women." Others maintain that Beruriah is sincerely admonishing Rabbi Yose for not heeding the advice of the passage, which is actually not offensive toward women because it deals with men's weakness. Consider Beruriah's character, and decide which explanation seems more plausible.

2. What does the story from Midrash on Proverbs illustrate about Beruriah's character? What do we learn about Jewish attitudes toward death and grieving?

3. The excerpt from *Eruvin* indicates that Beruriah guided students in their studies. How might she have accomplished this in the patriarchal era in which she lived? What views were her students likely to hold of her?

4. In *Berakhot*, Beruriah interprets a verse more compassionately than her husband, and Rabbi Meir accepts her interpretation. Does Beruriah's womanhood play a significant role in her choice of interpretation? Are women more likely to forgive others, to use compassion?

5. In *Avodah Zarah*, we read that Rabbi Meir went to Babylon: "Some say it was because of that incident [freeing his sister-in-law from a Roman brothel] that he ran to Babylon; others say because of the incident

about Beruriah." No "incident" about Beruriah is ever discussed in the Talmud or Midrash. Rashi, however, recounts that Beruriah committed adultery and Rabbi Meir then ran away to Babylon. In all likelihood, Rashi is recounting a legend from sources that have not been preserved. Why might this legend have gained currency?

Suggested Activities and Programs

1. Organize a debate on whether Beruriah may ascend into heaven after committing suicide. One side will defend Beruriah's actions and advocate for her, and the other side will denounce her and try to prevent her entrance into heaven. Consider Jewish views on suicide.*

2. In "Yentl the Yeshivah Boy," Isaac Bashevis Singer (1904–1991) wrote of a woman who, like Beruriah, ultimately could not be sustained in a world that did not accept her.** Ask a volunteer to read Singer's story and to briefly analyze its portrayal of a learned Jewish woman. As a group, rent the videotape of the 1983 film *Yentl* and discuss its portrayal together.

IV. LETTY COTTIN POGREBIN

Letty Cottin Pogrebin, born in 1939, was a founding editor of *Ms.* magazine, the ground-breaking feminist journal. Her activism and commitment have helped to change women's status in the United States and abroad. As a writer, Pogrebin has used her talents to reach thousands. She has written with a piercing directness about working women, motherhood, religion, sex, friendship, politics, family, and aging. In the early eighties Pogrebin co-authored *Free To Be You and Me*, a feminist work on child-rearing that achieved popular success throughout America. She continues to publish magazine and newspaper articles.

Pogrebin's contributions to Jewish feminism came relatively late in her life. Though raised in a religious home, Pogrebin rejected Judaism, in part because she rejected the practices of her father. Indeed for most of her adult life she distanced herself from Jewish religious organizations and institutions. Her return to Judaism is the subject of the autobiographical *Deborah, Golda, and Me: Being Jewish and Female in America*, published in 1991. In it Pogrebin explains that her alienation began at age fifteen, immediately after her mother died. Pogrebin and her

---

* Refer to Kalman J. Kaplan and Matthew B. Schwartz, eds. *Jewish Approaches to Suicide, Martyrdom, and Euthanasia* (Northvale, NJ: Jason Aronson, 1998) and Sidney Goldstein, *Suicide in Rabbinic Literature* (Hoboken, NJ: Ktav, 1989).

** The short story is available in several collections. It was first published in English translation by Farrar Straus & Giroux in 1964 in *Short Friday and Other Stories*.

father were observing *shiva*, the seven-day period of mourning, in their home, and as the time approached to recite the *min<u>h</u>ah* (afternoon) prayer service, only nine men were present. However, in order to recite the *kaddish* (mourner's prayer) aloud during the *min<u>h</u>ah* service, a quorum of ten men—a *minyan*—was needed. The young Letty asked if she—as her deceased mother's child and as a knowledgeable Jew—could count as the tenth member of the quorum, but her father summarily rejected her request, because women do not count in a *minyan*.

In *Deborah, Golda, and Me,* Pogrebin tells of both her withdrawal from organized Judaism and her return. She also tells of her attempts to reconcile Judaism and feminism, relating her personal stories to the struggles of Jewish women everywhere. Her book encourages Jewish women to break the boundaries that they feel exclude them from Judaism and Jewish life, and to achieve a greater sense of freedom and importance as women and as Jews.

by Hadassah Tropper and Claudia Chernov

SELECTIONS FROM *DEBORAH, GOLDA, AND ME: BEING JEWISH AND FEMALE IN AMERICA*

Kaddish

In New City, New York, a village largely inhabited by Orthodox Jews, there is a sign advertising a Talmud course: TALMUD FOR EVERYONE—MEN ONLY.

I have a perverse fondness for this sentence.... Men are "everyone," women are not....

"Jew" means man, because males are the only Jews who count—literally. I learned this when I was most vulnerable, when I wanted to count—to be counted as a Jew. It didn't matter that I was my father's intellectual heir, my mother's daughter, an educated Jewish student, and a bat mitzvah girl. None of it mattered. I may as well have been a Christian, Muslim, or Druze.

A strange man was called in to say *kaddish* for my mother, because he was more a "Jew" than I.

In those first weeks after losing my mother I needed to lean on my religion, crawl into its arms, rock myself to Hebrew rhythms as familiar to me as rain. But how could I mourn as a Jew if my *kaddish* did not count?

The answer is, I could not.[4]

Jewish Education

For a people whose ethos, whose very identity, is founded in *remembering,* we have forgotten too much about Jewish women. For a community that calls itself "the people of the book," we have left too many pages blank. The Jewish educational establishment has left us ignorant of Jewish women's past. Writers and historians have under-documented our women's achievements. The Jewish press has not done justice to women, with the exception perhaps of our actresses and organizational superstars....

My own Jewish schooling ... included ten years in afternoon Hebrew school and two years at the Yeshiva of Central Queens. In total, "they"—the keepers of memory, the transmitters of history—had me as a student for twelve years and in all that time they taught me about fewer than a dozen Jewish women....

The most outrageous false myth in Judaism is that women were not doing anything important. By whose definition? Even if most women were denied the opportunity of study, prayer, leadership and conquest, that doesn't mean they were not *being Jews*. Their spirituality and religiosity found expression in ways that kept them and their children affirmatively Jewish in every imaginable alien culture. They were doing hard work, vital work—God's work—creating Jewish life and nourishing Jewish families. If women had written the Bible, we would know about *that* work, and *that* work would be deemed "important." Even without the male standard of importance, where is the bare-bones record of women's existence from generation to generation? Where is women's Bible? Who decided that everything female was unimportant, even our names?

We may not be able to give names to the wives-of and daughters-of and other anonymous women who flit like shadows across the page of the written record, but, as I have noted, Jewish feminist scholars are trying to undo the damage on behalf of some women who have escaped invisibility. We must insist that the fruits of such research filter down to our young people, and that teachers make a particular effort to sift women's reality from the cast-off crumbs of memory and literature, and help young women ... to find sustenance in the gleanings.[5]

Antisemitism

The Jewish woman who does not take possession of her total identity, and make it count for something, may find that others will impose upon her a label she does not like at all.

That is what I discovered in 1975, when the delegates meeting in Mexico City at the first of three United Nations International Women's Decade Conferences passed a resolution that effectively identified all Jews as racists. The "Zionism is racism" resolution—called the declaration of Mexico—took me by surprise. I could not believe that supposed feminists who had been entrusted with the inauguration of a ten-year commitment to improving the status of all the world's women—and who were pledged to address the monumental problems of female infanticide, illiteracy, high mortality rates, abject poverty, involuntary pregnancies, domestic violence, and so on—could allow their agenda to be hijacked on behalf of this unspeakable PLO slogan....

Although it was ostensibly the Israelis who had been attacked as racists, I knew the arrow also was meant for me. I could stand under any damn sign I pleased, but to feminists who hate Israel I was not a woman, I was a *Jewish* woman. The men of the *minyan* might not consider me a Jew among Jews, but to many of those delegates in Mexico City, that's all I was. Now the question I had to answer was, *Why be a Jew for them if I am not a Jew for myself?*

Theodore Herzl, the founder of Zionism, was inspired to identify affirmatively with his people after witnessing French antisemitism in action at the infamous Dreyfus trial. In the context of feminism, my experience mirrored his. I'd like to be able to claim a more positive impetus for my reawakened Jewish persona—an impressive mentor or persuasive literary argument—but it was only feral Jew-hating that forced me to reconsider what I was and what I wanted to be. While I had believed that feminists fight side by side *as* women, *with* women *for* women, it seemed as if some of my "sisters" were not out to get the patriarchal militarists, multinational pornographers, or capitalist imperialists—they were using the resolutions of the United Nations and the foot soldiers of international feminism to get the Jews.

I know Zionists who are racists, just as I know racist feminists, but that didn't make Zionism racism any more than a few bigoted women made feminism racism. Moreover, one could say that Zionism is to Jews what feminism is to women. Zionism began as a national liberation movement and has become an ongoing struggle for Jewish solidarity, pride, and unity. Similarly, feminism, which began as a gender-liberation movement, has become an ongoing struggle for women's solidarity, pride, and unity.... Calling Zionism racism makes Jewish self-determination sound like an attack on non-Jews, which is comparable to calling feminism "anti-male," as if female self-determination were an attack on men.

The difference in the two "isms" is this: Many women resist identifying as feminists because it means espousing their own interests and they've been taught that appearing "selfish" is unfeminine, whereas apart from a few ultra-Orthodox sects and rebels on the extreme left, there are relatively few Jews who do not identify as Zionists. Hence, virtually every Jewish woman at the gathering in Mexico City and every Jew reading about the conference at home considered herself a Zionist and suffered deep injuries from the impact of that anti-Zionist statement. I was accustomed to hearing Israel defamed at the UN, but not in a gathering where *sisterhood* is supposed to be powerful. What was going on? Why was all that womanpower being directed against Jews?[6]

Questions for Discussion

1. Letty Cottin Pogrebin traces her alienation from Judaism to the time of her mother's death, when she did not count as one of the ten Jews required for reciting the mourner's *kaddish*. As Pogrebin notes, many American women have found that issues related to reciting *kaddish* have increased their commitment to Jewish feminism. Even today, in certain right-wing Orthodox congregations, women mourners are permitted to join in the *kaddish* only if they pray silently. Pogrebin states: "What men are saying when they silence women is that men, and only men, deserve God's attention. I cannot believe that God believes that." Discuss.

2. In Orthodox Judaism, men are required to recite *kaddish* aloud for eleven months following a parent's death. Today, many female mourners in left-wing or centrist Orthodox congregations have also begun reciting *kaddish*. However, for the Orthodox woman, *kaddish* remains optional. What can we make of the difference between women's choice and men's obligation? Should women and men both be equally obligated?

3. The antisemitism of the Mexico City women's conference shocked many Jewish participants. How could hatred of Jews arise in the context of women coming together to work for women? Does the appearance of antisemitism at the women's conference reveal a flaw in the feminist movement? A flaw in humanity as a whole? If the latter, why was feminism unable to conquer this flaw?

4. Pogrebin states that antisemitism reawakened her to Judaism. This common phenomenon is called "negative Judaism": Jews who feel distant to the Jewish people identify with Judaism when they witness or experience hatred of Jews. Pogrebin, because of antisemitism, identified herself as one of the Jewish people and became a Jewish activist. How do you view negative Judaism? How could "positive Judaism" become as effective as negative? In other words, what could unite Jews?

Suggested Activities and Programs

1. Request one or more volunteers to read *Deborah, Golda, and Me* in its entirety. (It is available in paperback from Anchor Books.) In it, Pogrebin grapples with her contradictory feelings of affiliation with and alienation from organized Judaism. As your group members read the book, have them record the aspects of Jewish life that attract Pogrebin and the aspects that cause her to turn away. Have the volunteers present their lists to the Rosh H̱odesh group, and then initiate a discussion on how group members reconcile the things they love and the things that disturb them in Jewish life.

2. Organize an education day on Jewish women and social change, including exploration of both ancient and modern Jewish women. Refer to pages 169–170 for a suggested schedule.

---

1. *The Pentateuch: T'rumath Tzvi* with a translation by Samson Raphael Hirsch and excerpts from The Hirsch Commentary, edited by Ephraim Oratz, English translation from the original German by Gertrude Hirschler (New York: Judaica, 1986), pages 588–589.

2. Mary Gendler, "The Restoration of Vashti" in *The Jewish Woman: New Perspectives*, ed. Elizabeth Koltun (New York: Schocken, 1973), pages 242–247. Reprinted from *Response* 18 (Summer 1973).

3. Cited in *Encyclopaedia Judaica*, volume 4, page 701.

4. Letty Cottin Pogrebin, *Deborah, Golda, and Me: Being Jewish and Female in America* (New York: Crown, 1991), pages 49–50.

5. Letty Cottin Pogrebin, *Deborah, Golda, and Me*, pages 139–141.

6. Letty Cottin Pogrebin, *Deborah, Golda, and Me*, pages 154–155.

BA'ALOT TESHUVAH

On September 28, 1997, 70,000 ultra-Orthodox Jewish men filled the seats at Madison Square Garden and other stadiums across America. They had gathered to celebrate the completion of the entire Talmud through study of one page every day for the previous seven and a half years. This sell-out event was a powerful testament to ultra-Orthodox or *haredi* Judaism's enduring strength. Through commemorating the years of Talmud study, the gathering also announced to the public that *haredi* Judaism offers its adherents the best pathway through life.

And where were the ultra-Orthodox women? At home—cooking, cleaning, taking care of the children, dealing with the household finances. Or they were out at work, earning the family's income. Most *haredi* women juggle housekeeping and child-rearing together with a full-time or part-time job. Only men are encouraged to study (to learn, as they say), and many ultra-Orthodox men spend the entire day hunched over a page of Talmud, debating the fine points of the text with a study partner. The *haredi* community prizes these *talmidim hakhamim*—wise scholars—for their dedication. The unmarried ones are keenly sought as prospective husbands. Men studying, women supporting the household—the *haredi* community maintains a separate sphere for each sex.

The modern Orthodox Jewish community also maintains separate spheres for women and men. However, modern Orthodoxy strikes a balance between the Jewish and the non-Jewish worlds, and so the modern Orthodox Jew defines men's and women's spheres more closely in accordance with the general American population. In contrast to the *haredim*, modern Orthodox Jews expect a husband to financially support his family. Typical is the man who wakes up at the crack of dawn to make time for both *shaharit* (the morning prayer service) and *daf yomi* (daily page of Talmud study) before commuting to his corporate office. Though many modern Orthodox wives contribute to the family's income, the husband is nearly always the higher wage earner. If the family has sufficient financial resources, the mother often drops out of the workforce to raise her children. Also in consonance with the general American population, the modern Orthodox have recently blurred the lines between men and women's educational spheres. For instance, a small but growing number of modern Orthodox women study Talmud. Like the *haredi* woman, however, the modern Orthodox woman is not required to attend synagogue on a daily basis, as is the Orthodox man, but she is expected to prepare lavish Shabbat and holiday meals.

If Orthodox Judaism in either form strikes you as gender-biased, you might be surprised to learn that to many women, Orthodoxy offers a rich, appealing, and pro-woman way of life. Many women raised in non-religious, half-heartedly religious, and even anti-religious homes have recently taken on the obligations of Orthodox Judaism and have been welcomed into Orthodox communities.

The Orthodox writer Sally Berkovic states: "In the coded language of the religious world, my community is divided into those who are *frum* [religious] from birth (FFB) and those who are *ba'alei teshuvah* (BT), a master of repentance: a Jew who was not born into the Orthodox world, yet makes a choice to lead a religious lifestyle."[1] A man entering Orthodoxy as an adult is called a *ba'al teshuvah*, and a woman is called a *ba'alat teshuvah*. The plurals are *ba'alei teshuvah*—masculine, which also includes men and women together—and *ba'alot teshuvah*—feminine. Colloquially, the newcomers are called BT. The penitent or returning label is something of a misnomer; its use today is generally restricted to Jews who are approaching Orthodox observance for the first time, not to Jews who repent and return to a community which they have left.*

---

*Reform, Conservative, and Reconstructionist Judaism also attract significant numbers of adherents from among Jewish adults who were raised in non-observant or minimally-observant homes. Occasionally such adults are, like the newly Orthodox, called *ba'alei teshuvah*. Usually, however, the non-Orthodox do not use any special label to classify newly religious adults. (A personal account by a newly religious Conservative Jew can be found in Lee Meyerhoff Hendler's *The Year Mom Got Religion: One Woman's Midlife Journey into Judaism*, published in 1998 by Jewish Lights of Woodstock, VT.) Perhaps because the phenomenon of increasing Jewish commitment is relatively common and also relatively flexible in non-Orthodox communities, it merits no separate designation. In addition, the comparatively large numbers of non-Jews who have chosen Judaism may seem a more noteworthy phenomenon in non-Orthodox synagogues.

In prior centuries, of course, the BT phenomenon would have been impossible. In order to choose Orthodoxy as an adult, one must have the freedom to choose one's religion and, even more important, one's parents must have had the freedom to reject religion or to choose non-Orthodox Jewish denominations. Until the last two centuries, these freedoms did not exist. Only in the late eighteenth century were Jews accepted into the civil life of Western Europe. The nineteenth century gave birth to Reform Judaism, which sought to fuse Jewish theology and practice with modern ethical thought and with modern scientific understanding. The reformers' changes forced those who were faithful to an unchanged Judaism to define their ideology more precisely and at the same time more narrowly. In rejecting fundamental change, Orthodox Judaism positioned itself as the authentic link to historic Judaism—from the time of Moses to the time of the *shtetl* to our own time. At least numerically, the lure of modernity remains stronger than the lure of authenticity. In 1990 the Reform movement was the largest Jewish denomination in the United States, while American Conservative Jews outnumbered Orthodox Jews by more than five to one.[2]

Swimming against this demographic tide are the *ba'alei teshuvah*. The BT phenomenon became prominent in the seventies with the opening of several schools designed especially for newcomers to religion. In Israel today, several Orthodox organizations still openly recruit young, unmarried Jews, usually among American tourists. In the United States, the Lubavitch Hasidim recruit aggressively, also mainly targeting unmarried Jews in their teens and twenties. Jews in large urban areas are no doubt familiar with the Lubavitch *mitzvah* mobiles. Young Hasidim stop women and ask them if they light Shabbat candles; they stop men and ask them if they have put on *tefillin*. In both Israel and America, interested young people are steered toward BT schools, which are segregated by sex. Many of the schools are residential, enabling students to learn every aspect of Orthodox Jewish life firsthand.

The modern Orthodox, in contrast, use more subtle recruiting tactics, but they are just as serious about the effort. Manhattan's Lincoln Square Synagogue, for example, is well-known for its programs educating newcomers on how to lead an observant Jewish existence.* Generally targeting Jews in their twenties to forties, the modern Orthodox strongly encourage both male and female *ba'alei teshuvah* to continue learning

---

* Educational programs designed for non-observant Jews and for Jews with little or no Jewish education are a mainstay of Conservative, Reform, Reconstructionist, and other Jewish (JCC's, Y's, etc.) recruiting efforts as well. These efforts are called outreach. In some cases outreach involves religious instruction (for instance, Beginners' Shabbat Services), and in some cases it involves social events; education on Jewish history, culture, or literature; or community service projects.

about Judaism, either through synagogue courses or at accredited Orthodox schools.

In addition to gaining a basic spiritual understanding of Judaism, the *ba'alat teshuvah*, both modern and *haredi*, is expected to take on the primary responsibilities of homemaking and (at some point) motherhood. She must master the myriad rules for keeping a kosher kitchen, dressing and behaving modestly, and maintaining family purity, yet her participation in synagogue ritual is strictly limited and in the ultra-Orthodox world her familiarity with Jewish texts is severely circumscribed.

Why would a single, contemporary woman—the beneficiary of feminism's struggle to liberate women from private and public subordination—choose the sex-based restrictions of Orthodoxy? Why would she reject the other streams of Judaism, which have granted women full participation in religious life, and choose the one branch that does not even call women up to the Torah at Shabbat services? In the following selections, *ba'alot teshuvah* offer some answers in their own words, and scholars and journalists who have studied the newly Orthodox present their conclusions.

by Leora Tanenbaum and Claudia Chernov

PIETY AND CHOOSING ORTHODOX JUDAISM

Psalm 119:1-15

Happy are those whose way is blameless,
    who follow the teaching of the Lord.
Happy are those who observe His decrees,
    who turn to Him wholeheartedly.
They have done no wrong,
    but have followed His ways.
You have commanded that Your precepts
    be kept diligently.
Would that my ways were firm
    in keeping Your laws;
      then I would not be ashamed
      when I regard all Your commandments.
I will praise You with a sincere heart
      as I learn Your just rules.
I will keep Your laws;
      do not utterly forsake me.

How can a young man keep his way pure?—
    by holding to Your word.
I have turned to You with all my heart;
    do not let me stray from Your commandments.
In my heart I treasure Your promise;
    therefore I do not sin against You.
Blessed are You, O Lord;
    train me in Your laws.
With my lips I rehearse
    all the rules You proclaimed.
I rejoice over the way of Your decrees
    as over all riches.
I study Your precepts;
    I regard Your ways;
    I take delight in Your laws;
    I will not neglect Your word.

Gerson Cohen (1982)

Rabbi Gerson Cohen (1924–1991) was Chancellor of the Jewish Theological Seminary, the foremost academic institution of Conservative Judaism. In an address on "the state of world Jewry," he strongly condemned the ultra-Orthodox residential schools for ba'alei teshuvah.

They are not appeals to the return of religion, much less the healing of breaches; they are appeals to magic ritual, to rank anti-intellectualism and superstition and, above all, to rebbe-worship. The *ba'alei teshuvah*, those young people who have ostensibly returned to the Jewish fold by enrolling in the diverse *yeshivot* that have been set up to serve them, in fact find their fulfillment in an anti-intellectual study of the Torah, in a rejection of the world, in a hero-worship and ritualism that we easily recognize—and condemn—in others. How different are they, after all, from the Moonies, the Hare Krishna, the Ayatollah Khomeini, or the Moral Majority? They are Jews, to be sure, but they are no source of strength for the Jewish people.[3]

Students at Bais Chana (1983)

Sociologist Lynn Davidman interviewed students living in Saint Paul, Minnesota, at the Bais Chana seminary established by Lubavitch Hasidim specifically for ba'alot teshuvah. *Davidman also interviewed women who had recently become religious through participation in a modern Orthodox synagogue in New York. Analyzing her research results, Davidman found a number of differences between the two groups of women. All of those who turned to* hasidic *Judaism were younger than 30, and a third were teenagers. Those who turned to modern Orthodoxy, however, were mostly between age 29 and 40. The modern*

Orthodox women, in consequence, had a higher level of secular education. Furthermore, several Bais Chana residents had tried other spiritual options, including Eastern religions and fundamentalist Christian sects, before turning to Judaism, whereas the modern Orthodox women generally had not tried other religions before Judaism.

Many of the ba'alot teshuvah, *both modern and ultra-Orthodox, criticized feminism, but the ultra-Orthodox rejection of feminism was especially fervent.**

Lisa: Society cries, "Women's lib! Be a modern woman! Don't get tied down and caught up in a rut of old-fashioned norms. Be fulfilled! Use birth control!" Being "just" a wife and mother, we are taught, isn't satisfying, even degrading. We must go to college, find careers, and find our own identity. I think that with all of this identity finding we have lost the true identity we had all along.... We *are*, first and foremost, women ... we are meant to cleave to a man and be one together with him; we *are* meant to raise a family and, yes, even find fulfillment in it! This was God's plan from the beginning, and nothing has changed as far as He's concerned. We, as "returning" Jewish women, must acknowledge this and say "no!" to society's cries.

Rivka: Women say they want to be freer, not attached, yet I think they're slaves to what society is saying about the whole thing and they're not really themselves. They should be wanting to be themselves.

Tamar: Women are intrinsically there for family, to serve. But I think the world at large has been misinformed. They think the woman raising the family is being subservient. Something to be ashamed of. On the contrary, I think it's one of the most responsible, most beautiful, most creative roles there is.... They think a woman who's working for IBM is happy? No, it's—there's always somebody that can do that, be an executive. There's always somebody that can take over my job being a nurse. But there is only one person that can raise a child like you.

A young woman: There is a connection between feminism and the *ba'al teshuvah* movement because those who don't find an answer to the problem of male-female relationships in the twentieth century are looking to Judaism for an alternative answer. Judaism looks on women not as sex objects but as something much higher, and so women are not treated as the playthings of men. They are taken more seriously. Therefore, some of the problems of feminism disappear and do not need solutions.[4]

---

* Lisa, Rivka, and Tamar are pseudonyms chosen by Lynn Davidman.

Lis Harris, *Holy Days* (1985)

Over the course of several years, literary journalist Lis Harris observed and interviewed a Lubavitch hasidic family. At their first meeting, Sheina* reveals that she grew up in a less-than-strictly-observant Orthodox family and only became hasidic as an adult, after raising five children. When her first marriage failed, she was introduced to Moshe, a widower and father of five, whose family had been Lubavitch Hasidim for generations. The two married and settled in Crown Heights, Brooklyn.

[Sheina stated:] "I've come to understand that, like all Jews, I'm here for a purpose."

"And that is?"

"To see the beauty and holiness in everyday things. To try to elevate ordinary life. The key is in the Torah and the way to get there has been shown us in a practical way by the *mitzvot* [commandments]. When the Jews accepted God's challenge to follow His ways, He gave us the *mitzvot* so that we'd know how to do it."

...

Sheina's acquiescence to the idea of an arranged marriage and acceptance of the hasidic form of courtship [involving only a few meetings] was, of course, the most radical step she had taken in her new life. Somewhere along the line, she had jettisoned the dearly held, if ill-defined, contemporary belief in romantic spontaneity, proven sexual compatibility, and tried-and-tested ability to get along in a day-to-day way as the basis for marriage.... Like the other transformations in her life, Sheina regarded the *shiddukh* [engagement; matchmaking] as another link to a world that would change the way she saw herself as a private person. As she recalled those days, it became clear to me that just as she had accepted the various rules that governed how she prayed, when she prayed, how she dressed, what food she ate, and what her ethical conduct should be, she accepted (and even liked) the restrictions and protocol of Orthodox courtship. In fact, they seemed to have appealed to her precisely because they were at odds with modern customs and practices. She sensed and was grateful for the fact that while everything was demanded of Orthodox men and women in terms of fulfilling their religious duties, far less was demanded of them than is demanded of most modern husbands and wives. The success or failure of any marriage depends on many complexities, of course, but most outsiders have observed that hasidic husbands and wives seem surprisingly content, partly because they are so passionately dedicated to the same suprapersonal goals, partly because they do not expect so much from each other. There are few Hasidim who expect their mates to be unfailingly exciting lovers,

---

*Sheina, Moshe, and Bassy are pseudonyms chosen by Lis Harris.

forever youthful admirers, or amateur therapists. If the excitement level has been minimized in <u>h</u>asidic courtships by relegating Eros to the back seat, so have the subsequent disappointments.

...

Bassy [Moshe's daughter, who taught kindergarten in a Lubavitch girls' school] had invited me to spend the morning in her classroom.... As we walked the children down to the lunchroom, I asked the little girl with the pearl earrings what she would like to be when she grew up. She pretended to think about the question, then grinned broadly, "A mother." A chorus of "me too's" echoed down the hallway. As it happened, I'd asked the same question of a kindergarten class at the boys' school. None of them wanted to be firemen, policemen, or astronauts. The boys' equally unanimous answer was, "A father."[5]

Akiva Tatz (1987)

Akiva Tatz, himself a ba'al teshuvah, *contrasts ultra-Orthodox and non-religious styles of dating. In his estimation, Orthodox Judaism, which he calls the Torah world, benefits women.*

During the transition to Torah living, Eve became sensitized to many things. One of them was the dignity of religious women. Walking through the religious neighborhood of Geulah, in Jerusalem, for example, she noticed a number of things that differ from nearby Jaffa Street. The women are well dressed and modestly covered no matter how hot the weather. Men avoid looking at a woman despite her modest appearance. Married couples engage in no physical contact in public. The women radiate a self-respect and fulfillment which come from having a strong and stable family, the security of a completely faithful relationship with a husband, and the kind of community that is supportive in every way. People in general have an air of purposefulness; they are engaged in the great work of achieving something idealistic, and external political and economic factors impinge on their state of mind only peripherally. There is a pervasive sense of peace, human dignity, and grace.

A few blocks away downtown, however, many women, married and unmarried alike, expose themselves with no shame for anyone who cares to look. Men stare openly at whatever exposed flesh happens to be passing. Dating couples relate explicitly, unabashed. Many older faces are worried and often reflect broken lives and dreams, clearly telling of years of disappointment; attachment to the material has proved cruelly unrewarding; many families are only empty shells, women have given away their power to generate large families in the illusory hope of having more materially or for some other false ideal; they age and are left with neither, and the faces tell it all. Young faces are often vacant or full of bravado, only the very youngest do not show the painful scars of having been cheaply used, and the ambience is harsh and mercenary.

[Eve] had long noted a sad paradox: Young women would speak in feminist terms about wanting to be seen and related to by men as a whole being, mind and body together and not simply as a "sex object," but society's norms dictate the kind of dress (and deportment) for women which result in the male's being presented primarily with the physical. The initial focus of his interest would therefore be the physical, the relationship would begin on the wrong basis and progress rapidly to include physical intimacy, often with a skew of misunderstanding if not downright deception: The girl would tend to impute to the male much more emotional involvement with her than he actually felt, his interest being more directly in the physical relationship than hers. This unhealthy relationship could be prevented only by maintaining a degree of chastity, but those girls who did were considered strange and, of course, were much less popular.

However, in the Torah world the "boy meets girl" story is radically different. First, the girl is modestly dressed—her body is not exposed. However, her attire is feminine—it is forbidden for women to wear men's clothing. So the male is presented not with a body but with an integrated person, attractive, feminine, and with dignity. Second, there is no physical contact, so the relationship is predicated on the level of personality. And third, since physical relations are forbidden premaritally, he has no ulterior motives and the relationship is a refined one from the beginning; the last thing in the male's mind is the woman as simply a sex object; ironically, an achievement of the feminist aim.[6]

Anne Roiphe, *Lovingkindness* (1987)

In her 1987 novel, Anne Roiphe portrays a non-observant Jewish mother and a newly religious daughter. The title of the book, Lovingkindness, *is an English translation of the Hebrew word* ḥesed.

"Mother?" she said.

"Yes, Andrea, where are you?"

"In Israel, Mother."

"Yes," I said, "have you been to the old city yet?"

"Yes," she answered. "I'm living there.... I am staying at the Yeshivah Rachel, I am different from when you last saw me.... Mother," she said, "don't be upset. I love you, I made my own decision, by myself. I am peaceful. I honor you, of course," she added.

This was the most upsetting phrase of all. I had never heard it or its sentiment from her before and I knew just what it meant.

"Good-bye," she said.

"Wait," I shouted as if it were my responsibility to carry my voice across the sea. "We have to talk. How do I reach you? Do you have a phone, an address? Do you need money?" Suddenly I was begging.

"Good-bye, Mother," she said cheerfully, sweetly.

There was something too kind in her tone. It made me sweat. I was always waiting for some definitive, end-of-the-line call. We've found your daughter in a ravine outside of Las Vegas with her throat cut, we've found your daughter dead of an overdose in a pickup truck with a Hell's Angel, we've found your daughter naked hallucinating on the LA freeway. I had anticipated a lot of phone calls. I had not thought of the Yeshivah Rachel.

Rachel—what was the Yeshivah Rachel? I called a friend and a friend of the friend told me, a new yeshivah, for women only, to teach them some Talmud, to teach them how to keep kosher. "But she doesn't cook at all," I said.

"They will teach her," the friend of the friend who knew all about it said. "They will turn your daughter into a real *ba'al teshuvah*, a returned, one of the found." I counted her still among the lost. "They will find her a husband," she said, "they will encourage her to have twelve children."

I laughed. Andrea had never picked up a shirt from the floor. She had never thrown a tissue into the wastebasket. She had never taken care of the kitten I had bought to encourage her to make the connection between obligation and affection.

She would not, I was sure of it, would not tend and clean and wipe. This will last two weeks and then she'll be off, I thought. And then what? I was distracted and unable to work....

DEAR MOTHER, Please call me Sarai, I have changed my name to one in keeping with my new life. I will not answer or read any letters addressed to Andrea. I honor you, of course. Love, Sarai....

DEAR MOTHER, Rabbi Cohen wants me to explain my new life to you.... I don't want you to think that everything is easy here. Sometimes I just can't concentrate. I still get this buzz in my head that makes me feel weird. When that happened before, I would go find someone to do something with, some exciting stuff. Here I go to Mrs. Cohen. She's usually in the kitchen, and she puts something in my hands to do, to cut, or stir, or pound. We make this incredible bread. We put the dough in big white bowls on the stove and it rises, I mean really rises. She tells me that God respects me. Once my hands were shaking and she held them in hers and told me how brave the Jewish women were in the desert, after they had fled from Egypt, when they wouldn't give their jewels or their mirrors to the men who wanted to build an idol. Did you know that?

Rabbi Cohen knows everything about the Talmud. You can ask him any question and he knows the answer. He goes to his books and turns the page right to the words he wants. He has an enormous memory. He says we must remember everything because the world is always trying to erase our footprints and our covenant shows us how to sanctify life on earth. We can only do that, he says, if we remember everything. Women don't have to remember as much. We create the room in which the work takes place. We are the sun, the moon, the stars, the ocean, the forest, and the field. We make the learning possible.[7]

Rabbi Tucker, Dean of the D'var Yerushalayim School for Women (1989)

The D'var Yerushalayim School in Israel was established to teach prospective ba'alot teshuvah *about Orthodox Jewish observance.*

I heard of two girls who were visiting [a *ba'alat teshuvah*] for Rosh Hashanah and asked their hostess, "How are you preparing for Rosh Hashanah?" She answered, "I made gefilte fish, and I made a chicken, and I made a *kugel*, and so forth, and I've cleaned the house." The girls were dumbfounded. They expected her to say that she studies two hours a day, that she davens three times a day. That's what they are expecting and hoping for. And they are turned off a bit. They scorn and laugh at their hostess, and that is very wrong, because a very important part of Rosh Hashanah is making the fish and making the chicken. That's an important part of family life. Some schools feel that a girl should study all day because she missed religious instruction for eighteen years and has to make up for it. We feel our girls are much more balanced religiously.[8]

Agi Bauer (1991)

In "Black" Becomes a Rainbow, *a memoir by the mother of a* ba'alat teshuvah, *Agi Bauer depicts her own transformation from hurt, anger, and outrage to acceptance and respect for her daughter Natalie's* choice. In the excerpt that follows, Natalie visits her parents' home in Australia. Natalie, a university graduate with advanced training in social work, has lived in Israel for the past three years, completely immersed in ultra-Orthodox life. In future chapters, Agi Bauer will describe Natalie's wedding, the births of Natalie's children, and the way in which she herself comes to appreciate and even admire ultra-Orthodox Judaism.*

[The newly religious] subject themselves to this incredible discipline [intensive learning about Orthodoxy], as they find this the only way in which to cope with a world that is too fast, too unjust, too promiscuous, and in fact too everything.... I will tell you what my own child said, as a perfect example: "I like waking up in the morning, knowing what God expects of me." This she can do only by adhering to a most rigorous set of laws and customs. In a world in which "anything goes" and the rule of law seems to have collapsed, it is understandable that people should seek to put some order in their lives. Strictly Orthodox Judaism, where every rule is carefully spelled out and life is neat and orderly, was apparently what Natalie wanted....

At first glance, Natalie [who had been living in Israel] looked as if she were still our own daughter. [However,] she now wore dresses with necklines high up to her chin, buttoned all the way up. She now wore

---

* Natalie is a pseudonym chosen by Agi Bauer.

stockings even on the hottest summer day. Her blouses all had long sleeves. She would not go to the beach anymore. Not to the beach or, for that matter, even to our own swimming pool. In our own home! *Home*— we couldn't imagine what this meant to her by now.

And then there was the matter of being kosher. Not just kosher, mind you, but *glatt* kosher—super kosher.... On the morning of Natalie's arrival, I began showing off about all the preparations I had made. She followed my guided tour (of her own home) as if she had never been there before. She inspected everything with a gracious nodding of her head. Triumphantly, I sat down in our family room for our first cup of coffee together.

Natalie's eyes followed my every move. Just as I was about to pour a drop of milk into her own (brand-new) cup of (kosher) coffee, she asked in a tone of voice that to my ears sounded slightly shrill: "Have you got the 'yeshivah milk' I asked you for?"

I must admit I had been found out. I was found guilty in the first hour. I had not done my homework diligently enough. "No problem," said this new Natalie in her new superior tone of voice, "I just won't drink any milk until I've fetched some of my own from the yeshivah."

Suddenly all of my good humor vanished. I was like a bull who saw red. I could not help raising my voice: "Surely you don't think anything will happen to you if you have a drop of our 'contaminated' milk?" I looked squarely into her gray eyes.

"Mummy," I heard *that* voice say, "you don't think I want to have an argument over such a little thing, and in the first hour that I'm at home?"

"*Who* is arguing and *who* is making a mountain out of a molehill?" I bellowed.

I could not believe my ears when I heard my ... daughter's super-calm voice admonishing me: "Mummy, please don't talk in such an ugly way. Let us not lose our heads over a drop of milk. Can't you see, to me it does not matter at all."

Maybe I was going crazy already, but I thought: How dare she stand there, so calm and so pious. And in the first hour of our being together! I can still see it clearly before my eyes: a child who would not have a drop of my milk in her coffee, but had to run to her *rebbe* to ask for *his* milk....

I had made the first of thousands of foolish remarks that ruined the whole of the three-week visit that followed. In retrospect, how sorry I am; I should have shut up, and just let her be. I should not have argued, not wasted our precious time together with trying to change a person who was changed already.[9]

Lynn Davidman, *Tradition in a Rootless World* (1991)

After studying ba'alot teshuvah *in both modern and ultra-Orthodox settings, Lynn Davidman concluded that the attraction to a stable, meaningful, and clearly defined way of life was critical in the women's attraction to religious Judaism.*

The women ... were on a quest for a clear articulation of their role as women, one that would place them in the center of nuclear families. The women's desires coincided with the centrality of the nuclear family in the world of Orthodox Judaism....

Many stated explicitly that the [Orthodox] community's clear delineation of separate roles for men and women was a welcome contrast to the blurring and confusion about these roles in secular society.[10]

David Landau, "Late Entries" (1993)

Landau, a prominent Israeli journalist, explores the haredim *in* Piety and Power: Inside the World of Jewish Fundamentalism. *He devotes one chapter to the education of* ba'alei teshuvah.

In most seminaries for *ba'alot teshuvah*, as in virtually all *haredi* girls' schools and women's seminaries ... women, as a matter of religious principle, are not taught Talmud. [In times past, Jews confined] their daughters' religious education—apart from rare and exceptional cases—to a smattering of Bible stories and prayers, and a solid curriculum of cooking and sewing. The very concept of a women's seminary is a twentieth-century innovation ... to stanch the flood of young women abandoning Orthodoxy in search of education. Today, all *haredi* groups have their girls' schools and seminaries. Some offer fairly broad secular curricula, with the result that many *haredi* women are better read and better educated [in non-Jewish subjects] than their menfolk.

In the most ultra-conservative women's institutions ... the traditional ban on religious learning is still largely enforced: texts as such—even of the Pentateuch—are not studied. Instead, material is distilled from the sources, translated into Yiddish, and taught in this digested form to the girls and young women.

In mainstream *haredi* seminaries ... the ban is interpreted as applying only to the Oral Law, that is the Talmud, but not to the Bible and its commentaries, nor to ethical and philosophical works, nor to books on practical *halakhah*. This is also the case, for instance, in Ohr Somayach's sister-school, the 400-student Neve Yerushalayim. [Both Ohr Somayach for men and Neve Yerushalayim for women are geared toward *ba'alei teshuvah*.]

"But if someone wants to study Talmud, nobody will stop her," says Rabbi David Bowden, head of the Girls' High School at Gateshead, England. This unwonted (relative) liberalism [may possibly] reflect a demand, not vociferous but nevertheless audible, on the part of some *ba'alot teshuvah* not to be excluded from the talmudic experience that is so central to <u>h</u>aredi life in general, and specifically to the <u>h</u>azarah beteshuvah (return in penitence) process of their husbands.[11]

Sally Berkovic (1997)

Sally Berkovic, a journalist, feminist, mother, and the wife of an Orthodox rabbi, attended an ultra-Orthodox seminary in Jerusalem when she was 18 and another in her native Australia when she was a university student. Raised in an observant Orthodox home, she differed from most seminary students, who sought—in addition to an intensive Jewish education—an entirely new life.

In 1972, the first yeshivah (or seminary, as they are usually referred to when discussing women) to cater for women from a secular background, or women willing to renew and dedicate their lives to a rediscovered Orthodoxy, was founded. In the women's seminaries [little emphasis is placed on text study, but] there is a distinct emphasis on personal development. *Musar shmoozes*, a meandering list of character traits to aspire to, and the means to acquire good character traits, are popular subjects. While being a good person is an important ethical imperative inherent in the Jewish religion, for the BT women, this translates into expecting women to adopt a demure and deferential role....

I watched with a combination of intense curiosity and admiration as those I knew slowly began to take on the rituals and mind-set of an Orthodox Jewish woman. I learned how to gauge how long a student had been there by her external appearance. Some arriving in jeans and a clingy short-sleeved top were transformed within a few weeks. Soon they were wearing the trademark long denim skirt and [running shoes] with short socks. A loose-fitting pale blue cotton shirt hung neatly, conveniently avoiding her breasts. Sometimes it appeared that these women were suddenly scared of their own bodies....

For some newly observant people, the switch to religion is no more than a sophisticated form of rebellious virtue. I remember Beth, a model student. In her own family, no matter how hard she tried, she could not satisfy her parents. She was never considered as attractive as her older sister, nor as academic or as sociable. But at [the Jerusalem seminary], she was valued for herself. Typically, Beth's family felt extremely rejected. They were convinced she had joined some weird cult. As very assimilated Jews, they had no real concept of Orthodox Judaism, and could not identify with the extreme zealots they would sometimes see on the news, throwing stones at skimpily-clad women passing through the religious neighborhoods of Jerusalem. Beth tried to explain that the seminary was not like this, but the more she tried to make them understand, the less they believed her. They wanted their little girl back, but [the seminary] made her realize she did not have to be that little girl any longer. It gave her an opportunity to construct a new personality and rewarded her for precisely those things her family did not value. Her rebellion was to become Orthodox. This rebellion undermined the materialism of her parents, and she blatantly told them she did not value the life goals they had struggled to achieve. There is a certain asceticism that only the rich can afford.[12]

Students at the Jewish Renaissance Center (1998)

Sarah Blustain in Lilith *magazine's "Right-Wing Women: Keeping Orthodoxy Safe from Feminists?" writes of recent outreach efforts by right-of-center Orthodox Jews. Non-observant Jewish women, she notes, are "drawn by the aggressive recruiting of the Jewish Renaissance Center,"[13] an ultra-Orthodox women's educational institute in New York City.* Lilith *interviewed several students who had adopted an Orthodox way of life as adults. Elizabeth Fried, a graduate of Harvard Business School and Yale Drama School, works as a costume designer. Dora Green, now a full-time mother of four, was formerly an investment banker with a prestigious career. These and other students "echo their teachers' diatribes as they turn against the women's movement."*

Elizabeth Fried: The role that feminism played for me was that I gave priority to my career ambition. I felt like I had to act like a man.... All these accomplishments and no spiritual or personal satisfaction. [Orthodox Judaism is] empowering, that's for sure. And even more empowering because of the separation [between men and women].

Dora Green: Feminism was a bill of goods that was sold that wasn't so advantageous to women.... Women became doctors and lawyers and Indian chiefs and got married and had children and who do you think is running their homes? You don't think that their husbands are worrying about whether there's toilet paper in the pantry, do you? [Orthodox feminists] are missing it. They're trying to be men, and they're not bringing to [Jewish life] what women can bring.[14]

Sarah Blustain (1998)

Though Blustain's commitment to feminism remains strong, she recognizes the issues raised by anti-feminist Orthodox Jewish women.

There is a warning here for secular feminists as well, and the questions that [right-wing Orthodox women are] asking are ones feminists might consider. Every day we hear stories of impossible choices women make between joining the "man's world" and remaining at home. Whether leaving a two-month-old child at day care or leaving their professions in order to care for children, these women are not encountering a world that activist feminism has succeeded in making hospitable.

The success of the Jewish Renaissance Center might serve as a needed heads-up to feminists who think their work is done. The women who are flocking to the Jewish Renaissance Center are expressing their dissatisfaction with their choices, and with the way our culture is judging them for having to make those choices. They are turning to an old system largely because it values *as the highest good* a woman's choice to fulfill her biological destiny.[15]

Questions for Discussion

1. Read Psalm 119, verses 1 to 15. Are those who follow God's teachings happy? If yes, why and in what way does observing God's decrees make a person happy? If no, why not? Discuss how these verses apply to *ba'alei teshuvah*.

2. What are the advantages to the ultra-Orthodox way of dating, as presented by Akiva Tatz and Lis Harris? What are the disadvantages?

3. The dean of the D'var Yerushalayim School for Women says that an "important part of Rosh Hashanah is making the fish and making the chicken." Discuss.

4. How would you characterize the daughter Andrea in the selection from Anne Roiphe's novel? How would you characterize the mother? Describe the mother-daughter relationship. Do you identify with the mother or with the daughter? How would you characterize Agi Bauer and her daughter Natalie? Describe their relationship. At the close of her memoir, Agi Bauer is close to her daughter, and she has a warm and loving relationship with her ultra-Orthodox grandchildren. She can look back and laugh at herself and her fury over the milk. Would Bauer's description of the incident have led you to predict this? Why or why not? What would you predict for Ann Roiphe's fictional characters?

5. In Chapter 3, we analyzed Jewish self-hatred. Is the *ba'alat teshuvah* exhibiting the opposite of Jewish self-hatred? In what way? Is the *ba'alat teshuvah* exhibiting another kind of self-hatred, perhaps American self-hatred? Perhaps Western civilization self-hatred? In what way?

6. A newly religious young woman states that by living an Orthodox Jewish life, "some of the problems of feminism disappear." In what ways does Orthodox Judaism address problems also addressed by feminism? In what ways does Orthodox Judaism fail to address problems addressed by feminism?

7. Both modern Orthodox and ultra-Orthodox Jews believe that differences in sex roles are necessary, and are based on natural and innate differences in the female and male character. Lis Harris, for instance, asked Moshe and Sheina to name the main difference between women and men. Moshe "answered unhesitatingly, 'Women rule the heart, men the intellect.' Sheina nodded in agreement."[16] Orthodox Jews are careful to note, however, that the woman's role is equal in dignity and worth to the man's. How do the selections in Chapter 7 support this "separate but

equal" doctrine? How do they fail to support it? Some feminists also believe that sex-based differences in character are innate, yet they do not conclude that separate male and female roles are necessary. Discuss. (Other feminists argue that sex-based differences are not innate; instead they are learned, a product of one's culture.)

Suggested Activities and Programs

1. Debate the late Chancellor Gerson Cohen's denunciation of the BT schools. Divide the group into two camps: those who agree that ultra-Orthodox schools resemble cults, and those who believe that ultra-Orthodox schools can be a valuable tool in combating assimilation and alienation from Judaism. Allow 15 minutes for each side to choose a speaker and set its priorities. Then have the two speakers present their arguments. Conclude by asking group members to think about a middle ground.

2. Request one or more members in your Rosh Hodesh group to choose one of the books excerpted in this chapter and to read it in its entirety. (Particularly recommended: Anne Roiphe's novel *Lovingkindness* and Lis Harris's portrait *Holy Days: The World of a Hasidic Family*.) Ask your volunteer(s) to present a summary of the book's themes and to initiate discussion.

3. Invite Jewish outreach professionals to speak about their work. If possible, invite a Lubavitch rabbi or rabbi's wife as well as an individual who works with the newly religious at a modern Orthodox synagogue. (Consider inviting non-Orthodox outreach professionals as well.)

4. Organize an education day on women in Orthodox Judaism. Use the following schedule as a guide.

Women and Orthodoxy

10:00 **Registration**

10:30 **Modesty—*Tzeniut***
Invite a knowledgeable Orthodox woman to speak about *tzeniut* and modest dress. (Refer to chapter 3.) The speaker should explain the religious basis for modest dress and for married women's hair covering, then briefly describe the varying dress codes among different groups of Orthodox women. The talk should also include personal reflections on *tzeniut*, with a particular focus on the ethical and spiritual values that are revealed through modesty. Conclude with a question-and-answer session.

12:00 **Lunch**

1:00   *Ba'alot Teshuvah*

Invite a *ba'alat teshuvah* to speak for 30 minutes. Have her describe her religious journey in personal terms. How does she differ from women raised in Orthodox families? What is her relationship today with her birth family? What was the most difficult part of adjusting to Orthodox Judaism? What was most compelling to her when she was first attracted to Orthodoxy, and what is most compelling today? Ask the speaker to address: differences between female and male roles in Orthodox Judaism, attitudes toward feminism, attitudes toward feminist Orthodox Judaism. Conclude with a question-and-answer session.

2:15   **Orthodoxy and Feminism**

Invite an Orthodox feminist to discuss her outlook, recent struggles, and changes in Orthodox attitudes toward women today. Discuss the bitter controversies caused by Orthodox women's prayer groups, the tremendous growth in educational opportunities for Orthodox women, and feminist Orthodox religious practices. Conclude with a question-and-answer session.

3:45   **Workshop and Conclusion**

As a conclusion to the Education Day, ask participants: What can the non-Orthodox learn from the Orthodox? Pass around paper and pencils, and ask each participant to write down three lessons she has learned today. (Orthodox participants should write down three insights or three questions for thought.) Go around the room and invite participants to share their thoughts. Write out the responses on a large poster (or request a volunteer to write the list). Discuss.

---

1. Sally Berkovic, *Straight Talk: My Dilemma as a Modern Orthodox Jewish Woman* (Hoboken, NJ: Ktav, 1999; originally published in London in 1997 as *Under My Hat*), page 146.

2. Barry A. Kosmin, Sidney Goldstein, Joseph Walsberg, Nava Lerer, Ariella Keysar, Jeffrey Scheckner, *Highlights of the CJF 1990 National Jewish Population Survey* (New York: Council of Jewish Federations, 1991), page 32.

3. Cited in M. Herbert Danzger, *Returning to Tradition: The Contemporary Revival of Orthodox Judaism* (New Haven: Yale University Press, 1989), page 301.

4. Lynn Davidman, *Tradition in a Rootless World: Women Turn to Orthodox Judaism* (Berkeley: University of California Press, 1991), pages 130–132, 134. Davidman lived with women at Bais Chana in Saint Paul, Minnesota, and conducted surveys and interviews in 1983. Her study of these and other newly Orthodox women was published in 1991.

5. Lis Harris, *Holy Days: The World of a Hasidic Family* (New York: Summit/Simon & Schuster, 1985), pages 19–20, 116–117, 194–195. *Holy Days* is now available in paperback from Touchstone.

6. Akiva Tatz, *Anatomy of a Search: Personal Drama in the* Teshuvah *Revolution* (Brooklyn: Mesorah, 1987), pages 80–81, 83.

7. Anne Roiphe, *Lovingkindness* (New York: Summit, 1987), pages 10–11, 15–16, 45–47.

8. Cited in M. Herbert Danzger, *Returning to Tradition: The Contemporary Revival of Orthodox Judaism* (New Haven: Yale University Press), page 138.

9. Agi L. Bauer, *"Black" Becomes a Rainbow: The Mother of a Baal Teshuvah Tells Her Story* (New York: Feldheim, 1991), pages 14–15, 45–47.

10. Lynn Davidman, *Tradition in a Rootless World*, pages 109, 126.

11. David Landau, *Piety and Power: Inside the World of Jewish Fundamentalism* (New York: Hill and Wang/Farrar, Straus and Giroux, 1993), pages 243–244.

12. Sally Berkovic, *Straight Talk*, pages 150–151, 155–156. Berkovic attended the Jerusalem seminary in 1978, and a seminary in Australia in the mid-eighties.

13. Sarah Blustain, "Right-Wing Women: Keeping Orthodoxy Safe from Feminists?" *Lilith* 23:4 (Winter 1998–99), page 10.

14. "Are These Women Speaking for Themselves?" *Lilith* 23:4 (Winter 1998–99), page 14.

15. Sarah Blustain, "Right-Wing Women," page 15.

16. Lis Harris, *Holy Days*, page 189.

WOMEN AND ISRAELI LAW

Israel, the land of milk and honey, was once also known as the land of sexual equality. Zionist posters featured an attractive Israeli woman working side by side with sun-browned men on a kibbutz. The Israeli army drafted both boys and girls. And the legendary Prime Minister Golda Meir led the country. The possibilities for the Israeli woman's advancement certainly seemed limitless. Yet the kibbutz woman more often scrubbed the kitchen than ploughed the land, the army woman was not trained to fight in combat, and Golda Meir never supported feminism. What went wrong?

Israel's early leaders, to be sure, had noble intentions. The Declaration of Independence pledged "complete equality of social and political rights to all its inhabitants, irrespective of religion, race, or sex," and the earliest acts of legislation passed by the Knesset promoted equality of the sexes. In 1949, the National Service Law was enacted, stipulating that both women and men would be conscripted into the army at age eighteen. Also in 1949, the Knesset passed the Compulsory Education Act, mandating schooling for both girls and boys between the ages of five and fourteen. (The law had far-reaching implications, since many of Israel's new citizens had come from countries in which education was not compulsory.) In 1951, the Israeli Knesset passed the Equality of Men and Women Law, equivalent to the United States' unratified Equal Rights Amendment, and, in 1964, it passed the Equal Pay Law.

The State of Israel also enables working mothers to care for their newborns without severe economic hardship. Mothers who have been

149

Iyar

employed for at least nine months prior to giving birth are entitled to three months of maternity leave at 80-percent pay. Once back on the job, the mother is granted a great deal of flexibility in her work schedule. Israel also has an extensive child care system, with the government subsidizing the cost depending on family size and income. In many ways, then, Israel ensures that its citizens can be mothers as well as workers. Furthermore, numerous Israeli women run their own businesses; head institutions; serve as high-ranking officers in the police, armed services, and judiciary; and occupy high civil service positions.

Nonetheless, the legislative acts guaranteeing workers flexibility and paid maternity leaves have served to entrench the notion of mother as primary caregiver. The conventional wisdom—influenced by Orthodox beliefs—is that all women will become mothers, and that as mothers their time will be devoted to child care. As a result, women are perceived as unreliable workers lacking in ambition. This is why, though women constitute 46 percent of the Israeli workforce, the vast majority are in middle-management or non-management positions.[1]

Half of state-employed lawyers are women, as are half of the doctors in government clinics, but women make up only a small fraction of the lawyers in private practice and the doctors teaching medicine at the university level.[2] There are a mere fourteen women out of 120 members in Israel's Knesset, a pitifully low number.* Finally, twice as many women as men are unemployed, yet many more women than men live below the poverty level.[3]

To counter some of these inequities, Israeli women have turned to the courts, on occasion bringing their cases all the way to the Supreme Court. In ruling on economic discrimination, Israeli courts have generally ruled in favor of women's equality. If the case hinges on religious issues, though, Israeli courts have generally not been receptive to feminist arguments. Israel, unlike the United States, has no separation between church and state. Thus, Israel has a system of government-run religious schools, government-funded synagogues, and local government councils to deal with religious matters. Israel's religious institutions are thus government agencies. One of their functions is the registering of births, marriages, divorces, and deaths. (Rabbis determine such issues for Jews, mullahs for Muslims, priests for Christians, and so on).

In Israel, Judaism is synonymous with Orthodoxy, and Orthodox Judaism upholds unequal legal status for women and men. (As a rule, Israeli rabbis—and indeed the Israeli public—believe that women and men are essentially different and that their different legal standings in

---

*Fourteen women serving as Members of Knesset is a record; the previous record was 12 women. Prior to the elections in the spring of 1999, only 9 women served as Members of Knesset.

religious matters simply reflect the fundamental differences in their natures.) In almost all cases, the unequal Jewish legal status of men and women puts the Israeli woman at a disadvantage. For instance, when a Jewish Israeli couple decides to divorce, they must conform to the Orthodox religious ritual. Accordingly, a divorce between Jewish Israelis is valid only when the husband hands the wife a *get*, a written divorce decree. Without a valid divorce, a woman remains forever married in the eyes of the law, hence unable to remarry. The situation is not analogous for the husband. Although the wife can refuse to accept the *get*, the husband may nonetheless remarry and start a new family. Israeli Jewish divorce law thus gives the husband power over the wife. A number of husbands deny their wives a *get* in order to extort money or gain custody of the children; others deny a *get* because of resentment and hatred. Such non-divorced women are known as *agunot*—chained women—because they remain bound to a dead marriage. Should the chained woman—*agunah*—fall in love again and decide to raise a new family despite the lack of a divorce decree and a new marriage certificate, her children would be illegitimate. In Jewish law, the children of *agunot* are *mamzerim*, bastards, who are barred from inheriting or marrying Jews. Religious courts have generally been reluctant to intervene when a husband refuses to hand his wife a *get*—yet they are the only courts authorized to intervene.

In this chapter, we will read the Israeli Supreme Court decisions in four precedent-setting cases. Two involve employment issues, and two involve the clash between Jewish and feminist ideals.

by Leora Tanenbaum

ALICE MILLER AND THE ISRAELI DEFENSE FORCES

The Israeli Defense Forces (IDF), once idealized as the apex of sexual equality, is in reality a male-dominated institution. Women receive scant combat training; they serve for less than two years as opposed to men's three years; and upon discharge they are not assigned to reserve duty. To the non-militaristic, these sex-based differences may seem a benefit rather than an injustice. But, as a feminist analyst writes, "because of the army's pivotal role in determining a person's status in civilian life, women's marginal role in the IDF helps translate into ... second-class status in civilian society."[4]

In 1994, one woman fought against her marginal role in the IDF. Alice Miller, then a 22-year-old South African immigrant, had long dreamed of admission to the Air Force pilot's course, which gives soldiers the opportunity to prove their qualifications for Air Force service, a military option that carries tremendous prestige. Women, however, were not allowed to take the course, because women were not allowed to serve as pilots. Miller fought against the restriction, ultimately arguing her case before the Supreme Court. In 1996, the Court found in her favor, ruling that women could be admitted to the course. In the end, Miller took the course but did not pass the rigorous examinations for the Air Force. However, as a result of her victory, one IDF unit called the Border Guard now offers women the opportunity to volunteer for a "back-breaking" combat course.[5] The Israel Women's Network, an organization that advocates on behalf of Israeli women, believes that Miller's victory paved the way for integration of more women into prestigious combat units.

by Leora Tanenbaum

Alice Miller versus Minister of Defense (1995)

In the Supreme Court sitting as the High Court of Justice:

Justice Matza: The enormous investment in the training of pilots is based on a long-term prospect. The candidates for the pilots' course agree to regular army service for a (predetermined) number of years beginning from the day of their ordination as pilots. They also undertake (voluntary) reserve duty, in annual installments that generally exceed the legal requirements, in keeping with a formula established by the Air Force according to necessity and the types of activities required. The legal regulations regarding the extent of women's required service—specifically their limited obligation regarding reserve duty, which is also contingent upon clear grounds for a complete exemption from service because of pregnancy or childbirth—make their incorporation into this organizational framework an impossibility. One may, indeed, require a female candidate for a pilots' course to agree to perform additional regular service, as is accepted for men candidates; so too one may require her to take upon herself voluntary reserve duty over and above her legal obligation. However, both of these are insufficient guarantees of orderliness and continuity in service. The temporary absence of a woman pilot during the course of her regular service, because of pregnancy or childbirth, is liable to upset the routine planned activity of the entire Air Force unit. However, the primary difficulty resides in the inability to rely on her promise to be steadfast in her performance of reserve duty when this is duty that she is not obligated to serve. For, should she fall pregnant or give birth, and declare her repudiation of her undertaking to volunteer, there is no legal way of obligating her to serve.

I find myself wondering whether or not these worries are well-founded. The basic supposition is that women who submit their candidacy for the pilots' course will be required, like male candidates, to agree to the required service and reserve duty. In general, one may assume that one who takes upon himself such an obligation will want to, and will be able to fulfill that obligation.... The majority of the women pilots in other countries regard military aviation as a profession and choose an army "career." But who is to say that the incorporation of women into the profession of aviation in the IDF will not produce a similar tendency. It is noteworthy that the process of incorporating women into the Air Forces of other countries, was carried out gradually [by means of limited and controlled experimentation; citing the experience of Canada and the United States].

Experimentation such as this, or similar to it, has not yet been tried in the IDF; and in my view, it ought to be arranged.... However, as long as the (Israeli) Air Force does not permit experimental participation of women in the course for the profession of aviation, while maintaining a systematic and intelligent follow-up of their performance in the course and in the units, we will never know whether, in the prevailing special (Israeli) circumstances, women may be successfully integrated into the Air Force crews....

This Court does not tend to intervene in professional-organizational decisions of the military authorities. However ... the violation of equality, through discrimination on the basis of sex, is a clear example of a case that justifies and compels intervention. Such is the case before us. The IDF cannot be heeded in its claim that women are disqualified for a certain task because they are women. The claim that the training of women for the functions of pilots is not worthwhile, despite their having the appropriate talents, is a jarring claim. It is not enough that we declare equality between the sexes, for the real test of equality is in its realization, in practice, as an *effective* social norm. This normative obligation also applies to the IDF. Everyone knows how great the influence of the ways of the army are on our entire way of life. And in entrenching the recognition of the importance of human rights, the IDF cannot remain outside the picture. It too must contribute its part.

[The respondent is ordered to allow the appellant to participate in the admission tests to the pilots' course, and to attend the course if she is found to be qualified. Thus, the Air Force will commence the experiment of incorporating women into the Air Force.]

Justice Dorner: In cases where woman's difference is a consideration relevant to the attainment of the object of the regulation, there exist a range of possible means for attaining that aim.

At the one extreme is the asymmetrical model of "special treatment." According to this model, women possess special characteristics and functions, which justify differentiating them from men, and *inter alia* rule out their employment in certain capacities. The worthy purpose—the smooth running of the relevant operations—is achieved therefore by closing the door to women requesting to carry out those same functions.

At the opposite extreme is the symmetrical model of "sex-blindness." This model demands the same treatment for men and women, and assumes that the members of both sexes have the same functional capabilities. According to this approach, pregnancy will be regarded as a disability comparable to an illness suffered by a man. The adoption of this model generally involves the structuring of the system according to the abilities of the male.... The special needs of women are not taken into account. According to this model, a company that has an interest in the optimal efficiency of a system will be permitted to close its doors to women, if it becomes clear that because of their needs and attributes the duration of their activity is likely to be shorter than that of men (and that includes women taking advantage of privileges granted them by law, in connection with pregnancy, childbirth and other similar female benefits). The symmetrical model is liable, therefore, to prevent or to narrow down to a substantial degree the employment of women in vital institutions....

To my mind, the solution to the difficulties raised by the models on the two extremes may be found in the intermediate model. According to this model, what is required in order to attain equality between the sexes is institutional structuring that takes into account the particular needs of women. The interest of upholding the dignity and standing of women, on the one hand, and the continued existence of society and the raising of children, on the other hand, require—as far as possible—not expropriating from women the possibility of realizing their potential and their aspirations simply because of their special natural functions, which would result in discrimination against them. The social institutions—including the legal regulations—must be adapted to the woman's needs.

This intermediary model, according to which every employer is required to take into account the fact that a woman's performance is liable to be interrupted because of pregnancy, nursing, and looking after children, is entrenched in Israel in labor legislation. So, for example, the Employment of Women Law, 1954, establishes a woman's right to maternity leave, the right to be absent from work during the period of the pregnancy, if there is a medical need, and the right to return to work after the birth following an absence of no longer than twelve months.

Naturally, the institution of the intermediary model costs money and encumbers the organization. These expenses must be carried—sometimes with the participation of Social Security—by the private employer. How much more so does this obligation apply to the State....

In addition, the harm in closing the course to women is greater than the benefit of the organizational considerations. Firstly, barring women from participating in the course violates their human dignity and degrades them. It even constitutes, if unintentionally, encouragement for the humiliating slogan: "the best guys to be pilots, the best girls for the pilots."

Secondly, the potential of half the population is not realized, thus harming society as a whole....[6]

Questions For Discussion

1. Justice Matza questions whether pregnancy and childbirth would cause a female pilot to be absent from the military and whether such absence would impair the activities of her unit. Ultimately, however, Matza rejects this concern. Is his concern valid? On what grounds does he reject it? Do any circumstances exist under which barring fertile woman would be justified?

2. Israel's military is necessary for the very existence of the State of Israel. Is equality of the sexes really a necessary goal? Discuss.

3. Justice Dorner proposes the "intermediate model" as a method that allows women to achieve equality with men, and as the method primarily used by Israeli society. Does American legislation generally follow the "special treatment," "sex blindness," or "intermediate model"? In what ways? Discuss the advantages and disadvantages—for women and for their employers—of each of the three models.

4. According to Justice Dorner, "society as a whole" is harmed when "the potential of half the population is not realized." List ways in which the society as a whole is harmed. (Consider as well the societal implications when *any* demographic group is excluded from particular fields of employment.)

NAOMI NEVO AND MANDATORY RETIREMENT AGE

Until 1987, Israeli law stipulated that the retirement age for men was 65 and the retirement age for women was 60. One woman, Naomi Nevo, contested this inequality. Nevo had worked for the Jewish Agency since 1962, first as a senior sociologist and then as chief sociologist in the Department of Settlement. Though she sought to continue working, she was forced to retire upon reaching age 60 in 1985. She filed a complaint with the National Court of Labor Relations, but her claim was rejected. Her case, supported by several women's organizations, then went all the way to the Supreme Court, and resulted in Nevo's victory. Meanwhile, the Knesset passed the Equal Retirement Age Law, granting all Israeli women equality in retirement.

by Leora Tanenbaum

Dr. Naomi Nevo versus The National Court of Labor Relations et alia (1990)

In the Supreme Court sitting as the High Court of Justice:

Justice Bach: To determine whether [the retirement law] is discriminatory, it must be examined in light of the following question: In the current case, is there a legitimate purpose for sexual distinction?

There are two purposes for setting a compulsory retirement age for elderly workers, and neither is illegal, on the face of it:

To give the worker rest from toil in old age.

To allow the employer to renew his staff and employ new and younger forces to replace the retired workers.

Is sexual distinction in the matter of retirement age relevant to realizing those purposes?

The attorney for the Respondent claims that [the retirement law] constitutes a privilege by granting a bonus to women. He contends that [it] even anticipates sexual equality by relieving women, since the earlier retirement age lessens the excessive burden of the woman worker who is also a mother and a spouse. His argument is that the obligation to retire at the age of 60 is accompanied by the right to receive a pension at that age. And he adds that, in his opinion (which he supports with the affidavit of a woman worker), many women are satisfied with that arrangement, and many women even ask to retire right after the date when they are entitled to full retirement rights.

I am not convinced by these arguments, not even by their combined weight, and I have concluded that the aforementioned distinction does indeed constitute discrimination. The following is the reasoning for my conclusion, which is partially based on the claims of the learned counsel for the Petitioner:

The distinction is not relevant for relieving a burden. There is nothing to support the argument that women need relief from their burden more than men when they reach the age of 60. When both male and female workers reach that age, the need for that distinction seems to vanish altogether. The fact that the life expectancy of women is higher than that of men may even indicate the opposite.

Early retirement does not constitute a positive preference, and has many negative implications. Retirement has negative social, personal, and emotional implications. In many cases, a person who retires from work because of advancing age feels that he is no longer participating in the creative life of society. He feels that he has been deprived of the satisfaction of action and of receiving compensations for his labor. This feeling is also reinforced by the attitude of society, which in many cases treats him like an "old person," who is no longer good for anything. Those are the most scathing words in our day, when average life expectancy has increased, and a person's health is also well-preserved in advanced age. Because of that, there is an increase in the number of years when an elderly person, of strong mind and body, is forced, despite his capacities, to retire from his activity in the labor market, and look on, often in frustration, at the active flow of life he can no longer participate in.

The forced early retirement of women also has negative economic implications. A woman who has not worked enough years to be entitled to a full pension loses five years in the accumulation of that pension. This is the situation of the Petitioner, who, at the age of 60, had accumulated 55.3 percent of the salary to set her pension; but if she had been allowed to retire at the age of 65, the rate would have increased to 69.3 percent.

The woman loses five years of salary. A full salary with benefits is much higher than a pension.

Often, just at the end of a person's years of employment, he reaches the apex of his career, and therefore also his highest salary. The loss in early retirement also derives from the loss of the higher salary and because the rate of pension—calculated according to the rate of salary at the time of retirement—is lower.

In functions requiring long academic preparation, like that of the Petitioner, people usually enter the labor market at a relatively late age. For the worker to realize his full early potential, he needs to exhaust the years of work at advanced ages.

The problematic nature of extracting the full early potential is more severe in the case of women. During the period of bearing and raising children, many women cannot devote the main part of their energy to work. Thus, they lose many years necessary to advance in their careers. The obligation of early retirement, therefore, is liable to affect women especially....

I do not find anything harmful in giving a woman the option to retire; that can be to the advantage of all parties concerned. But there is no justification for the arrangement that forces a woman to resign when a man, at the same age, employed at the same work, is entitled to continue working....

After a precise analysis of all the relevant claims, the court reaches the following conclusion:

For an employer to dismiss a woman employee after she has passed her sixtieth birthday pursuant to a policy of retiring men at the age of 65 and women at the age of 60 and on the grounds only that she is a woman who has passed the said age of 60 is an act of discrimination....

Many women may be satisfied with the existing situation, and consider it a right to be able to retire early. But, as said above, this right is offered as an option to retire at the age of 60, and granting this right is not to compel or justify forcing the woman to retire at that age against her will....

When the court comes upon a distinction between groups, it must examine very carefully whether this distinction is based on general stereotypes emanating solely from prejudice.

Establishing the discriminating distinction between men and women in the issue of retirement age can reinforce the notion that women cannot be equal in the labor market, and in fact that does affect equality of opportunity for women....

Justice Netanyahu: I find it sad that in Israel today it is not clear and self-evident that the compulsory retirement of women at an earlier age than men constitutes discrimination.

Ever since the generation of the founders and pioneers, to our own time, women have taken an equal part with men in activity in all areas of life and are no less able than men to do that, despite the additional impositions they have borne as wives and mothers.

As I see it, discrimination is expressed not only in the monetary loss caused by her retirement at an earlier age, but also, and in my opinion, mainly, that she is prevented—at an age when she is freer for it—to achieve, to excel, and to flourish in the realization of her various abilities and talents.

I join the opinion of my colleague, Justice Bach, that [the retirement law] is illegal because it is discriminatory.[7]

Questions for Discussion

1. Discrimination in Israel today may result from policies that were necessary at one time or from policies that still remain necessary. For example, employment inequities currently exist because of special protections for Israeli mothers. Did any logical reason once exist for women's earlier retirement age? Or was the law instituted because of prejudice against women, that is, because women were believed to be frailer and less competent than men?

2. Justice Bach states that two possible reasons for setting a compulsory retirement age are "to allow the employer to renew his staff and employ new and younger forces to replace the retired workers" and "to give the worker rest from toil in old age." Are either or both of these reasons legitimate?

3. In America today women tend to achieve professional success at a later age than men, primarily because they leave the workforce for lengthy periods to raise families. This fact, coupled with women's longer life expectancy, could be used to justify setting an earlier retirement age for men than for women. Discuss.

LEAH SHAKDIEL AND THE YERUHAM RELIGIOUS COUNCIL

The Leah Shakdiel case highlights the conflict between Israel's women's rights movement and its religious leadership. In 1986, Leah Shakdiel, a religiously observant, married woman and mother of three, was elected to the religious council of her Negev town, Yeruham. Israel's religious councils administer synagogues, *mikvaot* (ritual baths), and cemeteries; they also supervise dietary laws and hold other religious responsibilities. Israel's Ministry of Religious Affairs, however, refused to confirm Shakdiel's appointment, arguing that women could not serve on religious councils. Shakdiel and her many supporters then began a long fight for her confirmation. Two years after her election to the religious council, Shakdiel turned to the Supreme Court, which found that the discrimination against her clearly violated both the Israeli Declaration of Independence and the 1951 Women's Equal Rights Law. In 1988, Shakdiel began her term as the first Israeli woman to serve on a religious council. Several women now sit on religious councils in Israel.

How was Shakdiel able to overcome discrimination in the religious sphere? Israeli sociologist Susan Sered answers that Shakdiel was victorious precisely because her fight was *not* interpreted as a religious one by the Supreme Court. The Chief Justice was convinced "that the issue at hand in fact has nothing to do with religion—that traditional religious mandates are not being challenged!"[8] As an Orthodox woman, Shakdiel did not attempt to change the structure of the Yeru<u>h</u>am religious council, Sered explains; she simply wanted to participate in the existing structure.

by Leora Tanenbaum

Leah Shakdiel versus Minister of Religious Affairs et alia (1988)

In the Supreme Court sitting as the High Court of Justice

Justice M. Elon: The exclusion of a female candidate from appointment to a religious council, because she is a woman, clearly contradicts a fundamental principle of Israeli law, which prohibits discrimination on grounds of gender. This fundamental principle was laid down in the Declaration of Independence and is among those that have gone beyond recognition in the case law to become enshrined in legislation. I am referring to the Women's Equal Rights Law (1951), section 1 of which reads as follows:

> The law shall apply equally to man and woman with regard to any legal act; any provision of law which discriminates, with regard to any legal act, against a woman as woman, shall be of no effect.

President Justice Agranat: This court has held more than once that one must always distinguish ... between wrongful discrimination (hereinafter "discrimination") and permissible distinction. The principle of equality, which is none other than the converse side of the coin of discrimination, and which the law of every democratic country aspires to realize for reasons of justice and fairness, means equal treatment of persons between whom there is no substantial difference that is relevant for purposes of the matter in issue. If they are not treated equally there is discrimination. On the other hand, if the difference or differences between different people are relevant to the purpose under discussion, then it will be a permissible distinction if they are treated differently for that purpose, so long as the differences justify this....

Classic examples, in legislation and in the case law, of such distinctions stemming from real differences between men and women, are those relating to pregnancy, giving birth, and nursing....

Discrimination on the basis of religious-halakhic [Jewish legal] considerations is allowed in matters of marriage and divorce, but such considerations do not operate here....

We must still consider whether those grave fears expressed by the representative of the Minister of Religious Affairs, and in the decision of the Committee of Ministers, serve to outweigh the interest in the fundamental right of women's equality. For we adhere to the rule that fundamental rights are not absolute but relative, that their existence and preservation call for a proper balance between the different legitimate interests of two individuals or of the individual and the public, given that all the interests are founded in and protected by the law.

After due consideration and deliberation I conclude that given the issues and the facts in the present case, the scale does not tip in favor of those grave fears pleaded by the Respondents. Non-discrimination against a woman, because she is a woman, is a fundamental principle of the legal system in Israel. To warrant the subjection of this fundamental principle to such a balancing process, it should have been contended, at least, that a woman's membership on a religious council is forbidden from a halakhic point of view, with the result that such an appointment would bring the work of the religious council to a standstill. Had this argument been made, there would have been room to seek a balance and compromise between the two poles. For we are concerned here with a religious council which, although a statutory, administrative body and therefore subject to the statutory principles, is also a body whose functions, and its functionaries, are closely associated with the world of *halakhah* [Jewish law], and it would have been proper to try and bridge the two opposites.

[Justice Elon reviews the opinions of a number of religious experts concerning women's qualifications to participate in public communal activities and to hold public office. He concludes that most rabbinic authorities today hold that women may so participate and may hold such public office.]

There is an express rule in the Talmud, generally upheld in the halakhic codes, that a woman is not only exempt from studying the Torah but even forbidden to do so, this rule being derived from the biblical verse "and you shall teach them to your sons," and not your daughters. But the profound socio-ideological change experienced in latter generations has radically altered also the outlook on the issue of women studying Torah, and it has been determined that not only is there no longer any prohibition, but women are even obligated to study Torah; and not only do they study it for themselves, but they even teach it to the sons of others. And if this is the outcome of the controversy concerning women studying the Torah, then the issue of the election of women to public office should have the like outcome, *a fortiori*, since rabbinical scholars are of the opinion that the matter is not expressly prohibited in the talmudic *halakhah*, and some of the codifiers and *rishonim* [literally "firsts," meaning Jewish legal experts of approximately 1050 to 1450] differed from Maimonides's opinion that only a man may be appointed to a public office. And if so radical a departure as abrogation of the grave prohibition against women studying the Torah could result from social and ideological changes, why not a much less radical departure that permits a woman to serve on a religious council?

Justice A. Barak: The purpose of the Religious Services Law is to fix a framework for the provision of religious services to Jews. For this purpose a religious council is established, which sets a budget and organizes activities for the provision of religious services. All Jews, men and women, religious and secular, avail themselves of these services. It is sufficient to note that the council organizes burial services, which everyone needs, and marriage registration, which every Jew needs if he wishes to marry. Against the background of these activities we have ruled more than once that the qualifications for serving on a religious council are "secular" and not necessarily "religious." ...

Indeed, there is nothing in the Religious Services Law to indicate that only persons learned in matters of the faith and its law may serve on the religious council, and even a person who is not religious is competent, in principle, to serve on the council. There is nothing in the Law or in its purpose from which to deduce that the halakhic rules of competency are also the legislative standards, and, therefore, even if a woman is not competent to serve as a member of the council according to the *halakhah*, this does not mean that a woman is not competent to serve on the religious council under the Religious Services Law. The two competencies are entirely separate matters.

For all that, I am not contending that a religious consideration is extraneous to the Religious Services Law. It is only natural for religious considerations to be relevant to a statute dealing with the provision of religious services. Thus, for example, the religious council provides services in matters of dietary rules and ritual slaughter.... The question here is whether the religious laws that determine one's competency to serve as a member of the religious council are the laws that apply within the frame of the statute. To this my response is in the negative, because the statute is secular, it deals with religious services for all Jews—religious and secular alike—and the council itself is an administrative body, which must provide religious services in the most efficient way.... The assumption ought to be that all persons whose personal traits would enable them to perform the task in the optimal way, are competent to serve on the religious council.... Therefore, a woman is competent to serve as a member of the council, and her selection is dependent on her personal qualifications.[9]

Questions for Discussion

1. Justice Elon states that one must distinguish between "wrongful discrimination" (which is outlawed by the Women's Equal Rights Law) and "permissible discrimination." What does Elon see as "permissible discrimination"? Do you find Elon's distinction valid? If yes, can you think of other instances of permissible discrimination? If no, back up your reasoning.

2. According to Justice Elon, if *halakhah* did forbid women to hold public office yet Israeli law demanded equality, "there would have been room to seek a balance and compromise between the two poles." What sort of balance or compromise do you envision?

3. Justice Barak arrives at the same decision as Justice Elon, but his rationale is different. Distinguish between the logic used by the two men. Do you prefer one opinion to the other? If you were deciding this case, what would your rationale be for allowing Leah Shakdiel to serve on the Yeruham city council?

THE WOMEN OF THE WALL AND JEWISH PRAYER

Leah Shakdiel won her battle to serve on the Yeruham religious council because, as Professor Susan Sered argues, she did not stake her claim on religious change. As we will see, the Supreme Court does not sympathize with women who agitate for change.

Women of the Wall, a group of women who pray together communally every month, are now legally prohibited from praying together at the Western Wall, the *Kotel*. The organization—a non-denominational group of Israeli and non-Israeli women (including many Americans)—first prayed together at the *Kotel* in December 1988. They wore *tallitot* (prayer shawls) and read from the Torah. Several months later, the Ministry of Religion prohibited all religious worship that offends worshippers' sensibilities at a holy site. Violators were subject to imprisonment. This ruling was framed explicitly to bar women from collective prayer at the Wall.

In 1989, several Israeli members of the Women of the Wall petitioned the Supreme Court to assure the rights of Jewish women to pray as a group at the *Kotel*. In 1990, several American supporters made a similar petition. In 1994, the Court decided on both petitions together. In his 126-page decision, Justice Menachem Elon wrote that even though women's group prayer had a valid basis in Jewish law, such prayer could not take place at the Western Wall because it ran counter to *minhag hamakom*—the established custom of the place.

Over the years, there have been numerous acts of violence by right-wing Orthodox men and women against the women who gathered to pray together at the Wall. In 1994 members of the National Board of Hadassah approached the Wall carrying their own Torah, and were verbally and physically attacked. The police escorted the women from the area. Ze'ev Rosenberg, director of the Religious Affairs Ministry, explained that the Hadassah members' presence had constituted contempt of court.

The Court subsequently recommended the appointment of a government commission. Its task was to find a way for Jewish women to worship together at the Wall without offending the sensibilities of the other worshippers. After three years of deliberation, the commission opted for the status quo, in which it is illegal for women to pray collectively at the Wall. The Women of the Wall protested, and the commission proposed that women pray at the southeastern corner of the Old City Wall, a site entirely outside the Jewish Quarter and even outside the Old City. The women refused this so-called compromise. The commission then suggested that they pray at Robinson's Arch, adjacent to the Western Wall. This area, however, consists of a large archaeological dig and tourist site, and the Women of the Wall refused this location as ill suited for prayer. (The Government is considering additional development of the Robinson's Arch site for tourists.) No acceptable compromise has been proposed.

According to the Women of the Wall and their supporters, no religious law prohibits women from praying together, reading from a Torah scroll, and wearing *tallitot* at the Wall. But according to their opponents, Jewish religious law does indeed prohibit the actions of Women of the Wall, because their behavior goes against *minhag hamakom*, and because established religious custom takes on the status of law. Hence, opponents argue, allowing women's group prayer would tamper with religious law.

by Leora Tanenbaum

Anat Hoffman et alia versus The Supervisor of the Western Wall et alia and Susan Alter et alia versus The Minister of Religion et alia (1994)

[The Women of the Wall and their supporters] represent:
Regarding the character of their prayers, since the women belong to different religious strains, although predominantly Orthodox, they decided to adopt the lowest common denominator, and to conduct prayers acceptable to all the strains.

In light of this decision, this group prays solely in accordance with Orthodox *halakhah*, as this will not offend the religious position of any of the participants. As a result, they hold prayers that are permitted by the *halakhah* as practiced by the Orthodox Jewish religious world.

In light of the above, the [Women of the Wall] insist that in their common prayers, which are held communally:

> (a) They do not call or consider themselves a *minyan* in any connection or for any purpose.
> (b) They do not read those prayers which are allowed only in the forum of a *minyan*. Thus they do not recite the *kaddish* or the *Barkhu* and the *hazzan* does not repeat the *Shmoneh Esrei*, and so on.
> (c) They do not follow orders for reading the Torah, and they do not recite the blessings or go up to read the Torah.

In essence, within a communal setting the prayer of the [Women of the Wall] is individual, by its nature and limitations, with the addition of two things that are fully permitted by *halakhah*—

> (a) They wrap themselves in a prayer shawl while praying.
> (b) They read from the Torah Scroll they carry....

Among their efforts to forge a deep and strong bond with Jerusalem, the Women of the Wall brought a Torah scroll to Jerusalem at the end of 1989 and left it there so that upon their return they might be able to read from it during their prayers.

The Women of the Wall requested to pray as described above at the services marking the beginning of the month of Kislev (February 29, 1989) beside the Wall wrapped in prayer shawls and reading from the Torah scroll they brought with them.

When the Women of the Wall learned that [Rabbi Getz, Supervisor of the Western Wall] was liable to prevent their above-described prayers, as he had done with a group of Israeli women whose Petition in the matter was heard by this Court [earlier, the Women of the Wall] postponed the date of their prayer to Thursday, November 30, 1989. And on November 26, 1989, they turned to [Rabbi Getz and General Commander, Israel Police] in the Old City with a copy sent to [the Minister of Religions] and [the Attorney General] so that the [Women of the Wall] would be able to take the necessary steps to prevent the disturbance of their proposed prayers. The letters were delivered to their destinations by November 28, 1989.

At the appointed hour for the prayer as above-described, the Women of the Wall came to the courtyard of the Wall carrying prayer shawls and a Torah scroll. However, a representative of [the Minister of Religion], based on the decision of [Rabbi Getz], prevented their entrance into the courtyard, claiming that since they were women they were not allowed to wear prayer shawls and to read from the Torah. [The Women of the Wall] were told that their entry into the courtyard of the Wall and their prayer there would be prevented by force....

With the prevention of their entrance to the courtyard of the Wall as described above ... their prayer did not disturb the peace, because it was never held at the Wall, near it, or in the courtyard to its left....

The Law on the Preservation of Holy Places of 1967 states as follows:

1. The holy places shall be guarded against desecration and all other injury and against any thing which might interfere with the free access of the members of the religion to their holy places or in their feelings toward those places....

2. A person who desecrates a holy place or injures it in any manner shall be subject to seven years imprisonment. A person who does any act which may interfere with access of members of religions to their holy places or with their feelings towards those same places shall be subject to five years imprisonment....

3. This law shall be in addition to any other law and not derogate from it....

4. The Minister of Religions is appointed to ensure performance of this law, and he may, after consultation with the representatives of the religions which are affected or upon their advice, and with the approval of the Minister of Justice, prescribe regulations to enforce it.

When the original Petition was filed ... the regulations prescribing the holy places for the Jews [stated]: Within the area of the holy places ... the following is forbidden:

1. Desecration of the Sabbath and Jewish festivals;
2. Inappropriate attire;
3. Establishing food stalls or stands, running a grocery, or any other business;
4. Providing religious services of any type without permission of the Supervisor;
5. Distribution of publications without permission of the Supervisor;
6. A speech, an oral declaration, or carrying placards or signs without permission of the Supervisor;
7. Begging and acceptance of contributions, except displaying boxes or charity boxes in the location which the Supervisor shall designate and for the purposes he specifies;
8. Slaughtering animals;
9. Eating, drinking, or conducting celebrations outside the permissible spots as the Supervisor shall designate;
10. Smoking;
11. Sleeping outside the permissible spots as the Supervisor shall designate;
12. Bringing in animals.

.... Every person within the boundaries of the holy places must obey the lawful instructions of the Supervisor.

The Supervisor may expel any person from a holy place if such person disturbs him in the performance of his duties or violates the instructions....

Since this was the wording of the regulations at the time [the Israeli members of the Women of the Wall's petition] was filed, the main argument of the [Women of the Wall] was that "the Preservation regulations do not prohibit women's prayers in the women's section, nor do they prohibit women reading from the Torah or wearing prayer shawls."

And thus they argued that the Supervisor of the Wall and the Chief Rabbis are not authorized "to impose prohibitions or pronounce verdicts that are not specified in the Preservation regulations, and if they do they exceeded their jurisdiction." The [Women of the Wall] thus argued that it was illegal to prevent them from praying at the Western Wall while reading from the Torah and wearing prayer shawls, and that the Israel Police had a duty to ensure their right to do so.

[However, after they submitted their petition, the State added an amendment to the regulations for Preservation of the Holy Places for Jews:] "The following [is forbidden:] conducting a religious ceremony contrary to the custom of the place, which offends the sensibilities of the praying public toward that place."

[The Women of the Wall then submitted an amended Petition.] In their amended Petition the Petitioners made detailed arguments against the validity of the above amendment.... They claim that the new regulations are fundamentally cancelled or, alternatively, should be declared invalid for various defects: extreme unreasonableness, invalid discrimination, extraneous considerations and aim ... and injury to fundamentals of justice....

They also argued that praying while wearing a prayer shawl and reading from the Torah does not fall within the prohibition set by the new regulations. The basis of this argument is that such prayer is not in contravention of the "custom of the place." ...

In its reply, the State stressed that the right of the [Women of the Wall to go to] the Western Wall, and their right to pray there is not in dispute. What is prohibited to the [Women of the Wall] is to pray there as they do, coming in a group, wearing prayer shawls, carrying a Torah scroll, and reading from it. This is prohibited because, when the [Women of the Wall] held their prayer service as described, they caused serious disturbances in the courtyard of the Wall, breached the public order, and damaged accepted forms of polite behavior.

In pursuance of the powers granted to him by the Law of the Preservation of Holy Places and after consulting with the Chief Rabbis of Israel and with the approval of the Minister of Justice ... the Minister of Religion issued regulations concerning Preservation of the Holy Places for Jews. In these regulations, procedures were determined to accomplish the purposes of the law, that is, not to desecrate or injure the holy places, and not to offend the sensibilities of those who pray at the place. These procedures guarantee that in the holy place, public order and proper forms of polite behavior shall be preserved. As part of these procedures [the regulations] prescribe a list of "prohibited acts" within the boundaries of the holy places. One of the prohibited acts is "conducting a religious ceremony that is not according to the custom of the place, which offends the sensibilities of the public that prays at the place."

The principle of stringently *maintaining the status quo* in the holy places exists to fulfill the obligation to maintain public order and polite behavior in the holy places. The Declaration of Independence of the State of Israel proclaims that it will guarantee freedom of religion and that "it will safeguard the holy places of all religions." This principle was upheld in reality by insisting on the maintenance of public order and courtesy in all the holy places, by preserving the status quo in those places....

According to the above, the regulation that is the subject of this Petition is valid, and the way the Petitioners conducted their prayers at the Wall should be examined accordingly. The State also argued that for the purpose of applying the instructions of the regulation to the [Women of the Wall], the question arises of whether the prayers as conducted by the [Women of the Wall] had ever been the custom of the place at the Western Wall. The answer to this question is negative, and the prayer *as conducted by the Petitioners at the Western Wall* is an affront to the sensibilities of those who pray there.[10]

Women of the Wall Update, May 23, 2000

As *Moonbeams* was going to press, the Women of the Wall achieved a victory. On May 22, 2000, the Israeli Supreme Court reversed its long-standing prohibition of women's group prayer at the Western Wall, and ruled that women can hold services, wear prayer shawls, and read aloud from the Torah. Anat Hoffman, a leader of Women of the Wall, remarked: "Today the Western Wall became part of the State of Israel." She also observed that families will be able to celebrate their daughters' becoming bat mitzvah at the Wall. The Supreme Court's ruling was condemned by Orthodox officials and rabbis. Moshe Gafni, an ultra-Orthodox legislator, called the decision a "shocking blow to observant and traditional Jews around the world, and a stab in their back."[11] Israel's Religious Affairs Minister said that he will submit a bill to the Knesset limiting the types of worship allowed at the Western Wall, thus countering the Supreme Court decision through legislation. Israel's battle over women's role in Judaism will certainly continue, with further controversy inevitable both at the Western Wall itself and in the Knesset.

Questions for Discussion

1. In deciding against the Women of the Wall, Justice Elon cites the importance of established religious custom—*minhag hamakom* and "the principle of stringently maintaining the status quo." Does adherence to

"the custom of the place" essentially bar all change? How, then, can a religious individual begin to change unjust religious practices?

2. How does Justice Elon justify the use of violence against the Women of the Wall?

3. Read the list of prohibitions at the Jewish holy sites. What do these items have in common? Are these prohibitions justified? Do any seem unjustified?

4. What are the implications of this decision for Israeli Jewish women at large? What are the implications for Jewish women throughout the world?

5. Professor Susan Sered states, "Significant advances in the status of women have already taken place: education for girls, votes for women, women working outside the home, and women serving in the Knesset." Sered notes that, on the one hand, in cases involving political or economic power, "women, backed up by the Supreme Court, negotiated mini-victories quite in keeping with Israeli secular norms. In the case involving sacred power, on the other hand, the Women lost."[12] Discuss your own experience of change in religious versus secular spheres. Is change within the sacred realm necessarily more disturbing? Are American Jews and Israeli Jews likely to have different answers? Why or why not?

Suggested Activities and Programs

1. Stage a mock trial. Choose one of the cases discussed above. Divide the group into a "pro" side and a "con" side. (If everyone chooses the same side, ask for volunteers to debate the other side for the sake of lively debate.) Allow 15 to 20 minutes for each group to organize its debating points and appoint a representative. Then hold the debate between the two representatives, allowing comments and assistance from other group members. The groups may refer to other cases (even if they were decided at a later date) in formulating their responses.

2. Support the Israel Women's Network (IWN), a non-profit, non-partisan organization that strives for equality and justice for women in Israel. IWN works against discrimination in the household and the workplace. To learn more about IWN, visit their Web site at www.iwn.org. To receive their quarterly newsletter, *Networking for Women*, which provides updates on the legal status of women in Israel and describes IWN activities, send a check for $50 to Friends of IWN, 20301 NE 30 Avenue, Unit 202, Aventura, FL 33180.

3. Rent and discuss *Women of the Wall*, a 30-minute documentary video. Eight Hadassah chapters (including San Diego; Richmond, VA; Minneapolis; and Atlanta) have already watched the video and used the accompanying discussion materials to explore women's roles and religious pluralism in Israel. For rental ($100) or purchase, contact Squeeze the Stone Productions at squeezestone@hotmail.com or telephone 212-865-4374.

4. The next time you are in Israel, pray together with Women of the Wall

on Rosh Ḥodesh. Though the women no longer pray as a group at the Western Wall, they do meet on the first of every Hebrew month, and all are welcome to join them in prayer. For more information, send email to mscb@pluto.mscc.huji.ac.il. Support Women of the Wall through their international organization, the International Committee for Women of the Wall, Inc. (ICWOW). Contributions to ICWOW can be sent care of Rabbi Helene Ferris, 215 Hessian Hills Road, Croton, NY 10520, and are tax-deductible to the extent allowed by law.

5. Organize an education day on Jewish women and social change, including exploration of both ancient and modern Jewish women. Use the following schedule as a guide.

Jewish Women at the Forefront of Social Change

10:00 **Registration**

10:30 **Heroines of Torah and Talmud—Miriam, Vashti, and Beruriah**

What did these women have in common? What can their lives teach us about our world today? Elaborate on their weaknesses as well as their strengths. (Refer to chapter 6.) Should we commemorate their lives in liturgy and rituals? If yes, how? If no, why not? Invite a Bible scholar or other Jewish expert to address these and other questions.

12:00 **Lunch**

1:00 **Israeli Women and the Law**

In Israel today, a number of courageous women are fighting within the legal system for women's rights. Invite a guest speaker—if at all possible, an Israeli feminist activist—to assess the legal battles over women's equality in Israel. Explore any or all of the Supreme Court battles presented in Chapter 8, or analyze other legal and social battles in Israel.

2:30 **American Jewish Feminists**

Many founders of the modern feminist movement are Jews, among them Betty Friedan, Andrea Dworkin, Phyllis Chesler, and Shulamith Firestone. Letty Cottin Pogrebin, author of *Deborah, Golda, and Me*, describes the intersection of feminism and Judaism in her own life. (Refer to chapter 6.) Invite a Jewish feminist sociologist or historian as guest speaker. Why did Jews play such a significant role in modern feminism? What role has Judaism played in the lives of the early feminists? Why have Jewish feminists—who in their own estimation are fighting injustice—been consistently decried as selfish? Discuss also antisemitism within the women's movement (refer to pages 124–126) and the impact of Jewish feminism on young women today.

4:00 **Conclusion**

Have a Hadassah volunteer bring the Education Day to a close. Many contemporary events deserve our attention and compel us to speak against injustice. What is your Hadassah chapter or region doing to intervene? Describe some of current projects, and enlist support for Hadassah's work. For instance: the Read*Write*Now! Partners Tutoring Program (National Community Education and Outreach at 212-303-8042); the First Amendment, First Watch: Religion in the Public Schools program (National American Affairs/Domestic Policy at 212-303-8136); the *Pikuah Nefesh* organ donation program (National Women's Health at 212-303-8094); or the Healthy Women Healthy Lives program (National Women's Health at 212-303-8094).

---

1. Sue Fishkoff, "The Status of Women in Israel: Myth vs. Reality," *Na'amat Woman* March/April 1998, page 10.

2. Alice Shalvi, *Women in Israel* (New York: New Israel Fund, 1994), page 10.

3. Shalvi, page 10.

4. Fishkoff, page 10.

5. Jolie Greiff, "Women Warriors: The Controversy over Combat in the Israeli Army," *The Reporter* (of Women's American ORT), Winter 1996, pages 9–12.

6. *Israel Law Review*, 32:1, winter 1998 (Jerusalem: Hebrew University Faculty of Law), pages 164–167, 173–175, 177. For the Court's complete verdict, in English translation, read pages 157–178.

7. *Dr. Naomi Nevo vs. The National Court of Labor Relations, et alia.* 749 (4) P.D. 44. Excerpts from Supreme Court decision were translated into English by Barbara Harshav.

8. Susan Sered, "Women and Religious Change in Israel: Rebellion or Revolution," *Sociology of Religion* 58:1 (1997), page 6.

9. *Selected Judgments of the Supreme Court in Israel* 8 (Tel Aviv: Israel Bar Publishing), pages 206–209, 242, 248–249. For the Court's complete verdict, in English translation, see pages 186–254.

10. *Anat Hoffman et alia versus The Supervisor of the Western Wall et alia and Susan Alter et alia versus The Minister of Religion et alia.* 48 (2) P.D. 265. Excerpts from Supreme Court decision were translated into English by Barbara Harshav.

11. Joel Greenberg, "Israeli High Court Rules for Women's Services at the Western Wall," *The New York Times,* May 23, 2000, page A6.

12. Sered, "Women and Religious Change in Israel," page 19.

WOMEN RABBIS

If you are a Reform, Reconstructionist, or Conservative Jew, you probably don't raise an eyebrow at the thought of a female rabbi—at least not any more. Since 1972, when a woman was first ordained at an American seminary, Jews in the United States have become accustomed to women delivering a sermon, donning a *tallit*, reading from the Torah, leading a congregation in prayer, answering questions on ethics, officiating at weddings and funerals, and offering spiritual guidance.

Yet the fight for ordination lasted almost a century. In 1890, a young woman named Ray Frank, who worked as a Sabbath school principal, preached to the Jews of Spokane, Washington, and urged them to establish a synagogue. Her sermon inspired the small community, and Frank became a well known preacher, invited to speak at pulpits throughout the West. She went on to study at Reform Judaism's Hebrew Union College (HUC) at Cincinnati, but said that she did not desire to become a rabbi. The subject of much press attention, Ray Frank was proclaimed "a latter-day Deborah," "the Jewess in the pulpit," and even (inaccurately) "the only female rabbi."[1]

In 1903, Hadassah's future founder Henrietta Szold met with Solomon Schechter, president of Conservative Judaism's Jewish Theological Seminary, to discuss the possibility of studying there. Schechter agreed—as long as Szold could assure him that she sought only education and not ordination.

In 1921, Martha Neumark enrolled in the undergraduate program that, for men, would ultimately lead to graduate study and ordination at Hebrew Union College. Her request for a High Holiday student preaching assignment led to a two-year-long debate on women's ordination. In the end, the HUC Board of Governors denied Martha Neumark the rabbinical degree, awarding her instead a teaching certificate.

In 1935, Regina Jonas of Germany, who had earlier completed course work at Berlin's liberal rabbinical seminary, was privately ordained. Germany had little history of feminist activism, so a woman rabbi was perhaps even more revolutionary there than in America. After ordination, Jonas worked primarily as a teacher, but she occasionally gave sermons and led congregations before being deported to Theresienstadt in 1942. She was murdered in Auschwitz in 1944.

In the United States in 1939, Helen Levinthal, daughter and granddaughter of rabbis, became the first American woman to complete the entire course of study in a rabbinical school. However, the Jewish Institute of Religion in New York (at that time liberal but non-denominational) denied her ordination. Instead she was granted the Master of Hebrew Literature degree, as well as a special Hebrew certificate. Levinthal's academic achievement was widely covered in the American and the Anglo-Jewish press, and many reporters speculated that women's rabbinic ordination would surely occur soon.

By mid-century innovations such as Sisterhood Sabbaths and speaking invitations to prominent Jewish women, had made American Reform and Conservative Jews comfortable with the idea of women's lectures, inspirational messages, and even sermons. In 1950, Rabbi William Ackerman died, after having served as spiritual leader of Temple Beth Israel in Meridian, Mississippi, for the previous 26 years. Knowing that finding a new rabbi would be difficult, the congregation turned to his widow, Paula Ackerman, asking her to serve as interim spiritual leader. For the next three years, Ackerman led weekly and holiday services, preached, and officiated at funerals, weddings, and confirmations. Like her predecessors, Ackerman was the subject of much media attention, and also like her predecessors she hoped that her example would inspire other women.

Nearly a quarter of a century would pass, however, before the Reform movement ordained a woman. In the late sixties, several women were enrolled at Hebrew Union College, some aiming for teaching degrees and a few aiming for the rabbinate. In 1972, Sally Priesand completed the course of study at HUC and became the first female rabbi in the United States. In 1974, Sandy Eisenberg Sasso became the first woman ordained at the Reconstructionist Rabbinical College in Philadelphia. The Conservative movement debated the issue from 1977 to 1983, and in 1983 voted in favor of admitting women to the rabbinical program of the Jewish Theological Seminary.* Amy Eilberg, who had

---

* Women's ordination was an extremely divisive issue. When the Jewish Theological

completed most of the course work previously, was ordained in 1985.

The Orthodox movement to date has refused to even consider women's ordination. Indeed the overwhelming majority of Orthodox Jewish men and women strongly oppose women's ordination. In addition to objections based on woman's domestic role and the community's expectations of male leadership, Orthodox Jews oppose women as rabbis because of *halakhah*, Jewish law.* According to traditional legal interpretation, a woman may not serve as a witness, and a woman is not obligated to pray at three specific times each day. Consequently, a woman may not officiate at weddings or divorces, which require a witness, and she may not lead communal prayers, which require a personal obligation for time-dependent prayer.

Nevertheless, several Orthodox feminists believe that women's ordination is on the horizon, and at least one Orthodox Jewish woman has applied to the rabbinic seminary of Yeshiva University. Meanwhile, as Orthodox Jewish women's educational and employment opportunities continue to grow, a number of "para-rabbinic" positions have been created, both in America and in Israel. Many of the duties that rabbis routinely perform are open to both women and men according to even the strictest interpretation of religious law: teaching, offering pastoral counseling, visiting the sick, comforting the bereaved, advising on ritual procedure. Increasingly, today's Orthodox women are seeking to perform such duties in their own careers.

As Orthodox Judaism begins to hear muted voices of support for women as spiritual leaders, other Jewish denominations are coming to terms with women's new roles. As feminist scholar Aviva Cantor notes, women rabbis "continue to struggle for full congregational acceptance, advancement, equal pay, and solo pulpits in large synagogues."[2] In the early nineties, a survey found that the income of women Reform rabbis was 5 to 25 percent lower than their male counterparts.[3]

Nonetheless, female rabbis believe that the rabbinate and indeed Judaism itself are enhanced by their womanhood. Stressing qualities such as inclusiveness and compassion, they assert that women rabbis have supplied a needed dimension to American Jewish life.

by Claudia Chernov and Leora Tanenbaum

Seminary did finally accept women rabbinical students, opponents left the Conservative movement and founded the Union for Traditional Judaism. The extremely small movement still exists today, and is centered in New Jersey.

* The issues of *halakhah* also occasioned the long debate in Conservative Judaism. Though Orthodox and Conservative interpretations of religious law agree on most aspects of dietary laws, Shabbat observance, and liturgical rules, differing only on certain points, the Orthodox and the Conservative interpretations of religious law on women's roles and responsibilities differ so profoundly that no Orthodox authority would consider the Conservative movement's decisions as guidelines.

WOMEN AND RELIGIOUS LEADERSHIP IN JEWISH LITERATURE

Judges 4:4–5

The biblical Book of Judges tells of Deborah, a spiritual leader and military advisor.

Deborah, wife of Lappidoth, was a prophetess; she led Israel at that time. She used to sit under the Palm of Deborah, between Ramah and Bethel in the hill country of Ephraim, and the Israelites would come to her for decisions.

Mishnah, *Shevuot* 4.1

The Mishnah prohibits women from serving as witnesses.

[The law governing an] oath of testimony applies to men and not to women, to those who are not related and not to those who are related, to those who are suitable [to bear witness] and not to those who are not suitable.

Babylonian Talmud, *Shevuot* 30a

The Sages of the Talmud explain the reasoning behind the Mishnah's prohibition.

How do we know [that women are ineligible as witnesses]? Because the Rabbis taught: "The two men shall stand" (Deuteronomy 19:17)—that verse refers to witnesses. [Hence witnesses must be men.]

Babylonian Talmud, *Kiddushin* 41b

According to Orthodox understanding of Jewish ritual law, a woman may not serve as shaliah *tzibbur (literally, agent of the congregation; prayer leader), because women are not obligated to pray at three specific times each day. The Talmud explains that only one who is obligated on his own behalf may act as an agent on behalf of others.*

Rabbi Yannai's dictum [stated,] "Just as you are members of the covenant, so must your agents be members of the covenant." For this, what need have I of a verse? It may be derived from Rabbi Hiyya bar Abba's dictum in Rabbi Yohanan's name! For Rabbi Hiyya bar Abba said in Rabbi Yohanan's name: "A [heathen] slave cannot become an agent to receive a divorce from a woman's husband, because he himself is not subject to the [Jewish] law of marriage and divorce!" [This shows that according to logic a person cannot act as an agent in situations in which the person cannot act as a principal.]

Babylonian Talmud, Megillah 23a

The Talmud allows women to publicly read from the Torah, but expresses disapproval.

Our Rabbis taught: All are qualified to be among the seven [who publicly read from the Torah on Saturday], even a minor and a woman, only the Sages said that a woman should not read in the Torah out of respect for the congregation.

Mary M. Cohen, "A Problem for Purim" (1889)

Feminist scholar Pamela Nadell, author of Women Who Would Be Rabbis: A History of Women's Ordination 1889–1985, *finds the first public support for women rabbis in Mary Cohen's 1889 essay. Cohen was the superintendent of Philadelphia's Hebrew Sunday School, and was active in many educational and charitable organizations. She was also a poet and essayist, writing frequently for the Anglo-Jewish and the American press. Although Cohen's proposal for women "ministers"—as rabbis were then known—was a radical innovation, she herself was a member of a traditional synagogue and in her writings argued against many of the changes instituted by Reform Judaism. Her 1889 essay begins with Lionel Martinez, a rabbinic student, inviting several friends to his home on the eve of Purim. Lionel suggests that the circle of friends discuss ways to improve the rabbinate.*

[Dora Ulman warns that her idea] "will shock you all considerably." [Dora asks:] "Could not—our *women*—be—ministers?"

All but Lionel were struck dumb. Even Jack's boasted calmness had taken flight; he sate in open-eyed surprise. Martinez said quickly: "Will you explain your idea or plan, Miss Dora?" He was, however, secretly a little astonished; he had not expected anything from her until later on, and then, "views" on sewing-schools.

[Dora argues] that there are trials in the lives of women that men do not and cannot understand [and women can preach about these trials better than men. She goes on to say:] "Women are created to the work of ministering just as they are to the painting of pictures, the writing of poems, or the molding of statues.... There are some among my friends ... who have a strong inclination for the work and only need due preparation and a little encouragement to properly qualify them; their example would no doubt bring forward other candidates."

[A young man asserts, "Many people] would laugh openly to see a woman in the pulpit."

[Isabel Harris counters:] "Every good cause is apt to meet with ridicule at first.... Are not some of our present preachers ridiculed? It would be no worse for women than for men."

[Lionel Martinez doubts that America's Jews are ready for female rabbis. He says:] "It would alarm them more than any previous novelty.

They will probably imagine that our present preachers are becoming too weak to hold the reins of spiritual influence. [In addition, many would make] the usual objection to women going out of their proper sphere."

[Dora replies:] "Fear of women out-doing men in ministerial work is just what would spur your sex on to better things, and thus give ours a higher ideal for which to strive. Competition is the safe-guard of the people.... If women have a gift for the ministry, they are more in their place in the pulpit than if they were doing plain sewing, teaching music, or attempting any other work than the one to which their nature and their conscience call them."[4]

Henrietta Szold (1897)

Henrietta Szold, who would go on to study at the Jewish Theological Seminary, participated in a symposium in 1897 on "Women in the Synagogue." All were asked to write a response to the question: "Should woman occupy the pulpit?" Szold answered yes. She added qualifications, though, that were extremely limiting, and that would, in effect, dissuade any actual woman from becoming a rabbi.

I believe that woman can best serve the interests of the synagogue by devoting herself to her home ... and by occupying the pulpit only when her knowledge of the law, history, and literature of Judaism is masterful, and her natural gift so extraordinary as to forbid hesitation, though even then it were the part of wisdom not to make a profession of public preaching and teaching, the old Jewish rule of not holding women responsible for religious duties performed at definite times having a deep-seated rational basis and wide applicability.... In other words, the Deborahs and Miriams need not hide their light under a bushel, but they and the world must be pretty sure that they are Deborahs and Miriams, not equally admirable Hannahs and Ruths.[5]

Rabbi Stephen S. Wise, letter to Lucile Uhry, 31 May 1919

Rabbi Stephen Wise (1874–1949) founded both the Free Synagogue and the Jewish Institute of Religion in New York City. In 1919 Lucile Uhry, then age 15 and a religious school student, wrote on women's fitness to serve as rabbis. Rabbi Wise, who later would encourage Helen Levinthal, wrote to her.

I am beginning to feel that if you are really in earnest and wish to study for the ministry, there is no reason why you should not. The fact that no woman has served as rabbi is no reason why no woman should so serve. If you were my child, as in a sense you are, and felt you wished to enter the ministry, I should urge you to go on and prepare yourself.[6]

Central Conference of American Rabbis (1922)

Because of Martha Neumark's enrollment at Hebrew Union College in 1921 and its attendant publicity, the rabbis attending the 1922 annual convention of the CCAR (the professional organization of Reform rabbis) voted on women's ordination. The measure was approved by a vote of 56 to 11.

We declare that woman cannot justly be denied the privilege of ordination.[7]

Rabbi Maurice Eisendrath (1970)

Despite theoretical support for women rabbis, none of the women who enrolled in Reform Judaism's seminary attained the wide support that would prove necessary for ordination. In the sixties, however, Sally Priesand and several other female students began their studies. By 1970, Priesand had received extensive press coverage and much public acclaim. Rabbi Eisendrath, president of the Union of American Hebrew Congregations (UAHC, the organization of Reform temples), in 1966 had urged lay leaders to support women's spiritual leadership. In 1970, he addressed the UAHC board of trustees.

Jokes [about women rabbis] are no longer funny, and no longer becoming to a movement whose self-image is one of liberal thought, just action, equality, and moral motivation.... We must stop dragging our feet on this subject and stop mouthing the same old tired bromides and act now to get women out of what many of them call "slave labor, kitchen squad" activities and into the mainstream of our work.[8]

Lucy Dawidowicz (1977)

The push for Conservative women's ordination began in earnest in the seventies, alongside widespread press coverage of Sally Priesand's Reform ordination in 1972 and Sandy Eisenberg Sasso's Reconstructionist ordination in 1974. During the years that the Conservative movement struggled with women's ordination, many scholars voiced opinions pro and con. Those who opposed women's ordination pointed, of course, to Jewish law. But social factors concerning women's roles figured even more prominently, as they did for Lucy Dawidowicz (1915–1990), the great Holocaust historian and a prominent right-wing essayist.

Even more forbidding [than women's religious passivity] is the threat of female power, female usurpation of the synagogue. Women are efficient; they can organize, raise funds, bring order out of chaos. They can turn the *shul* into a Hadassah chapter. Not that I disapprove of Hadassah, its activities, or its ladies. But I do not like the idea of their taking over the synagogue. To my mind, the assumption by a woman of rabbinic or priestly function in the synagogue undermines the very essence of Jewish tradition.[9]

Debra S. Cantor, Nina Beth Cardin, Stephanie Dickstein, Nina Bieber Feinstein, Sharon Fliss, Carol Glass, and Beth Polebaum, Letter to the Faculty of the Jewish Theological Seminary, December 6, 1979

During the seventies, several young women who had once dreamed of becoming Conservative rabbis enrolled instead at the Reform and Reconstructionist seminaries. A few others studied Talmud at the Jewish Theological Seminary, hoping to earn the credits that would some day be applied toward their rabbinic degrees. In 1979, Debra Cantor wrote this letter to the Jewish Theological Seminary faculty. It was signed by Cantor and six other women who hoped to enter the rabbinic degree program.*

We are seriously committed to Jewish scholarship and to the study of Jewish texts. Although some of our specific practices vary, we are all observant women who are committed to the halakhic system.

We wish to serve the Jewish community as professionals in a variety of educational and leadership capacities. We are interested in teaching, writing, organizing, counseling, and leading congregations. Although we realize that these tasks can be performed by people who are not rabbis, we desire to receive rabbinical training, and the title "rabbi," because we feel that with this authority we can be most effective in the Jewish community. We believe that our efforts are sorely needed and that there are many communities where we would be fully accepted and could accomplish much toward furthering a greater commitment to Jewish life.

We are fully aware that there are a number of complicated halakhic issues related to Jewish women. We feel that these issues should be addressed carefully, directly, and within the scope of the halakhic process. This process, however, should not delay the admission of women to the Rabbinic School. We wish above all to learn and to serve God through our work in the Jewish community.[10]

Blu Greenberg, "Will There Be Orthodox Women Rabbis?" (1984)

Blu Greenberg, regarded as the leading spokeswoman for Orthodox Jewish feminism, is a prominent lecturer and author.

In 1972, I read an article about the forthcoming ordination of Rabbi Sally Priesand at Hebrew Union College. I was, to put it mildly, horrified. Someone had crossed the line. "It is against *halakhah*," I argued. "Other things I can understand, but women as rabbis—never!"

Yet over time I went from asking, "What on earth is this woman doing?" to "What is she doing?" to "Why is she doing it?" to "Why not?"

My questions changed their nature and tone over the course of several

---

* At least five of the seven women who signed the letter have been ordained as rabbis.

years. I had to digest each new task that she, and then other female rabbis, were performing. Teaching, yes; but officiating at a funeral? Why would anyone want a woman to officiate at a funeral? I asked myself. Why would any family, in its moment of bereavement, break with tradition? It took me three years to understand that, to a family in a moment of grief, it does not matter whether the source of consolation and of Jewish communal representation is male or female. Officiating at services—I had become adjusted to that for Reform Judaism, but to consecrate marriage? A stigma would forever be attached to this Jewish couple.

With great difficulty, I finally had to ask myself what was so terrible about a woman's being that she could not perform these functions? After all, performing marriage is a sacred function and not a sacramental one (such as the sacraments of Temple times performed only by men born into the priestly class). In fact, *halakhah* permits any lay Jew to perform these functions, such as marriage and funeral rites, as long as the proper procedures are followed. There is nothing intrinsic to the rabbinic role that a woman cannot do. Therefore, her exclusion was only a matter of gender, which evolved from a cultural rather than a religious base. The model of women rabbis taught me that perhaps the problem lay not with women but with community and its conditioning.[11]

Rabbi Laura Geller, "Encountering the Divine Presence" (1986)

Rabbi Laura Geller was ordained in 1976 at the Hebrew Union College-Jewish Institute of Religion in New York, becoming America's third woman rabbi. Ten years later she was invited to address the annual meeting of the Central Conference of American Rabbis.

In my second year at [rabbinical school] we learned *Berakhot* [tractate of the Babylonian Talmud] with our teacher Rabbi Julius Kravitz. I had never learned about all the occasions for a blessing—new clothes, new fruit, seeing the ocean, seeing a rainbow, being in the presence of a scholar, on hearing good news or even bad news—I was exhilarated! God is present at every moment; it is up to us to acknowledge God's presence. We do it through saying blessings. Rabbi Kravitz said, "There is no important moment in the lifetime of a Jew for which there is no blessing." [But] I realized that it was not true. There had been important moments in my lifetime for which there was no blessing ... like when I first got my period. There in the classroom overlooking 68th Street I became again the thirteen-year-old girl running to tell her mother she had just got her period. And I heard again my mother tell me that when she got her first period my grandmother slapped her.... And, as I thought back to that time, I understood that there should have been a blessing—*she'asani isha, sheheheyanu* [thank you, God, for having made me a woman]—because holiness was present at that moment.

God had been present all along but I had never noticed. Perhaps I wasn't looking, or perhaps I was looking in the wrong places. If I had been looking I would have looked to a great and powerful wind to tear the mountain and shatter the rocks, to the earthquake or to the fire ... but instead, I needed to listen to the gentle whisper, the still small voice....

A blessing would have gently taught me what it means to be a woman, would have invisibly instructed me how miraculous the human body is, would have drawn me closer to my mother, my grandmothers, and all the women whose lives made mine possible. A blessing would have named the divinity present in this moment of transformation, this moment of connection. On 68th Street I suddenly realized that my experience is Jewish experience. There is a Torah of our lives as well as the Torah that was written down.[12]

Rabbi Nina Beth Cardin (1990)

Rabbi Cardin was interviewed by a Lilith *reporter in 1990. She was asked about ways in which women had redefined the rabbi's role.*

The push now is to change the image of the rabbi: to speak near the congregation, not from above. It's no longer the distant holy man, but rather that of a hand-holder, an educator to inspire and teach.... The idea is to empower the congregant to be a more active member of the Jewish community.[13]

Rabbi Amy Eilberg (1991)

Rabbi Eilberg was the first woman ordained by the Conservative movement. In a 1990 interview by Lilith, *she spoke about her first job out of the seminary. "My rabbinate was a first person rabbinate.... Women value experience as highly as intellect. My own story is as significant as any fact," she noted.[14] In an interview a year later, Rabbi Eilberg spoke of the difficulties she had faced. For instance, she told reporter Debra Nussbaum Cohen that congregants had debated whether she could be allowed to cross her legs when seated on the* bimah *(platform).*

Congregants are always more focused on the body of the woman rabbi than on the male rabbi. They discuss what she wears, whether her shoes are open or closed toe. It's a reflection of the deep place that is touched when women take on the mantle of leadership.[15]

Judith Hauptman, "Women and the Conservative Synagogue" (1992)

Judith Hauptman is a professor of Talmud at the Jewish Theological Seminary. She also served as the first female Dean of the Seminary. In 1992 she wrote a brief history of the changes that had occurred in Conservative Judaism as women became increasingly involved in religious life.

The issue that proved most difficult for the Conservative movement to come to terms with was the ordination of women. Allowing a woman to fill the pivotal role of religious leader of the synagogue seemed a greater break with the past than allowing women to count in the *minyan*, which, halakhically speaking, was far more radical. For almost ten years this issue was debated....

Both sides agreed that most contemporary rabbinic functions, such as religious role model, teacher, and preacher, could be filled by women without making any halakhic adjustments. Although women did not engage in all of these activities in talmudic society, there were no explicit laws preventing them from doing so. The only objections raised to ordaining women involved the ancillary rabbinic roles—leading prayer services and serving as a witness at weddings and divorces. The opponents of ordination noted that the Conservative rabbi of today is frequently called upon to serve as *shaliah tzibbur* [agent or leader for the congregation's prayer], often as the only competent prayer leader present in the *minyan*. It followed that if women were ordained, they too would find themselves pressed into service; however, the minority claimed, *halakhah* does not allow a woman to serve as a *shaliah tzibbur*; Mishnah *Megillah* 4.3 states that only men may count in the quorum of ten for prayer, and only men—who are themselves obligated to pray—may discharge the prayer responsibilities of others.

This objection to ordaining women overlooks the fact that the Talmud explicitly requires women to pray and in no way distinguishes their obligation from that of men (Mishnah *Berakhot* 3.3; Babylonian Talmud *Berakhot* 20b).[16]

Rabbi Emily Faust Korzenik, "On Being A Rabbi" (1992)

Rabbi Emily Faust Korzenik is spiritual leader of a congregation in Stamford, Connecticut.

Coming to a rabbinical career as an older person and as a woman also means that ... my way of being a rabbi has been shaped as much by my life as a wife and mother, a high school history teacher, and a social and political activist, as by rabbinical study and preparation itself.

People often ask me if I experience discrimination as a rabbi because I am a woman. From its inception, the Reconstructionist movement accepted women as peers. [In that milieu of equality] I began to form my desire to become a rabbi. It was a milieu that made discrimination against women elsewhere in the Jewish religious world seem incomprehensible and, therefore, something to be overcome.

There have been disquieting moments, of course. A young woman doctor asked me to officiate at her wedding, and then she discovered her Israeli fiancé and his family would not be comfortable with a woman rabbi. She asked if I would co-officiate with a man. I replied that if I was not rabbi enough to perform the ceremony, I preferred not to participate.

She wanted to satisfy her fiancé but she meant to be kind. Didn't I understand that the "social customs" were different in Israel? I did not remind her that "social customs" had kept women from becoming doctors until not long before her own entry into that profession.[17]

Nancy S. Hausman, "On Becoming A Cantor" (1992)

Nancy Hausman serves as cantor of a congregation in New Jersey.

My parents raised me to believe that I could do anything I wanted to do. Partway through my junior year in college ... cantorial school seemed just the right career for me, a person who loves Judaism and who also loves to sing. I entered Hebrew Union College–Jewish Institute of Religion's School of Sacred Music in the fall of 1974. I was part of a class of three women and five men—there was a grand total of forty-five students in the School of Sacred Music....

Our professors, mostly cantors, were still not sure how to teach women the traditional *nusah* [melodies of prayers] so every class was an experimental one for both them and us. However, they were all very positive; no exclusionary practices took place.

I do, however, remember negative comments from some of the male students about the female students. Some of the men were afraid that the women would take all of the jobs, leaving them with no employment. Others complained that salaries would suffer because occupations considered "women's" jobs are traditionally underpaid in our society. These kinds of comments made me angry, but as far as I can ascertain, these fears were unjustified.[18]

Rabbi Sally J. Priesand, "Looking Backward and Ahead" (1992)

Rabbi Priesand, America's first female rabbi, was ordained in 1972 by Hebrew Union College–Jewish Institute of Religion. Since 1981, she has served as rabbi of Monmouth Reform Temple in Tinton Falls, New Jersey. She delivered the following sermon just before the twentieth anniversary of her ordination.

It sounds corny to say that I love being a rabbi, but the truth is that I do and I can't imagine doing anything else....

Among the many lessons my congregants have taught me, three are foremost in my mind today. I think of them now because I see reflected in them the gifts that feminism has given to all of us over the past twenty years. First, we have gained a broader understanding that the rabbi's primary task is to help other Jews become more responsible for their own Jewishness. In today's language, that's called empowerment, and nothing in my rabbinate gives me greater joy than to see my congregants study Torah, observe *mitzvot*, and do Judaism for themselves.

[Moving away from ideas of] hierarchy and power toward new

opportunities for networking and partnership ... is not unique to feminism, but the women's movement has served as catalyst, encouraging us to rethink previous models of leadership in which the rabbi maintained complete control and did everything for members of the congregation.

The second area in which we see the impact of feminism is that of theology. Like most of you, I too grew up with the image of God as King, omnipotent and clearly male. My congregation has given me the opportunity, through experience and study, discussion and experimentation, to discover new models of divinity, to know that God embodies characteristics both masculine and feminine, to fashion for myself, and hopefully for them, a meaningful theology....

The third lesson I have learned from my congregation is this: success doesn't mean bigger. Twenty years ago, I thought the ultimate goal was to become a rabbi of a large congregation; indeed, as the first woman to be ordained, I thought it was my obligation.... Fortunately, for my own well-being, my congregation taught me to reject that notion.

Life is not measured by wealth or power, material possessions or fame. Life is counted in terms of goodness and growth. Someone once said that our purpose in living is not to get ahead of other people, but to get ahead of ourselves, always to play a better game of life. That's what success is all about. Have we done our best? Are we continuing to grow?[19]

Francine Klagsbrun (1993)

In celebration of its 1983 decision to admit women rabbinical students, the Jewish Theological Seminary hosted a two-day conference ten years later. Thirty-five Conservative women rabbis (from a total, at that time, of 50) participated in "Women in the Rabbinate: Dynamics of Change." Francine Klagsbrun, who had served on the Commission for the Study of the Ordination of Women, was one of the speakers.

What we need to be doing is cultivating both sides of our natures.... Male rabbis need to allow themselves to be open and accessible; female rabbis need to allow themselves to be seen as rigorous and meticulous in their scholarship, savvy about financial matters in their synagogues, strong administrators. Respect comes and will continue to come from being able to look up to the rabbi not as a social worker or therapist, but as an authority who can bring authentic, learned Jewish perspective to an issue.[20]

Rabbi Debra Cantor (1993)

Also speaking at the "Women in the Rabbinate: Dynamics of Change" conference, Rabbi Cantor warned her colleagues to protect themselves against the expectations of being "superwomen."

Our calling, however lofty, does not demand that we sacrifice our lives in the process of serving God and Israel. Self-destruction, the neglect of family and friends, workaholism, these are pernicious late-twentieth-century American values. They are not Jewish values.[21]

Haviva Ner-David (1999)

In America, two Orthodox synagogues have instituted communal leadership positions for women. In 1998 the Lincoln Square Synagogue in Manhattan and the Hebrew Institute of Riverdale in the Bronx each hired a young woman to serve as a congregational intern. The two women—Julie Stern Joseph and Sharona Margolin Halickman—both have extensive Jewish education, are married, and are in their mid-twenties. Both serve as spiritual leaders, working primarily in adult education and in counseling. The title of their position remains somewhat unsatisfactory, because the word "intern" implies apprenticeship, yet neither woman serves as an apprentice. Other suggestions have included morateinu, *the Hebrew feminine for "our teacher"; and* rabbanit, *which traditionally has meant "rabbi's wife," but could now be broadened to include women who are themselves religious leaders. Out of the question in Orthodox Judaism, however, is the simple and straightforward "rabbi."*

In 1993 Haviva Krasner-Davidson applied to the Rabbi Isaac Elchanan Theological Seminary of Yeshiva University. (She later moved to Israel, and shortened her name to Ner-David.) In a Moment *magazine article written shortly after submitting her application, she explained her motivations. Even though enrolling in a women's educational institution could, theoretically, enable her to master the same material that a male rabbinical student masters, her certificate would be less meaningful than his ordination. He could go on to become the head of a yeshivah or the principal of a day school, but she could aspire only to classroom teaching—and that for less pay than her male counterpart.*

Yeshiva University never responded to Ner-David's application. She is currently preparing for private Orthodox ordination in Jerusalem. But even with ordination, she is unlikely to find employment in an Orthodox congregation, and, as she noted in her 1993 article, no Orthodox school would treat her equally to a male rabbi in either pay or level of responsibilities. Ner-David's situation is unique, but Ray Frank was also unique in her time. Ner-David, like her predecessors, hopes that her example will inspire future generations.

The title "rabbi" means something. It carries with it connotations of authority, morality, commitment to Judaism and a certain mastery of texts. Even the most learned and pious Orthodox woman can never aspire to receiving a title that will gain her the same degree of power and respect in the Jewish community. Nothing is comparable to a rabbinical degree if you want to teach Torah, offer religious counseling, and be involved in the halakhic process.[22]

Chana Henkin, *Yo'atzot Halakhah*—Fortifying Tradition Through Innovation (1999)

In Israel as well as the United States, Orthodox women are assuming new spiritual responsibilities. Nishmat, the Jerusalem Center for Advanced Torah Study for Women, graduated its first class of eight yo'atzot halakhah, *female halakhic consultants, in the Fall of 1999. As Chana Henkin, the founder and dean of Nishmat, explains, the women studied a specialized curriculum in the religious laws of* taharat hamish-pahah, *family purity. These laws involve a woman's ritual immersion in a* mikvah *each month following the cessation of her menstrual period. The consultants' role is to advise women who have questions on menstruation and family purity rules. Rabbi Dr. Norman Lamm, president of Yeshiva University, addressed the first* yo'atzot halakhah *at their graduation. He observed that formal training of women as consultants in Jewish ritual law is "a revolutionary change for the good" that "adds* kedushah *[holiness] to* Am Yisrael *[the people of Israel]."*[23]

Eight women completed the first two-year course qualifying them to serve as halakhic consultants to women, and 16 have begun the second class. The program consists of more than 1,000 hours of the classic rabbinic curriculum of *hilkhot niddah* (laws of ritual purity) with supplementary training in women's medicine. In selecting the first class we looked for sincere religious commitment, talmudic scholarship, and leadership qualities. The average academic level of our fellows was midway between M.A. and Ph.D. (in Jewish scholarship).

What prompted me to take this action? Years of work in *taharat hamishpahah* and communal leadership made me aware that many observant women will simply not consult a rabbi with an intimate question. In some cases, the husband asks on behalf of his wife. In most cases, the question is not asked at all. I have been informed even by rabbis' wives, both in Israel and in the United States, that they themselves would never bring an undergarment to a rabbinical expert with a question.* Dignified observance requires that a woman feel comfortable about the consultation, and that the *halakhah* be explained patiently, clearly, competently, and in detail—a procedure with which most women and, in fact, many rabbis, are not at ease because of their ingrained sense of modesty.

Our *yo'atzot halakhah* are not replacing rabbis nor do they aspire to be rabbis. They can, however, determine which questions require a ruling by a qualified *posek* (rabbinic authority on Jewish law). The assumption

---

* For example, is the staining on the undergarment, occurring midway in the woman's menstrual cycle, caused by blood from the uterus? If so, the woman must refrain from sexual activity until she can again visit the *mikvah* after waiting the appropriate number of days.

that a learned woman will attempt to flex her talmudic muscles and rule on her own, instead of turning to a higher authority when warranted, could not be more mistaken.

Women halakhic consultants are an evolution, not a revolution. The problem of women's discomfort with bringing highly personal questions to a rabbi is not a new problem, but the solution is a breathtakingly new solution.[24]

Deena Zimmerman (1999)

Dr. Deena Zimmerman, a New York-born pediatrician who now lives in Israel, is one of the eight graduates of the Nishmat Center program.

Could this lead to women being [Orthodox] rabbis? That brings up the question of what is a full-fledged rabbi, and that question isn't totally answered.... Could women be trained as rabbis in 20 years, starting from this model? Maybe, but that's not the point of this program. [Nishmat's goal] is to help women in the halakhic process—to have women *involved* in the halakhic process. That's far more important than the title given to it.... There is a feeling of awe, something like finishing medical school, when you realize how much responsibility you've been given. You have a lot of authority and hope you'll use it wisely.[25]

Questions for Discussion

1. List several reasons why the Rabbis of the Mishnah excluded women from acting as witnesses.

2. Review from the Talmud's statement on public reading of the Torah. What can we learn about women in the synagogue of that era?

3. Fifty years passed between 1922, when the Central Conference of American Rabbis voted that "woman cannot justly be denied the privilege of ordination," and 1972, when an American woman first enjoyed that privilege. List several reasons for the fifty-year wait.

4. Describe your own initial reactions to women rabbis. Did you first learn of women rabbis through personal experience or through the media? Did your reactions change over time? How do you react to female rabbis today, more than 25 years after the first American woman was ordained?

5. As Blu Greenberg describes, some changes that at first appear shocking later appear normal. Besides female rabbis, what other changes fit Greenberg's description? Consider changes in both Jewish practice and women's roles. Describe your own progression (if any) from outrage to acceptance.

6. In an essay written in 1984, ten years after her ordination as the first woman Reconstructionist rabbi, Sandy Eisenberg Sasso asked: "What have women done in over a decade as rabbis?" She answered: "In part,

they have accomplished what rabbis have always accomplished. They have spoken out for justice in synagogues and communities; they have taught in university lecture halls and living room parlors; they have touched people's lives in immeasurable ways," but "they have done more. They have challenged presuppositions about Judaism and about God. They have taught us new ways of speaking and listening and of relating. They have given us new symbols to point to new realities."[26] Based upon the excerpts from Rabbis Laura Geller, Nina Beth Cardin, Amy Eilberg, and Sally J. Priesand, describe how women have challenged presuppositions about Judaism; have taught Jews new ways of speaking, listening, and relating; and have introduced new symbols pointing to new realities. Describe as well your reactions to these changes.

7. During the many years that women's ordination was debated by Reform and Conservative Jews, many argued that women rabbis would cause the men to lose their authority and to forfeit the respect of their congregations. Furthermore, as Cantor Nancy Hausman wrote about male cantorial students, many also feared that "salaries would suffer because occupations considered 'women's' jobs are traditionally underpaid in our society." To what extent are fears of loss of respect, authority, and salary justified and to what extent unjustified?

Suggested Activities and Programs

1. Invite a female pulpit rabbi to speak on her experiences as a rabbi, both positive and negative. A rabbi from another neighborhood might feel more comfortable than a local rabbi in discussing negative aspects of her work.

2. Invite an Orthodox feminist to discuss women's new leadership roles within Orthodox Judaism, and/or to give an overview of the obstacles based upon Jewish religious law that prevent women from entering the Orthodox rabbinate.

3. Assign one participant to present a summary of Pamela S. Nadell's comprehensive and insightful *Women Who Would Be Rabbis: A History of Women's Ordination, 1889–1985* (Boston: Beacon Press, 1998), and to initiate discussion on some of Nadell's concepts. These include: rising expectations for women, media presence, belief in exceptionality, lack of a support group, and comparison to Christian denominations.

4. Organize an education day on Judaism and feminism. Use the following schedule as a guide.

Feminist Judaism—How Are We Doing?

10:00 **Registration**

10:30 **Women at Prayer**
Women have changed the face of American Jewish congregations in a way that few would have envisioned even 25 years ago. One highly visible change is women wearing *tallitot* as they pray on Shabbat (refer to chapter 2). These women, however, are generally in their mid-thirties or older. Few young women (other than rabbinical students) take on the obligations that older religious feminists so greatly desired. Though we may question whether our granddaughters will wear *tallit* or *tefillin*, other innovations seem likely to last—gender-neutral translations of Hebrew prayers and Saturday morning bat mitzvah ceremonies with Torah reading, for example. Invite a rabbi or scholar of religion to speak about the impact of feminism on synagogue practices in America: Which recent changes were introduced—or reinforced—by Jewish feminism? Which innovations have caused the most resistance? Will any of today's changes endure? Which ones? Invite women to respond to the speaker with personal stories (for instance: first *aliyah*, laying *tefillin*, adult bat mitzvah).

12:00 **Lunch**
During the lunch hour, have a local vendor display women's *kippot* and *tallitot* (usually more colorful and stylized than conventional *kippot* and *tallitot*). Allow Education Day participants the opportunity to try on the ritual garments and make purchases.

1:00 **Women Rabbis**
Have a Hadassah volunteer moderate a panel discussion between three speakers: (1) a woman working as a congregational rabbi; (2) an woman rabbi working outside the pulpit; and (3) an Orthodox feminist who will explain women's new religious leadership options as well as opposition to women rabbis. (If possible, invite two women rabbis from two different denominations. For instance, a Conservative rabbi who serves as a hospital chaplain and a Reform rabbi who serves as spiritual leader of her congregation.) Allot each speaker 15 minutes to discuss the changes in religious leadership that she has experienced and her outlook on future changes and concerns. Conclude with a question-and-answer session.

2:30   Women's Ceremonies

It's a girl! No, there won't be a *bris*, but today we have a wealth of ceremonies to honor her birth and enter her into the covenant with God and the Jewish people. Other new Jewish ceremonies include prayers recited at first menstruation, after a caesarian section, and after a miscarriage. Invite a woman rabbi (or a knowledgeable Hadassah member) to describe some of the new ceremonies and explain why they are needed. After the presentation, facilitate a discussion among all participants: Can we write Jewish women's rituals ourselves? What makes a ritual Jewish? What rituals do women need today?

4:00   Conclusion

1. Cited in Pamela S. Nadell, *Women Who Would Be Rabbis: A History of Women's Ordination 1889–1985* (Boston: Beacon, 1998), page 40. Nadell cites Reva Clar and William M. Kramer, "The Girl Rabbi of the Golden West: The Adventurous Life of Ray Frank in Nevada, California and the Northwest," *Western States Jewish History* 18 (1986): pages 99–111, 223–236, 336–351, which chronicles the extensive press coverage of Frank's career.

2. Aviva Cantor, *Jewish Women/Jewish Men: The Legacy of Patriarchy in Jewish Life* (New York: HarperSanFrancisco/HarperCollins, 1995), page 418.

3. Debra Nussbaum Cohen, "Women Rabbis Still Struggling," *Forward*, August 16, 1991, page 20. Cohen cites a survey on women's and men's incomes conducted by the Central Conference of American Rabbis, the umbrella organization of Reform rabbis.

4. Mary M. Cohen, "A Problem for Purim," *Jewish Exponent*, 15 March 1889, page 1. Cited in Pamela S. Nadell, *Women Who Would Be Rabbis*, pages 2–3.

5. Henrietta Szold, *Reform Advocate*, 20 February 1897, page 9. Cited in Pamela S. Nadell, *Women Who Would Be Rabbis*, pages 53–54.

6. Stephen S. Wise, letter to "My dear Lucile," 31 May 1919, courtesy of Jeremy U. Newman (an heir of Lucile Uhry Newman). Cited in Pamela S. Nadell, *Women Who Would Be Rabbis*, pages 94–95.

7. *Central Conference of American Rabbis Yearbook* 32 (1922), page 51. Cited in Pamela S. Nadell, *Women Who Would Be Rabbis*, pages 71 and 130.

8. "Report of Maurice N. Eisendrath to Board of Trustees, UAHC, NY," 13 December 1970, American Jewish Archives, Cincinnati, Ohio, Ms. Col. #167, Maurice N. Eisendrath Papers, Box 2/6 Sermons and Papers. Cited in Pamela S. Nadell, *Women Who Would Be Rabbis*, page 159.

9. Lucy Dawidowicz, *The Jewish Presence: Essays in Identity and History* (New York: Holt, Rinehart, and Winston, 1977), pages 52–53. Cited by Susannah Heschel in the Introduction to *On Being a Jewish Feminist* (New York: Schocken, 1983), page xx.

10. Cited in Sylvia Barack Fishman, "The Impact of Feminism on American Jewish Life," *American Jewish Year Book*, 1989 (Philadelphia: Jewish Publication Society, 1989), page 53.

11. Blu Greenberg, "Will There Be Orthodox Women Rabbis?" *Judaism* 33:1 (Winter 1984), pages 24–25.

12. Laura Geller, "Encountering the Divine Presence," an address delivered in 1986 and published in *Central Conference of American Rabbis Yearbook*, 1987. Reprinted in *Jewish Women's*

Spirituality: A Sourcebook, eds. Ellen M. Umansky and Dianne Ashton (Boston: Beacon, 1992), page 244.

13. Quoted in Julie Gross, "Reworking the Rabbi's Role," *Lilith* Fall 1990, page 17.

14. Quoted in Julie Gross, "Reworking the Rabbi's Role," page 18.

15. Quoted in Debra Nussbaum Cohen.

16. Judith Hauptman, "Women and the Conservative Synagogue," *Daughters of the King: Women and the Synagogue*, Susan Grossman and Rivka Haut, eds. (Philadelphia: Jewish Publication Society, 1992), page 173.

17. Emily Faust Korzenik, "On Being a Rabbi," *Daughters of the King*, pages 251–252.

18. Nancy S. Hausman, "On Becoming a Cantor," *Daughters of the King*, pages 253–254.

19. Sally J. Priesand, "Looking Backward and Ahead," *A Treasury of Favorite Sermons by Leading American Rabbis*, ed. Sidney Greenberg (Northvale, NJ: Jason Aronson, 1999), pages 197–199.

20. Quoted in Naomi Danis, "*Kol Ishah:* Celebrating Ten Years of Women as Conservative Rabbis," *Lilith*, Fall 1992, page 6.

21. Quoted in Naomi Danis.

22. Haviva Ner-David, 1999 adaptation from Haviva Krasner-Davidson, "Why I'm Applying to Yeshivah U." *Moment*, December 1993, page 55.

23. Cited in Michele Chabin, "The New 'Poseks': Orthodox Women," *The Jewish Week*, October 8, 1999, page 35.

24. Adapted from Chana Henkin, "*Yo'atzot Halakhah*—Fortifying Tradition Through Innovation," *Jewish Action,* Winter 5760/1999, pages 17–18.

25. Cited in Michele Chabin.

26. Sandy Eisenberg Sasso, "Women in the Rabbinate: A Personal Reflection," *Reconstructionist* volume 49, number 5 (March 1984), page 20.

AFTERWORD

And now we have it, *Moonbeams: A Rosh Hodesh Study Guide*! Between the covers of this book there is a world of study and prayer, a world that helps bring us closer to the Almighty. Women studying together is a powerful concept that transcends generations and previous levels of education. Rosh Hodesh, the monthly celebration that mirrors the rhythm of a woman's essence, beckons us to study. The topics are more than interesting; they have the power to change a lifelong paradigm of the place of women within Judaism and ultimately to change lives. We consider, debate, and reflect such issues as modesty and medical ethics, fertility and feminism, all through a Jewish prism. The moon, its light and phases, predictable, consistent, eternal, connects the ancient with the present. As we bask in its glow, we learn and our lives are enriched.

Once more Hadassah senses the spiritual search of American Jewish women. Once more Hadassah acts in an appropriate, responsive way. Each month we grow stronger in our bonds to each other and to our commitment to study. Each month our knowledge grows and, like the sun to the moon, reflects upon and influences our lives and, through us, the lives of those we love. Hadassah's founder Henrietta Szold was right on point when she said, "In the life of the spirit, there is no end that is not a beginning." As we search for a higher spiritual meaning, we end each month a little bit closer to that ideal and begin the next eager for more.

Sandra King, Chair
Hadassah National Jewish Education

ROSH HODESH PRAYER

Rosh Hodesh, the festival of the new moon, has long been observed with a feast and special prayers. Rosh Hodesh can fall on any day of the week, including Shabbat. Sometimes the festival lasts for one day; other times it lasts two days. When in doubt, consult a Jewish calendar.

Because many *Moonbeams* groups will combine study with prayer, we provide you with outlines for typical weekday Rosh Hodesh services. The outlines are intended as guides for those experienced in Jewish prayer. For those who are new to prayer, we recommend that you recruit a prayer leader. Speak with your local Hadassah Jewish Education Chair for recommendations, or consult with a rabbi or cantor of a local synagogue.

We have chosen *Siddur Sim Shalom,* edited by Rabbi Jules Harlow and published in 1985, as our prayer book. *Siddur Sim Shalom,* published by the Rabbinical Assembly and the United Synagogue of America, is the standard daily *siddur* of the Conservative movement. Feel free, however, to use another *siddur.* (Refer to pages 201–202 for recommendations of prayer books.) And, when reading from the *siddur,* feel free to change masculine references to feminine or gender-neutral ones.*

---

*For examples of gender-neutral translations of the traditional liturgy, refer to the English-language prayers in *Siddur Sim Shalom For Shabbat and Festivals.* This 1998 *siddur* also includes the *Amidah* with matriarchs. (The Rabbinical Assembly is currently preparing gender-neutral translations for the weekday liturgy as well.)

For a Rosh Hodesh service, your group will benefit if several members (as well as the prayer leader) are familiar with the proper *nusah*—arrangements, melodies, and rhythms of the prayers—and with the typical places to read aloud and to read silently. Each group, however, can determine these, as well as the amounts of Hebrew and of English. The goal is member participation.

WEEKDAY PRAYER SERVICES

In *Siddur Sim Shalom*, Hebrew prayers are found on even-numbered pages, and English-language translations (as well as transliterations of selected prayers) are found on the facing odd-numbered pages. In general, the page numbers in the following outlines correspond to the Hebrew prayers.

Ma'ariv

Ma'ariv *is the evening service, and in synagogues it is typically held immediately after* minhah. *Rosh Hodesh begins at nightfall (as do all Jewish festivals), and so we begin by outlining the* ma'ariv *service.*

Read pages 200–226 in *Siddur Sim Shalom*. On page 216, in the *Amidah*, include the paragraph for Rosh Hodesh, *ya'aleh veyavo*.

If you do not have a *minyan** leave out the *barkhu* (two lines on page 200), *hatzi kaddish* (bottom of page 208), *kaddish shaleim* (on page 222), and *kaddish yatom* (the mourner's *kaddish* on page 226).

Shaharit

Shaharit *is the morning service and the longest prayer service of the day. On Rosh Hodesh it includes several special components, including reading from the Torah (Numbers 28:1–15) and the Rosh Hodesh musaf service. Musaf literally means addition, and it is recited in remembrance of the additional sacrifice offered on Rosh Hodesh at the Temple in Jerusalem. (Shabbat and festival* shaharit *services also include* musaf.)

The beginning of the service (before page 10 in Siddur Sim Shalom*) is fairly flexible. Many congregations sing* mah tovu *(page 2). Others allow time for private meditation.*

Tallit *and* tefillin *are worn at all weekday* shaharit *services.*

The service officially begins on page 10 of *Siddur Sim Shalom* with the series of blessings marked with the square. The service continues through the bottom of page 14, and on pages 16 to 18 one of the selections is generally read, concluded by the short paragraph at the bottom of page 18. If you have a *minyan*, page 20 follows.

---

*A *minyan* is a quorum of ten Jewish adults. Orthodox Judaism defines the *minyan* as

On pages 22 to 32 the proper Psalm for the day is recited in addition to the Psalm for Rosh Hodesh, which begins on page 34. This is followed by *mizmor shir* on page 50. If you have a *minyan*, mourners recite the *kaddish* on page 52.

Continue with pages 54 though the top half of page 60. Pages 80 to the top half of page 94 follow. If you have a *minyan*, recite the *hatzi kaddish* on the bottom of page 94, and proceed to the *barkhu* at the top of page 96.

All then read from the middle of page 96 through page 120. The only addition to the *Amidah* is *ya'aleh veyavo* on page 114. If you do not have a *minyan*, omit the repetition of the *Amidah* and the *kedushah*. (The *kedushah*, page 108, is only recited with a *minyan*. The *Amidah*, however, can always be done silently.) Omit pages 124 through 136.

After the *Amidah* recite from *Hallel*, page 380 to 389, omitting the top portions of pages 382 and 384 (the paragraphs that are not recited on Rosh Hodesh). If you have a *minyan*, recite *kaddish shaleim*, page 392.

If you have a *minyan*, continue with the weekday Torah service, page 138, and the reading of four *aliyot* from *Parshat Pinhas* Numbers 28:1–15. The breakdown is: 1–3; 3–5; 6–10; 11–15. (When Rosh Hodesh falls on a Monday or Thursday, Numbers 28:1–15 preempts the regular Torah portion.) Conclude the Torah service with the *hatzi kaddish*, page 146, and return the Torah to the Ark, page 150.

If you do not have a *minyan* present, the Torah passage can simply be studied or read from a Bible.

Sing *Ashrei*, pages 152 to 154. Omit *lamenatze'ah* on the bottom of page 154, and continue with *uva letzion*, pages 156 to the top portion of page 158. Remove *tefillin*.

Continue with the Rosh Hodesh *musaf* service. If you have a *minyan*, begin with the *hatzi kaddish* on page 428.

For all, the standard *musaf Amidah* is found on pages 486 to 505. If a *minyan* is not present, do not repeat the *Amidah* aloud and do not sing the *kedushah* aloud. (When a *minyan* is present, read the weekday text of the *kedushah* on page 488.)

If you have a *minyan*, follow the *musaf Amidah* with *kaddish shaleim* that begins on page 158.

All read *Aleinu* on page 160.

If you have a *minyan*, conclude with the mourner's *kaddish* on page 162.

---

ten male Jews age 13 or older. As a result, Orthodox women's prayer groups never recite those portions of the liturgy that require a *minyan*. Conservative, Reconstructionist, and Reform Judaism define the *minyan* as ten Jews, either male or female, age 13 or older. Many Reform congregations, however, do not require a *minyan* for communal prayer.

Minhah

Minhah *is the last service of the Hebrew day. Though it is usually recited with the* ma'ariv *service of the next day, you may recite* minhah *alone.*

Minhah is found on pages 164 to 198 in *Siddur Sim Shalom.* On page 178, in the *Amidah*, include the paragraph for Rosh Hodesh, *ya'aleh veyavo.* Omit pages 188 to 190, as well as the prayer entitled *takhanun*, page 192 and top of page 194. (*Takhanun*, a set of supplicatory prayers, is not recited on Rosh Hodesh.)

If you do not have a *minyan*, omit the *hatzi kaddish* (bottom of page 166), *kedushah* (page 170), repetition of the *Amidah* aloud, *kaddish shaleim* (page 194), and *kaddish yatom*, the mourner's *kaddish* (page 198).

Birkat Hamazon—Grace After Meals

At all meals during Rosh Hodesh, add *ya'aleh veyavo* and the appropriate *Harahaman* (May the Merciful) to the *Birkat Hamazon.*

SUPPLEMENTARY READINGS

We include suggestions for supplementary readings at *shaharit* on Rosh Hodesh. The readings may also be used during *ma'ariv* and *minhah* services.

Hannah's Prayer, from I Samuel 2:1–10

Read Hannah's prayer after the pesukei dezimrah *and before the* Shema *(after reading page 94 of* Siddur Sim Shalom*).*

And Hannah prayed:
My heart exults in the Lord;
I have triumphed through the Lord.
I gloat over my enemies;
I rejoice in Your deliverance.

There is no holy one like the Lord,
Truly, there is none beside You;
There is no rock like our God.

Talk no more with lofty pride,
Let no arrogance cross your lips!
For the Lord is an all-knowing God;
By Him actions are measured.

The bows of the mighty are broken,
And the faltering are girded with strength.
Men once sated must hire out for bread;

Men once hungry hunger no more.
While the barren woman bears seven,
The mother of many is forlorn.
The Lord deals death and gives life,
Casts down into She'ol and raises up.
The Lord makes poor and makes rich;
He casts down, He also lifts high.
He raises the poor from the dust,
Lifts up the needy from the dunghill,
Setting them with nobles,
Granting them seats of honor.
For the pillars of the earth are the Lord's;
He has set the world upon them.
He guards the steps of His faithful,
But the wicked perish in darkness—
For not by strength shall man prevail.

The foes of the Lord shall be shattered;
He will thunder against them in the heavens.
The Lord will judge the ends of the earth.
He will give power to His king,
And triumph to His anointed one.

Ruth's Vow, from Ruth 1:16-17

Ruth vows to remain with Naomi. Read from the Book of Ruth before the Amidah *(after reading page 104 of* Siddur Sim Shalom*).*

But Ruth replied, "Do not urge me to leave you, to turn back and not follow you. For wherever you go, I will go; wherever you lodge, I will lodge; your people shall be my people, and your God my God. Where you die, I will die, and there I will be buried. Thus and more may the Lord do to me if anything but death parts me from you."

Miriam's Song, from Exodus 15:20-21

Read of Miriam the prophetess before Hallel (after reading page 120 of Siddur Sim Shalom *and before turning to page 380).*

Then Miriam the prophetess, Aaron's sister, took a timbrel in her hand, and all the women went out after her in dance with timbrels. And Miriam chanted for them:

Sing to the Lord, for He has triumphed gloriously;
Horse and driver He has hurled into the sea.

Meditation for the New Moon, by Ruth Lerner

Recite the "Meditation for the New Moon" before the Torah reading. (If you have a minyan, recite it after reading page 392 of Siddur Sim Shalom and before turning to page 138. If you do not have a minyan, recite it after reading page 388 and before reading Numbers 28:1–15 from a Bible.)

There are as many ways to view the new moon
as there new days in our lives.

to view a moon
a poet's moon
you need only three things:
a silent spot inside you
a willingness to wait in the dark
and a wily nature that refuses to accept the "Man-in-the-Moon"
as the ultimate authority.

here is one way to observe the new moon:
settle upon a path from which to grasp
the handle of white gold waiting above
find a quiet spot inside your sight.

in the darkness, close your eyes
and cover them, as if blessing the *shabbos* candles

"Praised are You, O *Shekhinah*
who parts the days of the month
calls attention to our covenant and helps us to be
a light upon the earth."

then, slowly open your eyes
and behold the beginning
of time.[1]

The *Tekhine* of the Matriarchs, by Sarah Rebecca Rachel Leah Horowitz

Tekhines are prayers written in Yiddish, primarily for and by women. "The Tekhine of the Matriarchs" was written in the early eighteenth century by Sarah Rebecca Rachel Leah Horowitz, one of the classic writers of Yiddish prayers for women, and we have included an excerpt from the translation by Chava Weissler. Recite the tekhine before the musaf service. (If there is a minyan, read the excerpt after page 428 in Siddur Sim Shalom and before turning to page 486. If there is no minyan, read the excerpt after page 158 before turning to page 486.)

God, Lord of all the worlds,
You created in six days
Heaven and earth and all that is firmly planted
By means of ten sayings.
And on the seventh day, you rested from all those sayings,
And you commanded the holy people
To rest from all words,
Except as they occupy themselves
With the business of heaven and the secret mysteries.
And ignorant folk and women
Should busy themselves in their homes, in the easy language,*
With what they are obligated to do according to the
    commandments.

And thus you have given us festivals for joy
And new moons for remembrance;
And when we were in Jerusalem, city of beauty,
The seat of the dwelling house of our Mother the *Shekhinah*,
    of all beauty,
The heads of the community would consecrate the new moon
    according to eyewitnesses.**
But in this era of exile
Nothing is left to us except the blessing of the new moon.
And it is a time appropriate for supplication, when the
    appointed time has come to bless the new moon.
We spread out our hands to our merciful Father in heaven:
Cause us to return as in days of yore,
For the endurance of the tender young kid§ is failing
As in the noon-day heat.
Our joy, our festivals, and our new moons have ceased.
We are like orphans without a father
And like sheep without a shepherd.

The enemy has stretched out his hand over all that is precious,
And there is none to say, Restore!
God of vengeance, shine forth from Mount Paran!
He who answered our fathers
He will answer us on this new moon,
And that by the merit of the ancient mountains and hills.

---

*"The easy language" refers to Yiddish.

**During the time of the Sanhedrin, the beginning of each month would be decided according to the reports of eyewitnesses who had seen the new moon. This procedure is described in the Mishnah, *Rosh Hashanah* 2:5–7.

§"The tender young kid" refers to the children of Israel.

Sarah, for whose sake you commanded, "Touch not my
anointed ones."

So may it be for her descendants; may all who touch them
be destroyed.

Rebecca, who caused the blessing to come to us; may it soon
be fulfilled for us.

Rachel, whom you promised, "and your children will come
back to their own country;" cause us to return quickly for
her sake.

Leah, whose eyes were weak for fear she would fall to the lot of
the wicked one,* for the sake of her merit, cause our eyes to
shine out of the darkness of exile. The foolish dove has had
her fill of the sword; all the day she is crushed and violated.

The daughter of Abraham our father is under the law of the
exile which degrades her;

The daughter of Abraham dwells under harsh masters; this
one says,

Strike! and his fellow says, Let me be like him.

Wash us thoroughly, for we have already suffered double in
our rebellion.

And renew and bring this month upon us for joy;

Days, months which change from evil to good.

Pride of our power, exalt our horn**;

Give us our bride-price, a good gift without trouble and distress,

By the merit of Jacob, the chosen one among the Patriarchs,

May you multiply his good merit.²

Blessed, Majestic and Terrible, by Merecina of Gerona

*This Hebrew song was composed in the fifteenth century by the lady
Merecina, Rabbanit from Gerona, and was translated by Peter Cole. The
song frequently alludes to biblical passages. Read the song before singing*
Aleinu. *(The* Aleinu *begins in the middle of page 160 of* Siddur Sim
Shalom.)

Blessed, majestic and terrible
you established the Torah in Israel;
happy are they who seek your shelter,
they do not forget the Lord's will.

---

*"The wicked one" refers to Esau. According to a legend in the Talmud (*Bava Batra*
123a), Leah's weak eyes were caused by her incessant weeping, based on her assumption that as the older daughter of Laban, she was destined for Isaac's firstborn, Esau.

**"Horn" is an idiomatic expression in Hebrew for honor.

Salvation is far from the evil...
  though they've known of your Learning and Law;
the sowers in tears will soon exult
  they trust in Him who enables.

It has spread abroad—
  quickly plead, O Lord, my cause
with those who say from Gehenna: Give...
  Our God determines who will prevail.

He is seen, he strikes, and then heals,
  applies the balm before what comes;
exhausts alike the weak and strong,
  and restores well-being to Israel.

I will say what I must, and tell
  the truth to him who taunts me.
Keep slander far away from me;
  Grant peace to the people of Israel.[3]

PRAYER BOOKS

A number of Conservative congregations use the *siddur* translated and arranged by Ben Zion Bokser (published in 1983 by Behrman House). For *ma'ariv*, read pages 95 to 100 and 83 to 94; for *shaharit*, read pages 4 to 80 together with *Hallel* on pages 149–154 and Rosh Hodesh *musaf* on pages 190–199; and for *minhah*, read pages 81 to 94.

The ArtScroll Siddur (published 1987 by Mesorah) has recently come into broad use in Orthodox congregations.[4] For *ma'ariv*, read pages 256 to 283; for *shaharit*, read pages 12 to 181 together with the *Hallel* and Rosh Hodesh *musaf* on pages 632 to 653; and for *minhah*, read pages 232 to 255.

Some Orthodox congregations use *Ha-Siddur Ha-Shalem Daily Prayer Book*, translated and annotated by Philip Birnbaum (Hebrew Publishing Company, 1977). For *ma'ariv*, read pages 189 to 220; for *shaharit*, read pages 49 to 156 together with *Hallel* and Rosh Hodesh *musaf* on pages 565 to 584; and for *minhah*, read pages 157 to 188.

Gates of Prayer: The New Union Prayerbook, published in 1975 by the Central Conference of American Rabbis, offers a basic Reform afternoon, morning, and evening service, as well as four alternative selections that can be recited for evening or morning services (pages 29–114). For *Shaharit*, recite *Hallel* on page 487, and for all services conclude with one of the four versions of *Aleinu* (pages 615–621) and *kaddish* (pages 629–630). In addition, *Gates of Prayer for Shabbat and Weekdays: A*

Gender Sensitive Prayerbook, edited by Chaim Stern, was published in 1994, and includes a weekday evening and morning service.

The Reconstructionist movement's prayer books also use gender neutral language. For weekdays, use *Kol Haneshamah: Daily* published by the Reconstructionist Press in 1996. *Ma'ariv* begins on page 260, *shaharit* on page 2, and *minhah* on page 218.

In addition to standard prayer books, a number of other books include Rosh Hodesh prayer services. Susan Berrin has compiled a Rosh Hodesh ceremony in *Celebrating the New Moon* (Northvale, NJ: Jason Aronson, 1996), on pages 207 to 213. She also includes "Focal Points for Each Month" as well as detailed listings of the Rosh Hodesh changes to weekday and Shabbat liturgy (see pages 214 to 257).

Marcia Falk's *The Book of Blessings: New Jewish Prayers for Daily Life, the Sabbath, and the New Moon Festival* (San Francisco: HarperCollins, 1996) includes original prayer services in Hebrew and English for Rosh Hodesh and related rituals. Refer to pages 323 to 413.

Penina V. Adelman's groundbreaking ritual guide *Miriam's Well: Rituals for Jewish Women Around the Year* (second edition published 1990 by Biblio Press) remains a key resource for Rosh Hodesh, with original stories, meditations, and prayer.

---

1. Ruth Lerner, "Meditation for the New Moon" in *Celebrating the New Moon: A Rosh Chodesh Anthology*, ed. Susan Berrin (Northvale, NJ: Jason Aronson, 1996), pages 182–183.

2. Sarah Rebecca Rachel Leah Horowitz, "The *Tkhine* of the Matriarchs," trans. Chava Weissler, in *The Defiant Muse: Hebrew Feminist Poems from Antiquity to the Present, A Bilingual Anthology*, ed. Shirley Kaufman, Galit Hasan-Rokem, and Tamar S. Hess (New York: Feminist Press of City University of New York, 1999), pages 71, 73.

3. Merecina of Gerona, "Blessed, Majestic and Terrible," trans. Peter Cole, in *The Defiant Muse: Hebrew Feminist Poems*, page 65.

4. *The Rabbinical Council of America Edition of The ArtScroll Siddur*, translation and commentary by Rabbi Nosson Scherman, co-edited by Rabbi Meir Zlotowitz (Brooklyn: Mesorah, 1987).

RECOMMENDED READING

Jewish Feminist Theory and Jewish Feminist Anthologies

Adler, Rachel. *Engendering Judaism: An Inclusive Theology and Ethics.* Philadelphia: Jewish Publication Society, 1998.

Berkovic, Sally. *Straight Talk: My Dilemma as a Modern Orthodox Jewish Woman.* Hoboken, NJ: Ktav, 1999.

Cantor, Aviva. *Jewish Women/Jewish Men: The Legacy of Patriarchy in Jewish Life.* San Francisco: HarperSanFrancisco, 1995.

Fishman, Sylvia Barack. *A Breath of Life: Feminism in the American Jewish Community.* Hanover, NH: University Press of New England, 1993.

Greenberg, Blu. *On Women & Judaism: A View From Tradition.* Philadelphia: Jewish Publication Society, 1998.

Grossman, Susan, and Haut, Rivka, eds. *Daughters of the King: Women and the Synagogue.* Philadelphia: Jewish Publication Society, 1992.

Hadassah International Research Institute on Jewish Women. *Nashim: A Journal of Jewish Women's Studies & Gender Issues.* (A one-year subscription, consisting of two issues of the journal *Nashim*, costs $25/individual; $45/institution; $20/student. Send check and mailing information to HIRIJW, Brandeis University, Mailstop 079, Waltham, MA 02054.)

Heschel, Susannah, ed. *On Being a Jewish Feminist.* New York: Schocken, 1983.

Kaye/Kantrowitz, Melanie, and Klepfisz, Irena, eds. *The Tribe of Dina: A Jewish Women's Anthology*, 2nd ed. Boston: Beacon, 1989. (Stories, memoirs, poems, vignettes.)

Koltun, Elizabeth, ed. *The Jewish Woman: New Perspectives*. New York: Schocken, 1978.

Levitt, Laura. *Jews and Feminism: The Ambivalent Search for Home*. New York and London: Routledge, 1997.

Ochs, Vanessa L. *Words on Fire: One Woman's Journey into the Sacred*. San Diego: Harcourt Brace Jovanovich, 1990. (American feminist memoir on studying with Israeli women scholars.)

Plaskow, Judith. *Standing Again at Sinai: Judaism from a Feminist Perspective*. New York: Harper & Row, 1990.

Schneider, Susan Weidman. *Jewish and Female: Choices and Changes in Our Lives Today*. New York: Touchstone, 1985.

Rudavsky, T. M., ed. *Gender and Judaism: The Transformation of Tradition*. New York/London: New York University Press, 1995.

Jewish Women's Prayers and Rituals

Adelman, Penina. *Miriam's Well: Rituals for Jewish Women Around the Year*, 2nd ed. New York: Biblio, 1996.

Broner, E. M. *Bringing Home the Light: A Jewish Woman's Handbook of Rituals*. San Francisco: Council Oak Books, 2000.

Broner, E. M. *The Telling*, including *The Women's Haggadah* by E. M. Broner and Naomi Nimrod. San Francisco: HarperSanFrancisco, 1993.

Berrin, Susan, ed. *Celebrating the New Moon: A Rosh Chodesh Anthology*. Northvale, NJ: Jason Aronson, 1996.

Cardin, Nina Beth. *The Tapestry of Jewish Time: A Spiritual Guide to Holidays and Life-Cycle Events*. New York: Behrman, 2000.

Cardin, Nina Beth. *Tears of Sorrow, Seeds of Hope: A Jewish Spiritual Companion for Infertility and Pregnancy Loss*. Woodstock, VT: Jewish Lights, 1999.

Falk, Marcia. *The Book of Blessings: New Jewish Prayers for Daily Life, the Sabbath, and the New Moon Festival*. San Francisco: HarperSanFrancisco, 1996.

Kaufman, Shirley, Hasan-Rokem, Galit, and Hess, Tamar S., eds. *The Defiant Muse: Hebrew Feminist Poems from Antiquity to the Present, A Bilingual Anthology*. New York: The Feminist Press at the City University of New York, 1999.

Klirs, Tracy Guren, ed. *The Merit of Our Mothers, Bizhus Imohos: A Bilingual Anthology of Jewish Women's Prayer*. Translated from Yiddish by Tracy Guren Klirs, Ida Cohen Selavan, and Gella Schweid Fishman. Annotated by Faedra Lazar Weiss and Barbara Selya. Cincinnati: Hebrew Union College Press, 1992.

Orenstein, Rabbi Debra, ed. *Lifecycles, Volume 1: Jewish Women on Life Passages and Personal Milestones*. Woodstock, VT: Jewish Lights, 1994.

Rapoport, Nessa. *A Women's Book of Grieving*. Linecuts by Rochelle Rubinstein Kaplan. New York: William Morrow, 1994.

Reimer, Gail Twersky, and Kates, Judith A., eds. *Beginning Anew: A Woman's Companion to the High Holy Days*. New York: Touchstone/Simon & Schuster, 1997.

Umansky, Ellen M., and Ashton, Dianne, eds. *Four Centuries of Jewish Women's Spirituality: A Sourcebook*. Boston: Beacon, 1992.

Weissler, Chava. *Voices of the Matriarchs: Listening to the Prayers of Early Modern Jewish Women*. Boston: Beacon, 1998.

Women's Clothing and Jewish Ritual Garments, Feminist Views

Berger, Aliza. "Wrapped Attention: May Women Wear *Tefillin*." In *Jewish Legal Writings by Women*. Micah Halpern and Chana Safrai, eds. Jerusalem: Urim, 1998. Pages 75–118.

Biale, Rachel. "Women and the *Mitzvot*." In *Women and Jewish Law: The Essential Texts, Their History, and Their Relevance for Today*, 2nd ed. New York: Schocken, 1995. Pages 10–43.

Cayam, Aviva. "Fringe Benefits: Women and *Tzitzit*." In *Jewish Legal Writings by Women*. Micah Halpern and Chana Safrai, eds. Jerusalem: Urim, 1998. Pages 119–142.

Golinkin, Rabbi David. "May Women Wear Tefillin?" *Conservative Judaism* 50:1 (Fall 1997).

Hauptman, Judith. "Ritual." In *Rereading the Rabbis: A Woman's Voice*. Boulder, CO: Westview, 1998. Pages 221–243.

Sered, Susan. *What Makes Women Sick? Maternity, Modesty, and Militarism in Israel*. Hanover, NH: University Press of New England, 2000.

Sered, Susan. "From the Female Perspective." In *Women as Ritual Experts: The Religious Lives of Elderly Jewish Women in Jerusalem*. New York: Oxford University Press, 1992. Pages 65–86.

Weiss, Avraham. *Women at Prayer: A Halakhic Analysis of Women's Prayer Groups*. Hoboken, NJ: Ktav, 1990.

Women's Clothing and Jewish Ritual Garments, Traditional Orthodox Views

Brayer, Menachem M. *The Jewish Woman in Rabbinic Literature, Volume I: A Psychosocial Perspective. The Jewish Woman in Rabbinic Literature, Volume II: A Psychohistorical Perspective.* Hoboken, NJ: Ktav, 1986.

Frankiel, Tamar. *The Voice of Sarah: Feminine Spirituality and Traditional Judaism.* San Francisco: HarperSanFrancisco, 1990.

Meiselman, Moshe. *Jewish Woman in Jewish Law.* New York: Ktav and Yeshiva University Press, 1978.

Jewish Self-Hatred

Arendt, Hannah. *Rahel Varnhagen: The Life of a Jewess, First Complete Edition.* Liliane Weissberg, ed. Richard and Clara Winston, trans. Baltimore: Johns Hopkins University Press, 1997.

Aschheim, Steven. *Brothers and Strangers: The East European Jew in German and German Jewish Consciousness, 1800–1923.* Madison: University of Wisconsin Press, 1982.

Baum, Charlotte, Hyman, Paula, and Michel, Sonya. *The Jewish Woman in America.* New York: Dial, 1976. (See "Pearls Around the Neck, A Stone Around the Heart: The Changing Image of the Jewish Woman in Literature" and "From Veneration to Vituperation: Jewish Women Today," pages 163–261.)

Fishman, Sylvia Barack. "I of the Beholder: Jews and Gender in Film and Popular Culture." Hadassah International Research Institute on Jewish Women at Brandeis University. To order one complimentary copy, contact the HIRIJW by phone at 781-736-2064, by fax at 781-736-2070, or by email at hrijw@brandeis.edu.

Hertzberg, Arthur, ed. *The Zionist Idea: A Historical Analysis and Reader.* Garden City, NY: Doubleday and Herzl Press, 1959. (Refer to Moses Hess, Joseph Hayyim Brenner, Joseph Klatzkin, Aaron David Gordon.)

Pogrebin, Letty Cottin. "From *Marjorie Morningstar* to *Dirty Dancing*: Finding Myself at the Movies." In *Deborah, Golda, and Me: Being Jewish and Female in America.* New York: Crown, 1991. Pages 256–271.

Roth, Philip. *Goodbye, Columbus and Five Short Stories.* New York: Vintage, 1987. (First published 1959.)

Roth, Philip. *Portnoy's Complaint.* New York: Touchstone, 1969.

Wertheimer, Jack. *Unwelcome Strangers: East European Jews in Imperial Germany.* New York: Oxford University Press, 1987.

Medical Ethics

Abraham, Abraham S. *Medical Halachah for Everyone: A Comprehensive Guide to Jewish Medical Law in Sickness and Health*, 2nd rev. ed. Jerusalem/New York: Feldheim, 1980.

Feldman, David M. *Health and Medicine in the Jewish Tradition: L'Hayyim—To Life*. New York: Crossroad, 1986.

Kahn, Susan. "Rabbis and Reproduction: The Uses of New Reproductive Technologies Among Ultraorthodox Jews in Israel." Hadassah International Research Institute on Jewish Women at Brandeis University. To order one complimentary copy of the paper, contact the HIRIJW by phone at 781-736-2064, by fax at 781-736-2070, or by email at hrijw@brandeis.edu.

Rosner, Fred. *Modern Medicine and Jewish Ethics*. Hoboken, NJ/New York: Ktav/Yeshiva University Press, 1986.

Reclaiming Our Jewish Foremothers

Antler, Joyce. *The Journey Home: Jewish Women and the American Century*. New York: Free Press, 1997.

Antonelli, Judith S. *In the Image of God: A Feminist Commentary on The Torah*. Northvale, NJ: Jason Aronson, 1995.

Aschkenasy, Nehama. *Eve's Journey: Feminine Images in Hebraic Literary Tradition*. Philadelphia: University of Pennsylvania Press, 1986.

Buchmann, Christina, and Spiegel, Celina, eds. *Out of the Garden: Women Writers on the Bible*. New York: Fawcett Columbine, 1994.

Dame, Enid; Rivlin, Lily; and Wenkart, Henny, eds. *Which Lilith? Feminist Writers Re-Create the World's First Woman*. Northvale, NJ: Jason Aronson, 1998. (Essays, stories, poems, and personal reflections on Lilith.)

Frankel, Ellen. *The Five Books of Miriam: A Woman's Commentary on the Torah*. New York: Grosset/Putnam, 1996.

Frymer-Kensky, Tikva. *In the Wake of the Goddesses: Women, Culture, and the Biblical Transformation of Pagan Myth*. New York: Free Press, 1992.

Goldstein, Rabbi Elyse. *ReVisions: Seeing Torah Through a Feminist Lens*. Woodstock, VT: Jewish Lights, 1998.

Henry, Sondra, and Taitz, Emily. *Written Out of History: Our Jewish Foremothers*. Fresh Meadows, NY: Biblio Press, 1990. (First published 1978.)

Labowitz, Shoni. *God, Sex and Women of the Bible: Discovering Our Sensual, Spiritual Selves.* New York: Simon & Schuster, 1998.

Moskowitz, Faye, ed. *Her Face in the Mirror: Jewish Women on Mothers and Daughters.* Boston: Beacon, 1994.

Orenstein, Rabbi Debra, and Litman, Rabbi Jane Rachel, eds. *Lifecycles, Volume 2: Jewish Women on Biblical Themes in Contemporary Life.* Woodstock, VT: Jewish Lights, 1994.

Pogrebin, Letty Cottin. *Deborah, Golda, and Me: Being Jewish and Female in America.* New York: Crown, 1991.

Weinberg, Sydney Stahl. *The World of Our Mothers: The Lives of Immigrant Jewish Women.* Chapel Hill: University of North Carolina Press, 1988.

Ba'alot Teshuvah

Aviad, Janet. *Return to Judaism: Religious Renewal in Israel.* Chicago: University of Chicago Press, 1983.

Bauer, Agi L. *"Black" Becomes a Rainbow: The Mother of a Baal Teshuvah Tells Her Story.* New York: Feldheim, 1991.

Danzger, M. Herbert. *Returning to Tradition: The Contemporary Revival of Orthodox Judaism.* New Haven, CT: Yale University Press, 1989.

Davidman, Lynn. *Tradition in a Rootless World: Women Turn to Orthodox Judaism.* Berkeley: University of California Press, 1991.

Harris, Lis. *Holy Days: The World of a Hasidic Family.* New York: Summit, 1985.

Kaufman, Debra Renee. *Rachel's Daughters: Newly Orthodox Jewish Women.* New Brunswick, NJ: Rutgers University Press, 1991.

Klinghoffer, David. *The Lord Will Gather Me In: My Journey to Jewish Orthodoxy.* New York: Free Press, 1999.

Roiphe, Anne. *Lovingkindness: A Novel.* New York: Summit, 1987.

Tatz, Akiva. *Anatomy of a Search: Personal Drama in the Teshuvah Revolution.* Brooklyn: Mesorah, 1987.

Women and Israeli Law

Reinharz, Shulamith. "Timeline of Women and Women's Issues in the Yishuv and Israel." Hadassah International Research Institute on Jewish Women at Brandeis University. To order one complimentary copy of the paper, contact the HIRIJW by phone at 781-736-2064, by fax at 781-736-2070, or by email at hrijw@brandeis.edu.

Swirksi, Barbara, and Safir, Marilyn P., eds. *Calling the Equality Bluff: Women in Israel*. New York: Pergamon, 1991.

Women Rabbis

Goldstein, Rabbi Elyse, ed. *A Woman's Torah Commentary: New Insights from Women Rabbis on the 54 Weekly Torah Portions*. Woodstock, VT: Jewish Lights, 2000.

Firestone, Rabbi Tirzah. *With Roots in Heaven: One Woman's Passionate Journey into the Heart of her Faith*. New York/London: Dutton/Penguin, 1998.

Nadell, Pamela S. *Women Who Would Be Rabbis: A History of Women's Ordination, 1889–1985*. Boston: Beacon, 1998.

Ner-David, Haviva. *Life on the Fringes: A Feminist Journey Towards Traditional Rabbinic Ordination*. Newton, MA: JFL Books, 2000.

Priesand, Rabbi Sally. *Judaism and the New Woman*. New York: Behrman, 1975.

ACKNOWLEDGMENT OF SOURCES

We gratefully acknowledge permission to use the copyrighted material listed below.

All selections from the Bible are reprinted from *The TANAKH: The New JPS Translation According to the Traditional Jewish Text*. Copyright © 1985 by The Jewish Publication Society. Reprinted with the permission of the publisher. (In some cases, the authors have adapted the JPS translations to correspond with accepted English translations of rabbinic commentary or other texts.)

The Babylonian Talmud, edited by I. Epstein, London, copyright © by The Soncino Press Ltd. Excerpts from the English translations of *Sanhedrin* 42a, 47a, 65b, and 67b, *Hullin* 11b and 60b, *Nedarim* 30b, *Kiddushin* 31a, 33b–34a, and 41b, *Shabbat* 118b, 140b, and 156b, *Menahot* 43a, *Sukkah* 11a, *Eiruvin* 53b–54a and 96a–96b. *Ketubot* 65a and 72a–72b, *Berakhot* 10a and 24a, *Yoma* 9b and 47a, *Baba Batra* 123a, *Baba Metzia* 87a *Yevamot* 63b, *Megillah* 12a–12b, 13a, and 23a, *Sotah* 9b, 11b, and 12a–13a, *Ta'anit* 9a, *Pesahim* 54a and 62b, and *Avodah Zarah* 18a–b, *Shevuot* 30a. All translations from the *gemara* are reprinted with the permission of the publisher. (In some cases, the authors have slightly adapted the Soncino translations to correspond with accepted English translations of the Bible or other texts.)

The Midrash Rabbah, edited by H. Freedman and Maurice Simon, London, copyright © by The Soncino Press Ltd., 1983. Excerpts from the English translations of *Exodus Rabbah* 15:6 and 15:9, *Ruth Rabbah* 4:6, and *Numbers Rabbah* 1:2 and 1.3, and *Esther Rabbah* 5:1. All translations from *The Midrash Rabbah* are reprinted with the permission of the publisher. (In some cases, the authors have slightly adapted the Soncino translations to correspond with accepted English translations of the Bible or other texts.)

Chapter 1: The History and Observance of Rosh Ḥodesh

The Zohar, edited by Maurice Simon, London, copyright © by The Soncino Press Ltd., 1983; *Zohar Bereishit*, 19b–20a and 169b, *Zohar Vayikra*, 77a. English translations used with the permission of the publisher. (Slightly adapted by authors.)

Chapter 2: *Kippah, Tallit,* and *Tefillin*

Louis Ginzberg, Responsum. Copyright © 1996 by The Jewish Theological Seminary. Reprinted with the permission of The Jewish Theological Seminary.

Ovadiah Yosef, *Yehaveh Da'at*. Copyright © 1972 by the Responsa Project, Bar-Ilan University. Reprinted with the permission of the Responsa Project.

Yosef Karo, *Shulḥan Arukh, Oraḥ Ḥayyim*; Rema (Moshe Isserles) to *Shulḥan Arukh, Oraḥ Hayyim*; Moshe Feinstein, *Igrot Moshe, Oraḥ Ḥayyim*; *Mekhilta* on *Parshat Bo*; Yeḥiel Epstein, *Arukh HaShulḥan, Oraḥ Ḥayyim*. Selections are from *Woman and the Mitzvot: A Guide to Rabbinic Sources*, Volume I, by Getsel Ellinson. Copyright © 1986 by the Department for Torah Education and Culture in the Diaspora, World Zionist Organization. Reprinted with the permission of the World Zionist Organization.

Eliezer Berkovits, *Jewish Women in Time and Torah*. Copyright © 1990 by Eliezer Berkovits. Reprinted with the permission of Ktav Publishing, Inc.

Chapter 3: Modesty

Moshe Feinstein, *Igrot Moshe, Yoreh De'ah, Oraḥ Ḥayyim*, and *Even HaEzer;* Jehiel Jacob Weinberg, *Seridei Eish*; and Ovadiah Yosef, *Yabia Omer*. Copyright © 1972 by the Responsa Project, Bar-Ilan University. Reprinted with the permission of the Responsa Project.

Susan Grossman and Rivka Haut, *Daughters of the King: Women and the Synagogue*. Copyright © 1992 by Susan Grossman and Rivka Haut. Reprinted with the permission of the Jewish Publication Society of America.

Susan Starr Sered, excerpts from "The Scrutizined Body," *What Makes Women Sick? Maternity, Modesty, and Militarism in Israeli Society*.

Chapter 4: Jewish Self-Hatred

Chapter 5: Medical Ethics

reprinted with the permission of the author and of *Lilith*, the award-winning independent Jewish women's magazine, lilithmag@aol.com; www.lilithmag.com. For subscriptions or a sample copy call toll free 1-888-2-LILITH (or in New York 212-254-5484).

Chapter 8: Women and Israeli Law

Alice Miller vs. Minister of Defense. 49 (4) P.D. 94. English translation copyright © 1998 by Israel Law Review. Reprinted with the permission of the publisher.

Dr. Naomi Nevo vs. The National Court of Labor Relations Et Alia. 749 (4) P.D. 44. Translated from the Hebrew for Hadassah by Barbara Harshav.

Leah Shakdiel vs. Minister of Religious Affairs Et Alia. 42 (2) P.D. 221. English translation copyright © 1992 by The Israel Bar-Publishing House. Reprinted with the permission of the publisher.

Anat Hoffman Et Alia versus The Supervisor of the Western Wall Et Alia and Susan Alter Et Alia versus The Minister of Religion Et Alia. 48 (2) P.D. 265. Translated from the Hebrew for Hadassah by Barbara Harshav.

Chapter 9: Women Rabbis

Debra S. Cantor, et alia, Letter to the Faculty of the Jewish Theological Seminary. Reprinted with the permission of Debra S. Cantor.

Blu Greenberg, "Will There Be Orthodox Rabbis?" Copyright © 1984 by Blu Greenberg. Reprinted with the permission of the author.

Laura Geller, "Encountering the Divine Presence." Copyright © 1986 by Laura Geller. Reprinted with the permission of the author.

Judith Hauptman, "Women and the Conservative Synagogue." Copyright © 1992 by Susan Grossman and Rivka Haut. Reprinted with the permission of the Jewish Publication Society of America.

Emily Faust Korzenik, "On Being a Rabbi." Copyright © 1992 by Susan Grossman and Rivka Haut. Reprinted with the permission of the Jewish Publication Society of America.

Nancy S. Hausman, "On Becoming a Cantor." Copyright © 1992 by Susan Grossman and Rivka Haut. Reprinted with the permission of the Jewish Publication Society of America.

Sally J. Priesand, "Looking Backward and Ahead." Copyright © 1999 by Jason Aronson, Inc. Reprinted with the permission of the publisher.

Haviva Ner-David, "Why I'm Applying to Yeshivah U." Copyright © 1993 by Haviva Krasner. Revised by the author in 1999. Reprinted with the permission of the author.

Chana Henkin, "*Yo'atzot Halakhah*—Fortifying Tradition Through Innovation." Copyright © 1999 by Chana Henkin. Reprinted with the permission of the author and *Jewish Action* magazine.

Appendix A

Ruth Lerner, "Meditation for the New Moon," in *Celebrating the New Moon: A Rosh Chodesh Anthology*, ed. Susan Berrin. Copyright © 1996 by Susan Berrin. Reprinted with permission of the author and editor, and reprinted by permission of the publisher, Jason Aronson, Inc., Northvale, NJ 1999.

Chava Weissler, translator of "The *Tekhine* of the Matriarchs" by Sarah Rebecca Rachel Leah Horowitz, in *Voices of the Matriarchs* by Chava Weissler. Copyright © 1998 by Chava Weissler. Reprinted by the permission of Beacon Press, Boston.

Merecina of Gerona, untitled poem [Blessed, Majestic, and Terrible], as translated by Peter Cole, is reprinted by permission of The Feminist Press at the City University of New York, from *The Defiant Muse: Hebrew Feminist Poems from Antiquity to the Present, A Bilingual Anthology*, edited by Shirley Kaufman, Galit Hasan-Rokem, and Tamar S. Hess. English translation © 1999 by Peter Cole.

Notes

NOTES

NOTES

Notes

NOTES

Notes

ABOUT HADASSAH

Hadassah, the Women's Zionist Organization of America, is dedicated to enhancing the quality of American Jewish life, to improving health care in Israel, and to forging stronger connections between America and Israel. Founded by Henrietta Szold in 1912, Hadassah continues to follow her exhortation: "Dream great dreams, and then take practical steps to make them a reality."

Hadassah's work ranges from international projects to individual enrichment, from the founding and maintaining of state-of-the-art hospitals in Israel to organizing adult bat mitzvah ceremonies throughout the Unites States.

Hadassah is the largest Zionist organization and the largest women's organization in America. Its more than three hundred thousand members come from all walks of American Jewish life to participate in Hadassah's programs. Examples of the educational programs include Hebrew classes, adult study groups on Jewish themes, preparation for adult bat mitzvah ceremonies, Jewish family education programs, and Zionist youth groups. Hadassah also works to increase health awareness and to advocate for political change on issues of importance to American Jewish women.

Hadassah's publications include an award-winning monthly magazine that deals with a broad variety of topics of concern to the American Jewish community. Hadassah also publishes educational books and the curricula for its educational programs.

Through its diverse programs, Hadassah encourages members to strengthen their partnership with Israel, enhance their own Jewish commitment, and realize their potential as a dynamic force in American society.

ADDITIONAL HADASSAH PUBLICATIONS

True to its roots as a study circle, Hadassah encourages its members to explore the many facets of Jewish history and culture, and to aid members in doing so the National Jewish Education Department publishes study guides and other resources on a wide variety of topics. Unless indicated otherwise, for purchase, call the National Hadassah Order Department at 1-800-880-9455.

Jewish Women Living the Challenge: A Hadassah Compendium

Carol Diament, editor; programming ideas by Claudia R. Chernov and Leora Tanenbaum
Collection of essays on Jewish women's issues, with extensive programming ideas. Order #R797. $15 Hadassah members, $20 non-members.

Ribcage: Israeli Women's Fiction

Carol Diament and Lily Rattok, editors
Study guide contains short stories in English translation. Order #R492. $10 Hadassah members, $15 non-members.

Jewish Marital Status

Carol Diament, editor
Anthology of essays offering Jewish viewpoints on dating, sex, intimate relationships, marriage, and the end of marriage. Special price $25. Call Hadassah National Jewish Education Department at 1-212-303-8167.

A Companion Guide to Jewish Marital Status

Ellen Singer
Programming and activities on *Jewish Marital Status*. Order #R226. $3 Hadassah members, $5 non-members.

Judaism and Ecology

Carol Diament, editor

Study guide on Jewish environmental values.
Order #R229. $7 Hasassah members,
$11 non-members.

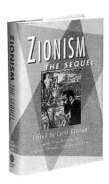

Zionism: The Sequel

Carol Diament, editor

Essays on the meanings of contemporary Zionism.
Part I, "The Israel-Diaspora Debate," introduced by
Gideon Shimoni, analyzes the relationship of diaspora
Jews to the State of Israel. Part II, "Zionism For and
Against Itself," introduced by Arnold Eisen, presents
personal statements from Israeli and American Jewish
thinkers—from the extreme Right to the extreme Left,
from the secular to the ultra-Orthodox, and more.
Order #R795. $18 Hadassah members,
$25 non-members.

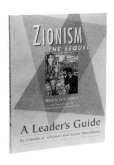

Zionism: The Sequel: A Leader's Guide

Claudia Chernov and Leora Tanenbaum

The *Leader's Guide* to *Zionism: The Sequel* provides
step-by-step instructions for leading a year-long study
group. Order #R915. $10.

Israeli and American Jews: Understanding and Misunderstanding

Carol Diament, editor

Study guide addresses the seemingly irreconcilable
differences between the two leading Jewish populations
of the world. Order #R222. $8 Hadassah members,
$12 non-members.

An American Zionist Tapestry

Lawrence Grossman

Study guide on the leaders of American Zionism. Order #R252. $4 Hadassah members, $6 non-members.

A Zionist Tapestry

Monty Penkower

Study guide presents the major thinkers and ideas of Zionism and their implications for contemporary Zionist thought and action. Order #R251. $4 Hadassah members, $6 non-members.

Images of Jerusalem: City of David in Modern Hebrew Literature

Rochelle Furstenberg

Study guide in honor of the 3000th anniversary of Jerusalem as the capital of the Jewish people. Order #R613. $10 Hadassah members, $13 non-members.

Reflections on Jerusalem: City of David in Classical Texts

N. Rothenberg, L. Tanenbaum, and S. Silverman

Study guide in honor of the 3000th anniversary of Jerusalem as the capital of the Jewish people. Order #R614. $6 Hadassah members, $9 non-members.

Understanding the Holocaust: How it Happened

Jack Wertheimer

Study unit focuses on the Holocaust itself and on the factors that permitted this tragedy to occur. Order #R221. $2 Hadassah members, $3 non-members.

The Talmud and You

Aaron Kirschenbaum

Two-book series on the Talmud's relevance to daily life. Order #R232 for Book 1 (Units I and II) and #R233 for Book 2 (Units III and IV). Each book $2 Hadassah members, $3 non-members.

Leader's Guide to the Book of Samuel

Naomi Sarlin

The first study guide in Hadassah's Bible series. Order #R199. $1.50 Hadassah members, $2.50 non-members.

Leader's Guide to the Book of Jeremiah

Aaron Kirschenbaum

Study the prophetic tradition in Judaism. Order #R197. $3 Hadassah members, $5 non-members.

Leader's Guide to the Book of Psalms

Nehama Leibowitz

Study one of Judaism's most beloved texts with our era's great Bible scholar. Order #R198. $3 Hadassah members, $5 non-members.

About JEWISH LIGHTS Publishing

People of all faiths and backgrounds yearn for books that attract, engage, educate and spiritually inspire.

Our principal goal is to stimulate thought and help all people learn about who the Jewish People are, where they come from, and what the future can be made to hold. While people of our diverse Jewish heritage are the primary audience, our books speak to people in the Christian world as well and will broaden their understanding of Judaism and the roots of their own faith.

We bring to you authors who are at the forefront of spiritual thought and experience. While each has something different to say, they all say it in a voice that you can hear.

Our books are designed to welcome you and then to engage, stimulate and inspire. We judge our success not only by whether or not our books are beautiful and commercially successful, but by whether or not they make a difference in your life.

We at Jewish Lights take great care to produce beautiful books that present meaningful spiritual content in a form that reflects the art of making high quality books. Therefore, we want to acknowledge those who contributed to the production of this book.

Stuart M. Matlins, Publisher

PRODUCTION
Marian B. Wallace & Bridgett Taylor

EDITORIAL
Sandra Korinchak, Emily Wichland,
Martha McKinney & Amanda Dupuis

COVER & TEXT PRINTING AND BINDING
Versa Press, East Peoria, Illinois

 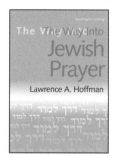 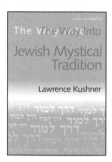 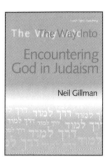

Spirituality & More

These Are the Words: *A Vocabulary of Jewish Spiritual Life*

by *Arthur Green*

What are the most essential ideas, concepts and terms that an educated person needs to know about Judaism? From *Adonai* (My Lord) to *zekhut* (merit), this enlightening and entertaining journey through Judaism teaches us the 149 core Hebrew words that constitute the basic vocabulary of Jewish spiritual life. 6 x 9, 304 pp, HC, ISBN 1-58023-024-5 **$21.95**

The Enneagram and Kabbalah: *Reading Your Soul*

by *Rabbi Howard A. Addison*

Combines two of the most powerful maps of consciousness known to humanity—The Tree of Life (the *Sefirot*) from the Jewish mystical tradition of *Kabbalah*, and the nine-pointed Enneagram—and shows how, together, they can provide a powerful tool for self-knowledge, critique, and transformation. 6 x 9, 176 pp, Quality PB, ISBN 1-58023-001-6 **$15.95**

Embracing the Covenant
Converts to Judaism Talk About Why & How

Ed. and with Intros. by *Rabbi Allan L. Berkowitz* and *Patti Moskovitz*

Through personal experiences of 20 converts to Judaism, this book illuminates reasons for converting, the quest for a satisfying spirituality, the appeal of the Jewish tradition and how conversion has changed lives—the convert's, and the lives of those close to them.
6 x 9, 192 pp, Quality PB, ISBN 1-879045-50-8 **$15.95**

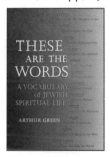    

Shared Dreams: *Martin Luther King, Jr. and the Jewish Community*
by Rabbi Marc Schneier; Preface by Martin Luther King III
6 x 9, 240 pp, HC, ISBN 1-58023-062-8 **$24.95**

Mystery Midrash: *An Anthology of Jewish Mystery & Detective Fiction*
Ed. by Lawrence W. Raphael; Preface by Joel Siegel, ABC's *Good Morning America*
6 x 9, 304 pp, Quality PB, ISBN 1-58023-055-5 **$16.95**

The Jewish Gardening Cookbook: *Growing Plants & Cooking for Holidays & Festivals*
by Michael Brown 6 x 9, 224 pp, HC, Illus., ISBN 1-58023-004-0 **$21.95**

Wandering Stars: *An Anthology of Jewish Fantasy & Science Fiction* Ed. by Jack Dann; Intro. by Isaac Asimov 6 x 9, 272 pp, Quality PB, ISBN 1-58023-005-9 **$16.95**

More Wandering Stars
An Anthology of Outstanding Stories of Jewish Fantasy and Science Fiction
Ed. by Jack Dann; Intro. by Isaac Asimov 6 x 9, 192 pp, Quality PB, ISBN 1-58023-063-6 **$16.95**

A Heart of Wisdom: *Making the Jewish Journey from Midlife through the Elder Years*
Ed. by Susan Berrin; Foreword by Harold Kushner
6 x 9, 384 pp, Quality PB, ISBN 1-58023-051-2 **$18.95**; HC, ISBN 1-879045-73-7 **$24.95**

Sacred Intentions: *Daily Inspiration to Strengthen the Spirit, Based on Jewish Wisdom*
by Rabbi Kerry M. Olitzky and Rabbi Lori Forman
4½ x 6½, 448 pp, Quality PB, ISBN 1-58023-061-X **$15.95**

Spirituality

My People's Prayer Book: *Traditional Prayers, Modern Commentaries*

Ed. by *Dr. Lawrence A. Hoffman*

This momentous, critically-acclaimed series is truly a people's prayer book, one that provides a diverse and exciting commentary to the traditional liturgy. It will help modern men and women find new wisdom and guidance in Jewish prayer, and bring liturgy into their lives. Each book includes Hebrew text, modern translation, and commentaries *from all perspectives* of the Jewish world. Vol. 1—*The Sh'ma and Its Blessings*, 7 x 10, 168 pp, HC, ISBN 1-879045-79-6 **$23.95**
Vol. 2—*The Amidah*, 7 x 10, 240 pp, HC, ISBN 1-879045-80-X **$23.95**
Vol. 3—*P'sukei D'zimrah* (Morning Psalms), 7 x 10, 240 pp, HC, ISBN 1-879045-81-8 **$23.95**
Vol. 4—*Seder K'riyat Hatorah* (Shabbat Torah Service), 7 x 10, 240 pp, ISBN 1-879045-82-6 **$23.95**
(Avail. Sept. 2000)

Voices from Genesis: *Guiding Us through the Stages of Life*

by *Dr. Norman J. Cohen*

In a brilliant blending of modern *midrash* (finding contemporary meaning from biblical texts) and the life stages of Erik Erikson's developmental psychology, the characters of Genesis come alive to give us insights for our own journeys. 6 x 9, 192 pp, HC, ISBN 1-879045-75-3 **$21.95**

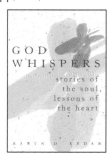

God Whispers: *Stories of the Soul, Lessons of the Heart*
by Rabbi Karyn D. Kedar 6 x 9, 176 pp, Quality PB, ISBN 1-58023-088-1 **$15.95**;
HC, ISBN 1-58023-023-7 **$19.95**

Being God's Partner: *How to Find the Hidden Link Between Spirituality and Your Work*
by Rabbi Jeffrey K. Salkin; Intro. by Norman Lear AWARD WINNER!
6 x 9, 192 pp, Quality PB, ISBN 1-879045-65-6 **$16.95**; HC, ISBN 1-879045-37-0 **$19.95**

ReVisions: *Seeing Torah through a Feminist Lens* AWARD WINNER!
by Rabbi Elyse Goldstein 5½ x 8½, 208 pp, HC, ISBN 1-58023-047-4 **$19.95**

Soul Judaism: *Dancing with God into a New Era*
by Rabbi Wayne Dosick 5½ x 8½, 304 pp, Quality PB, ISBN 1-58023-053-9 **$16.95**

Finding Joy: *A Practical Spiritual Guide to Happiness* AWARD WINNER!
by Rabbi Dannel I. Schwartz with Mark Hass
6 x 9, 192 pp, Quality PB, ISBN 1-58023-009-1 **$14.95**; HC, ISBN 1-879045-53-2 **$19.95**

The Empty Chair: *Finding Hope and Joy—*
Timeless Wisdom from a Hasidic Master, Rebbe Nachman of Breslov AWARD WINNER!
Adapted by Moshe Mykoff and the Breslov Research Institute
4 x 6, 128 pp, Deluxe PB, 2-color text, ISBN 1-879045-67-2 **$9.95**

The Gentle Weapon: *Prayers for Everyday and Not-So-Everyday Moments*
Adapted from the Wisdom of Rebbe Nachman of Breslov by Moshe Mykoff and
S. C. Mizrahi, with the Breslov Research Institute
4 x 6, 144 pp, Deluxe PB, 2-color text, ISBN 1-58023-022-9 **$9.95**

"Who Is a Jew?" *Conversations, Not Conclusions* by Meryl Hyman
6 x 9, 272 pp, Quality PB, ISBN 1-58023-052-0 **$16.95**; HC, ISBN 1-879045-76-1 **$23.95**

Jewish Meditation

Discovering Jewish Meditation
Instruction & Guidance for Learning an Ancient Spiritual Practice
by *Nan Fink Gefen*

Gives readers of any level of understanding the tools to learn the practice of Jewish meditation on your own, starting you on the path to a deep spiritual and personal connection to God and to greater insight about your life. 6 x 9, 208 pp, Quality PB, ISBN 1-58023-067-9 **$16.95**

Meditation from the Heart of Judaism: *Today's Teachers Share Their Practices, Techniques, and Faith*
Ed. by *Avram Davis*

A "how-to"guide for both beginning and experienced meditators, drawing on the wisdom of 22 masters of meditation who explain why and how they meditate. A detailed compendium of the experts' "best practices" offers advice and starting points. 6 x 9, 256 pp, Quality PB, ISBN 1-58023-049-0 **$16.95**; HC, ISBN 1-879045-77-X **$21.95**

The Way of Flame
A Guide to the Forgotten Mystical Tradition of Jewish Meditation
by *Avram Davis* 4½ x 8, 176 pp, Quality PB, ISBN 1-58023-060-1 **$15.95**

  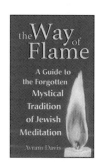 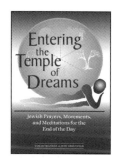 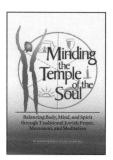

Entering the Temple of Dreams: *Jewish Prayers, Movements, and Meditations for the End of the Day* by *Tamar Frankiel* and *Judy Greenfeld*

Nighttime spirituality is much more than bedtime prayers! Here, you'll uncover deeper meaning to familiar nighttime prayers—and learn to combine the prayers with movements and meditations to enhance your physical and psychological well-being. 7 x 10, 192 pp, Illus., Quality PB, ISBN 1-58023-079-2 **$16.95**

Minding the Temple of the Soul: *Balancing Body, Mind, and Spirit through Traditional Jewish Prayer, Movement, and Meditation*
by *Tamar Frankiel* and *Judy Greenfeld*

This new spiritual approach to physical health introduces readers to a spiritual tradition that affirms the body and enables them to reconceive their bodies in a more positive light. Focuses on traditional Jewish prayers, with exercises, movements, and meditations. 7 x 10, 184 pp, Quality PB, Illus., ISBN 1-879045-64-8 **$16.95**; Audiotape of the Blessings, Movements and Meditations (60-min. cassette), JN01 **$9.95**; Videotape of the Movements and Meditations (46-min. VHS), S507 **$20.00**

Spirituality—The Kushner Series

Honey from the Rock, Special Anniversary Edition
An Introduction to Jewish Mysticism
by *Lawrence Kushner*

An insightful and absorbing introduction to the ten gates of Jewish mysticism and how it applies to daily life. "The easiest introduction to Jewish mysticism you can read."
6 x 9, 176 pp, Quality PB, ISBN 1-58023-073-3 **$15.95**

Eyes Remade for Wonder
The Way of Jewish Mysticism and Sacred Living
A Lawrence Kushner Reader

Intro. by *Thomas Moore*

Whether you are new to Kushner or a devoted fan, you'll find inspiration here. With samplings from each of Kushner's works, and a generous amount of new material, this book is to be read and reread, each time discovering deeper layers of meaning in our lives.
6 x 9, 240 pp, Quality PB, ISBN 1-58023-042-3 **$16.95**; HC, ISBN 1-58023-014-8 **$23.95**

Invisible Lines of Connection
Sacred Stories of the Ordinary
by *Lawrence Kushner* AWARD WINNER!

Through his everyday encounters with family, friends, colleagues and strangers, Kushner takes us deeply into our lives, finding flashes of spiritual insight in the process.
6 x 9, 160 pp, Quality PB, ISBN 1-879045-98-2 **$15.95**; HC, ISBN 1-879045-52-4 **$21.95**

    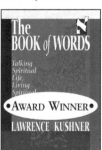

The Book of Letters
A Mystical Hebrew Alphabet AWARD WINNER!
by Lawrence Kushner
Popular HC Edition, 6 x 9, 80 pp, 2-color text, ISBN 1 879045-00-1 **$24.95**; *Deluxe Gift Edition*, 9 x 12, 80 pp, HC, 2-color text, ornamentation, slipcase, ISBN 1-879045-01-X **$79.95**; *Collector's Limited Edition*, 9 x 12, 80 pp, HC, gold-embossed pages, hand-assembled slipcase. With silkscreened print. Limited to 500 signed and numbered copies, ISBN 1-879045-04-4 **$349.00**

The Book of Words
Talking Spiritual Life, Living Spiritual Talk AWARD WINNER!
by Lawrence Kushner 6 x 9, 160 pp, Quality PB, 2-color text, ISBN 1-58023-020-2 **$16.95**; 152 pp, HC, ISBN 1-879045-35-4 **$21.95**

God Was in This Place & I, i Did Not Know
Finding Self, Spirituality & Ultimate Meaning
by Lawrence Kushner 6 x 9, 192 pp, Quality PB, ISBN 1-879045-33-8 **$16.95**

The River of Light: *Spirituality, Judaism, Consciousness*
by Lawrence Kushner 6 x 9, 192 pp, Quality PB, ISBN 1-879045-03-6 **$14.95**

Theology/Philosophy

A Heart of Many Rooms
Celebrating the Many Voices within Judaism
by *Dr. David Hartman* AWARD WINNER!

Named a *Publishers Weekly* "Best Book of the Year." Addresses the spiritual and theological questions that face all Jews and all people today. From the perspective of traditional Judaism, Hartman shows that commitment to both Jewish tradition and to pluralism can create understanding between people of different religious convictions.
6 x 9, 352 pp, HC, ISBN 1-58023-048-2 **$24.95**

A Living Covenant: *The Innovative Spirit in Traditional Judaism*
by *Dr. David Hartman* AWARD WINNER!

Winner, National Jewish Book Award. Hartman reveals a Judaism grounded in covenant—a relational framework—informed by the metaphor of marital love rather than that of parent-child dependency. 6 x 9, 368 pp, Quality PB, ISBN 1-58023-011-3 **$18.95**

The Death of Death: *Resurrection and Immortality in Jewish Thought*
by *Dr. Neil Gillman* AWARD WINNER!

Does death end life, or is it the passage from one stage of life to another? This National Jewish Book Award Finalist explores the original and compelling argument that Judaism, a religion often thought to pay little attention to the afterlife, not only offers us rich ideas on the subject—but delivers a deathblow to death itself. 6 x 9, 336 pp, Quality PB, ISBN 1-58023-081-4 **$18.95**; HC, ISBN 1-879045-61-3 **$23.95**

   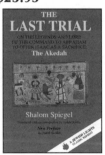 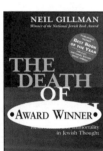

Aspects of Rabbinic Theology by Solomon Schechter; New Intro. by Dr. Neil Gillman
6 x 9, 448 pp, Quality PB, ISBN 1-879045-24-9 **$19.95**

The Last Trial: *On the Legends and Lore of the Command to Abraham to Offer Isaac as a Sacrifice* by Shalom Spiegel; New Intro. by Judah Goldin
6 x 9, 208 pp, Quality PB, ISBN 1-879045-29-X **$17.95**

Judaism and Modern Man: *An Interpretation of Jewish Religion* by Will Herberg; New Intro. by Dr. Neil Gillman 5½ x 8½, 336 pp, Quality PB, ISBN 1-879045-87-7 **$18.95**

Seeking the Path to Life AWARD WINNER!
Theological Meditations on God and the Nature of People, Love, Life and Death
by Rabbi Ira F. Stone
6 x 9, 160 pp, Quality PB, ISBN 1-879045-47-8 **$14.95**; HC, ISBN 1-879045-17-6 **$19.95**

The Spirit of Renewal: *Finding Faith after the Holocaust* AWARD WINNER!
by Rabbi Edward Feld
6 x 9, 224 pp, Quality PB, ISBN 1-879045-40-0 **$16.95**

Tormented Master: *The Life and Spiritual Quest of Rabbi Nahman of Bratslav*
by Dr. Arthur Green
6 x 9, 416 pp, Quality PB, ISBN 1-879045-11-7 **$18.95**

Your Word Is Fire: *The Hasidic Masters on Contemplative Prayer*
Ed. and Trans. with a New Introduction by Dr. Arthur Green and Dr. Barry W. Holtz
6 x 9, 160 pp, Quality PB, ISBN 1-879045-25-7 **$14.95**

Theology/Philosophy

Torah of the Earth: *Exploring 4,000 Years of Ecology in Jewish Thought*

In 2 Volumes   Ed. by *Rabbi Arthur Waskow*

Major new resource offering us an invaluable key to understanding the intersection of ecology and Judaism. Leading scholars provide us with a guided tour of ecological thought from four major Jewish viewpoints. Vol. 1: *Biblical Israel & Rabbinic Judaism*, 6 x 9, 272 pp, Quality PB, ISBN 1-58023-086-5 **$19.95**; Vol. 2: *Zionism & Eco-Judaism*, 6 x 9, 336 pp, Quality PB, ISBN 1-58023-087-3 **$19.95**

Broken Tablets: *Restoring the Ten Commandments and Ourselves*

Ed. by *Rabbi Rachel S. Mikva*; Intro. by *Rabbi Lawrence Kushner*;
Afterword by *Rabbi Arnold Jacob Wolf*   **AWARD WINNER!**

Twelve outstanding spiritual leaders each share profound and personal thoughts about these biblical commands and why they have such a special hold on us.
6 x 9, 192 pp, HC, ISBN 1-58023-066-0 **$21.95**

Evolving Halakhah: *A Progressive Approach to Traditional Jewish Law*

by *Rabbi Dr. Moshe Zemer*

Innovative and provocative, this book affirms the system of traditional Jewish law, *halakhah*, as flexible enough to accommodate the changing realities of each generation. It shows that the traditional framework for understanding the Torah's commandments can be the living heart of Jewish life for all Jews.   6 x 9, 480 pp, HC, ISBN 1-58023-002-4 **$40.00**

  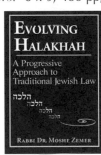  

God & the Big Bang
Discovering Harmony Between Science & Spirituality **AWARD WINNER!**
by Daniel C. Matt
6 x 9, 216 pp, Quality PB, ISBN 1-879045-89-3 **$16.95**; HC, ISBN 1-879045-48-6 **$21.95**

Israel—A Spiritual Travel Guide **AWARD WINNER!**
A Companion for the Modern Jewish Pilgrim
by Rabbi Lawrence A. Hoffman 4¾ x 10, 256 pp, Quality PB, ISBN 1-879045-56-7 **$18.95**

Godwrestling—Round 2: *Ancient Wisdom, Future Paths* **AWARD WINNER!**
by Rabbi Arthur Waskow
6 x 9, 352 pp, Quality PB, ISBN 1-879045-72-9 **$18.95**; HC, ISBN 1-879045-45-1 **$23.95**

Ecology & the Jewish Spirit: *Where Nature & the Sacred Meet* Ed. and with Intros.
by Ellen Bernstein 6 x 9, 288 pp, Quality PB, ISBN 1-58023-082-2 **$16.95**;
HC, ISBN 1-879045-88-5 **$23.95**

Israel: *An Echo of Eternity* by Abraham Joshua Heschel; New Intro. by
Dr. Susannah Heschel 5½ x 8, 272 pp, Quality PB, ISBN 1-879045-70-2 **$18.95**

The Earth Is the Lord's: *The Inner World of the Jew in Eastern Europe*
by Abraham Joshua Heschel 5½ x 8, 112 pp, Quality PB, ISBN 1-879045-42-7 **$13.95**

A Passion for Truth: *Despair and Hope in Hasidism* by Abraham Joshua Heschel
5½ x 8, 352 pp, Quality PB, ISBN 1-879045-41-9 **$18.95**

Life Cycle & Holidays

How to Be a Perfect Stranger, In 2 Volumes
A Guide to Etiquette in Other People's Religious Ceremonies

Ed. by *Stuart M. Matlins & Arthur J. Magida* **AWARD WINNER!**

What will happen? What do I do? What do I wear? What do I say? What should I avoid *doing, wearing, saying? What are their basic beliefs? Should I bring a gift?* In question-and-answer format, *How to Be a Perfect Stranger* explains the rituals and celebrations of America's major religions/denominations, helping an interested guest to feel comfortable, participate to the fullest extent possible, and avoid violating anyone's religious principles. It is not a guide to theology, nor is it presented from the perspective of any particular faith.
Vol. 1: *America's Largest Faiths,* 6 x 9, 432 pp, HC, ISBN 1-879045-39-7 **$24.95**
Vol. 2: *Other Faiths in America,* 6 x 9, 416 pp, HC, ISBN 1-879045-63-X **$24.95**

Putting God on the Guest List, 2nd Ed.
How to Reclaim the Spiritual Meaning of Your Child's Bar or Bat Mitzvah

by *Rabbi Jeffrey K. Salkin* **AWARD WINNER!**

The expanded, updated, revised edition of today's most influential book (over 60,000 copies in print) about finding core spiritual values in American Jewry's most misunderstood ceremony.
6 x 9, 224 pp, Quality PB, ISBN 1-879045-59-1 **$16.95**; HC, ISBN 1-879045-58-3 **$24.95**

For Kids—Putting God on Your Guest List
How to Claim the Spiritual Meaning of Your Bar or Bat Mitzvah
by Rabbi Jeffrey K. Salkin 6 x 9, 144 pp, Quality PB, ISBN 1-58023-015-6 **$14.95**

Bar/Bat Mitzvah Basics
A Practical Family Guide to Coming of Age Together
Ed. by Cantor Helen Leneman 6 x 9, 240 pp, Quality PB, ISBN 1-879045-54-0 **$16.95**;
HC, ISBN 1-879045-51-6 **$24.95**

The New Jewish Baby Book AWARD WINNER!
Names, Ceremonies, & Customs—A Guide for Today's Families
by Anita Diamant 6 x 9, 336 pp, Quality PB, ISBN 1-879045-28-1 **$16.95**

Hanukkah: The Art of Jewish Living
by Dr. Ron Wolfson 7 x 9, 192 pp, Quality PB, Illus., ISBN 1-879045-97-4 **$16.95**

The Shabbat Seder: The Art of Jewish Living
by Dr. Ron Wolfson 7 x 9, 272 pp, Quality PB, Illus., ISBN 1-879045-90-7 **$16.95**
Also available are these helpful companions to *The Shabbat Seder*: Booklet of the Blessings and Songs, ISBN 1-879045-91-5 **$5.00**; Audiocassette of the Blessings, DN03 **$6.00**; Teacher's Guide, ISBN 1-879045-92-3 **$4.95**

The Passover Seder: The Art of Jewish Living
by Dr. Ron Wolfson 7 x 9, 352 pp, Quality PB, Illus., ISBN 1-879045-93-1 **$16.95**
Also available are these helpful companions to *The Passover Seder*: Passover Workbook, ISBN 1-879045-94-X **$6.95**; Audiocassette of the Blessings, DN04 **$6.00**; Teacher's Guide, ISBN 1-879045-95-8 **$4.95**

Life Cycle

Jewish Paths toward Healing and Wholeness
A Personal Guide to Dealing with Suffering
by *Rabbi Kerry M. Olitzky*

"Why me?" Why do we suffer? How can we heal? Grounded in the spiritual traditions of Judaism, this book provides healing rituals, psalms and prayers that help readers initiate a dialogue with God, to guide them along the complicated path of healing and wholeness.
6 x 9, 192 pp, Quality PB, ISBN 1-58023-068-7 **$15.95**　　　(Avail. Aug. 2000)

Mourning & Mitzvah: *A Guided Journal for Walking the Mourner's Path through Grief to Healing*
by *Anne Brener, L.C.S.W.*; Foreword by *Rabbi Jack Riemer*; Intro. by *Rabbi William Cutter*

For those who mourn a death, for those who would help them, for those who face a loss of any kind, Brener teaches us the power and strength available to us in the fully experienced mourning process. 7½ x 9, 288 pp, Quality PB, ISBN 1-879045-23-0 **$19.95**

Tears of Sorrow, Seeds of Hope
A Jewish Spiritual Companion for Infertility and Pregnancy Loss
by *Rabbi Nina Beth Cardin*

A spiritual companion that enables us to mourn infertility, a lost pregnancy, or a stillbirth within the prayers, rituals, and meditations of Judaism. By drawing on the texts of tradition, it creates readings and rites of mourning, and through them provides a wellspring of compassion, solace—and hope. 6 x 9, 192 pp, HC, ISBN 1-58023-017-2 **$19.95**

Lifecycles
V. 1: *Jewish Women on Life Passages & Personal Milestones* AWARD WINNER!
Ed. and with Intros. by Rabbi Debra Orenstein
V. 2: *Jewish Women on Biblical Themes in Contemporary Life* AWARD WINNER!
Ed. and with Intros. by Rabbi Debra Orenstein and Rabbi Jane Rachel Litman
V. 1: 6 x 9, 480 pp, Quality PB, ISBN 1-58023-018-0 **$19.95**; HC, ISBN 1-879045-14-1 **$24.95**
V. 2: 6 x 9, 464 pp, Quality PB, ISBN 1-58023-019-9 **$19.95**; HC, ISBN 1-879045-15-X **$24.95**

Grief in Our Seasons: *A Mourner's Kaddish Companion*
by Rabbi Kerry M. Olitzky 4½ x 6½, 448 pp, Quality PB, ISBN 1-879045-55-9 **$15.95**

A Time to Mourn, A Time to Comfort: *A Guide to Jewish Bereavement and Comfort*
by Dr. Ron Wolfson 7 x 9, 336 pp, Quality PB, ISBN 1-879045-96-6 **$16.95**

When a Grandparent Dies
A Kid's Own Remembering Workbook for Dealing with Shiva and the Year Beyond
by Nechama Liss-Levinson, Ph.D.
8 x 10, 48 pp, HC, Illus., 2-color text, ISBN 1-879045-44-3 **$15.95**

So That Your Values Live On: *Ethical Wills & How to Prepare Them*
Ed. by Rabbi Jack Riemer & Professor Nathaniel Stampfer
6 x 9, 272 pp, Quality PB, ISBN 1-879045-34-6 **$17.95**

Healing/Wellness/Recovery

Jewish Pastoral Care
A Practical Handbook from Traditional and Contemporary Sources
Ed. by *Rabbi Dayle A. Friedman*

This innovative resource builds on the classic foundations of pastoral care, enriching it with uniquely Jewish traditions and wisdom. Gives today's Jewish pastoral counselors practical guidelines based in the Jewish tradition. 6 x 9, 352 pp, HC, ISBN 1-58023-078-4 **$34.95** (Avail. Nov. 2000)

Healing of Soul, Healing of Body
Spiritual Leaders Unfold the Strength & Solace in Psalms
Ed. by *Rabbi Simkha Y. Weintraub, CSW*, for The National Center for Jewish Healing

A source of solace for those who are facing illness, as well as those who care for them. Provides a wellspring of strength with inspiring introductions and commentaries by eminent spiritual leaders reflecting all Jewish movements. 6 x 9, 128 pp, Quality PB, Illus., 2-color text, ISBN 1-879045-31-1 **$14.95**

Self, Struggle & Change: *Family Conflict Stories in Genesis and Their Healing Insights for Our Lives*
by *Dr. Norman J. Cohen*

How do I find wholeness in my life and in my family's life? Here a modern master of biblical interpretation brings us greater understanding of the ancient text and of ourselves in this intriguing re-telling of conflict between husband and wife, father and son, brothers and sisters. 6 x 9, 224 pp, Quality PB, ISBN 1-879045-66-4 **$16.95**; HC, ISBN 1-879045-19-2 **$21.95**

    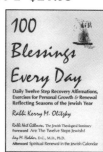

Twelve Jewish Steps to Recovery: *A Personal Guide to Turning from Alcoholism & Other Addictions . . . Drugs, Food, Gambling, Sex . . .* by Rabbi Kerry M. Olitzky & Stuart A. Copans, M.D. Preface by Abraham J. Twerski, M.D.; Intro. by Rabbi Sheldon Zimmerman; "Getting Help" by JACS Foundation 6 x 9, 144 pp, Quality PB, ISBN 1-879045-09-5 **$13.95**

One Hundred Blessings Every Day: *Daily Twelve Step Recovery Affirmations, Exercises for Personal Growth & Renewal Reflecting Seasons of the Jewish Year* by Rabbi Kerry M. Olitzky, with selected meditations prepared by Rabbi James Stone Goodman, Danny Siegel, and Gordon Tucker. Foreword by Rabbi Neil Gillman, The Jewish Theological Seminary of America; Afterword by Dr. Jay Holder, Director, Exodus Treatment Center 4½ x 6½, 432 pp, Quality PB, ISBN 1-879045-30-3 **$14.95**

Recovery from Codependence: *A Jewish Twelve Steps Guide to Healing Your Soul* by Rabbi Kerry M. Olitzky; Foreword by Marc Galanter, M.D., Director, Division of Alcoholism & Drug Abuse, NYU Medical Center; Afterword by Harriet Rossetto, Director, Gateways Beit T'shuvah 6 x 9, 160 pp, Quality PB, ISBN 1-879045-32-X **$13.95**; HC, ISBN 1-879045-27-3 **$21.95**

Renewed Each Day: *Daily Twelve Step Recovery Meditations Based on the Bible* by Rabbi Kerry M. Olitzky & Aaron Z. *Vol. I: Genesis & Exodus*; Intro. by Rabbi Michael A. Signer; Afterword by JACS Foundation. *Vol. II: Leviticus, Numbers and Deuteronomy*; Intro. by Sharon M. Strassfeld; Afterword by Rabbi Harold M. Schulweis
Vol. I: 6 x 9, 224 pp, Quality PB, ISBN 1-879045-12-5 **$14.95**
Vol. II: 6 x 9, 280 pp, Quality PB, ISBN 1-879045-13-3 **$14.95**